Massachusetts Environmental Law Handbook

Fourth Edition

Theda Braddock

Bernan Press

Lanham • Boulder • New York • London

Published by Bernan Press
An imprint of The Rowman & Littlefield Publishing Group, Inc.
4501 Forbes Boulevard, Suite 200, Lanham, Maryland 20706
www.rowman.com

86-90 Paul Street, London EC2A 4NE

British Library Cataloguing in Publication Information available

Library of Congress Cataloging-in-Publication Data available

Names: Braddock, Theda, author.
Title: Massachusetts environmental law handbook / Theda Braddock.
Description: Fourth edition. | Lanham, Maryland : Bernan Press, [2022] | Series: State environmental law handbooks | Includes bibliographical references and index.
Identifiers: LCCN 2022027920 (print) | LCCN 2022027921 (ebook) | ISBN 9781641434270 (paperback) | ISBN 9781641434287 (epub)
Subjects: LCSH: Environmental law–Massachusetts.
Classification: LCC KFM2754 .M38 2022 (print) | LCC KFM2754 (ebook) | DDC 344.744/046–dc23/eng/20220729
LC record available at https://lccn.loc.gov/2022027920
LC ebook record available at https://lccn.loc.gov/2022027921

Contents

Chapter 1

Massachusetts Environmental Agencies

EXECUTIVE OFFICE OF ENERGY AND ENVIRONMENTAL AFFAIRS

Environmental laws in Massachusetts are implemented primarily by the Massachusetts Executive Office of Energy and Environmental Affairs ("EOEEA") which was established by M.G.L. c. 21A, §1. The Office is headed by a secretary who is appointed by the Governor and has overall responsibility for implementing state environmental requirements. EOEEA includes the following five agencies, each of which is headed by a commissioner: (a) the Department of Environmental Protection, (b) the Department of Environmental Management, (c) the Department of Food and Agriculture, (d) the Department of Fisheries, Wildlife, and Environmental Law Enforcement, and (e) the Metropolitan District Commission. These agencies are described below.

EOEEA also encompasses several offices, commissions, and other entities. Those entities that most often handle environmental matters affecting commercial and industrial activities are described in this chapter. They include the Massachusetts Environmental Policy Act Office, the Office of Coastal Zone Management, the Water Resources Commission, the Office of Grants and Technical Assistance, the Office of Law Enforcement (commonly known as the "Massachusetts Environmental Police"), the Office of Geographic and Environmental Information, and Natural Resources Damages Assessment and Restoration. EOEEA also has six agencies under its direction: the Department of Conservation and Recreation ("DCR"), the Massachusetts Department of Agricultural Resources ("MDAR"), the Department of Fish and Game

("DFG"), the Department of Public Utilities ("DPU"), and the Department of Energy Resources ("DOER").

MASSACHUSETTS ENVIRONMENTAL POLICY ACT OFFICE

The Massachusetts Environmental Policy Act ("MEPA"), M.G.L. c. 30, §§61 to 62I, provides for review of state agency actions and private projects involving such action. The statute is implemented by the MEPA Unit of the Executive Office of Energy and Environmental Affairs. MEPA regulations specify the agency actions and project impacts that trigger environmental impact review requirements and contain detailed provisions regarding the review process. EOEEA publishes notice of all submissions requiring MEPA review in the *Environmental Monitor.*

The MEPA Office also quantifies greenhouse gas emissions and identifies measures to avoid, minimize, or mitigate such emissions. In 2021 the Legislature passed "An Act Creating a Next-Generation Roadmap for Massachusetts Climate Policy,"[1] which set specific greenhouse as emission limits for Massachusetts with an ultimate goal of "at least net zero statewide greenhouse gas emissions; provided however, that in no event shall the level of emissions in 2050 be higher than a level 85 percent below the 1990 level." The Act also set interim emission limits, increased offshore wind procurement, increased the renewable energy portfolio for retail electricity suppliers, promotes solar energy, and created several new environmental justice programs, among many other provisions.

COASTAL ZONE MANAGEMENT OFFICE

The federal Coastal Zone Management Act, 16 U.S.C. §§1451 to 1465 is administered in Massachusetts by the Massachusetts Coastal Zone Management ("CZM") Office. The CZM Office reviews federal funding, permitting, and construction activities that may affect the ocean and coastal zone in order to ensure that these activities are consistent with state coastal zone management policies.

MASSACHUSETTS WATER RESOURCES AUTHORITY

The Massachusetts Water Resources Authority ("MWRA") was established by Chapter 372 of the Acts of 1984 to manage the metropolitan Boston water supply as well as the sewage collection, treatment, and disposal system for metropolitan Boston. Although it is part of EOEEA, MWRA is autonomous and is not funded by taxes. Instead, it receives its revenues from bond sales, grants, administrative penalties, and the sale of water and/or sewer services to about sixty Massachusetts communities. MWRA regulations provide for the issuance of sewer discharge permits within communities served by the Authority.

DEPARTMENT OF AGRICULTURAL RESOURCES ("MDAR")

MDAR has four divisions: Agricultural Conservation and Technical Assistance, Agricultural Markets, Animal Health, and Crop and Pest Services. MDAR was established by M.G.L. c. 20 and includes the Pesticide Board, which was established pursuant to the Massachusetts Pesticide Control Act, M.G.L. c. 132B, to oversee implementation of that statute. The Board's regulations are set forth at 333 C.M.R. 2.01 to 13.10.

DEPARTMENT OF CONSERVATION AND RECREATION ("DCR")

DCR's primary function is to protect, promote, and enhance the natural, cultural, and recreational resources of the Commonwealth. It has three divisions: MassParks, the Engineering Division, and the Division of Water Supply Protection.

DEPARTMENT OF AGRICULTURAL RESOURCES ("MDAR")

MDAR, through its four divisions: Agricultural Conservation and Technical Assistance, Agricultural Markets, Animal Health, and Crop and Pest Services; supports, regulates, and enhances agricultural diversity and promotes economically and environmentally sound food safety and animal health, and fosters agriculture's role in energy conservation and production.

DEPARTMENT OF FISH AND GAME ("DFG")

DFG, formerly the Department of Fisheries, Wildlife, and Environmental Law Enforcement, has numerous responsibilities in connection with the protection of wildlife in the Commonwealth. Among these responsibilities is implementation of the Massachusetts Endangered Species Act, M.G.L. c. 131A, under which DFG's Division of Fisheries and Wildlife is responsible for identifying endangered and threatened species[2] and significant habitats of such species and reviewing projects that would alter such habitats. The Division of Marine Fisheries manages and regulates all commercial and non-commercial fisheries in state coastal waters and federal waters within 200 miles, including conservation of marine mammals. DFG's former Riverways Program and CZM's Wetlands Restoration Program merged into DFG's new Division of Ecological Restoration ("DER") to restore and protect the health of rivers, wetlands, and watersheds within the Commonwealth.

DEPARTMENT OF PUBLIC UTILITIES ("DPU")

DPU oversees electric power, natural gas, and water industries.

DEPARTMENT OF ENERGY RESOURCES ("DOER")

DOER develops and implements policies and programs to ensure the adequacy, security, diversity, and cost-effectiveness of the energy supply in Massachusetts. The Renewable and Alternative Energy Division within DOER strives to increase wind and solar power production.

OTHER STATE AGENCIES AND ENTITIES WITH ENVIRONMENTAL RESPONSIBILITIES

Department of Environmental Protection

The Department of Environmental Protection ("MassDEP") has primary responsibility for administering state environmental regulatory programs.[3] Most permitting and site-specific work is conducted from the four Regional Offices located in Wilmington, Worcester, Springfield, and Lakeville.[4] MassDEP is operationally organized around three areas: air and waste, water resources, and waste site cleanup. It is further divided into bureaus: the Bureau of Waste Prevention (regulates air pollution, solid waste recycling and disposal, toxic materials, underground storage tanks and hazardous waste), the Bureau of Water Resources (on an integrated watershed-based approach, issues surface and groundwater discharge permits, sets drinking water standards, protects wetlands and rivers, issues licenses in tidelands and waterways, and overseas well drillers), the Bureau of Waste Site Cleanup (oversees hazardous waste cleanups and, through the regional offices, responds to chemical and hazardous waste spills), the Bureau of Policy and Planning including Geographic Information Systems, Internet Strategy Unit, the Performance Partnership Agreement and Program Planning, the Office of Research and Standards, the William F. Wall Experiment Station, and the Information Technology Office. The Office of General Counsel performs legal services on regulations, policy, compliance, and enforcement. A separate Office of Appeals and Dispute Resolution works to facilitate settlement of adjudicatory appeals and conducts hearings if no settlement is reached. Another office, the Office of Municipal Partnerships and Governmental Affairs works with other government agencies. Finally, the Office of Permit and Regulatory Ombudsman and Special Projects coordinates large projects involving multiple parts of MassDEP.

LOCAL GOVERNMENT BODIES WITH ENVIRONMENTAL RESPONSIBILITIES

Although Massachusetts environmental laws and regulations authorize the state agencies discussed herein to carry out many environmental mandates, a number of laws and regulations also provide for local involvement in the regulatory process.

NOTES

1. Acts of 2021, Chapter 8.
2. Massachusetts Endangered Species Act, M.G.L. c. 131A; 321 C.M.R. 10.00.
3. See https://perma.cc/4AAH-AQL9.
4. Forms and guidance documents are available at https://perma.cc/9HBB-8Q77.

Chapter 2

Enforcement of Commonwealth Environmental Requirements

This chapter provides an overview of the enforcement of Massachusetts environmental laws in the administrative and judicial context. While such efforts generally are the responsibility of the Massachusetts Department of Environmental Protection ("MassDEP" or the "Department"), this discussion also addresses the U.S. Environmental Protection Agency ("EPA"), which retains the right, and often acts upon its authority, to enforce MassDEP-promulgated regulations. This chapter further addresses the increasingly common efforts of environmental groups, *ad hoc* alliances, and neighbors who attempt to enforce Massachusetts (or federal) environmental requirements in lieu of MassDEP (or EPA).

MassDEP has issued a series of enforcement-related policies and guidance. In addition to confirming MassDEP's multimedia, whole-facility approach, these policies emphasize monetary penalties as an integral part of the Commonwealth's compliance program.[1] Such policies stress, for example, that some form of sanction should be the rule rather than the exception: "[T]he use of administrative penalties should be considered a relatively routine sanction, not an extreme 'last resort' step," and that neither a verbal warning nor a warning letter typically is an appropriate enforcement response.[2] MassDEP also has followed EPA's lead by developing policies associated with supplemental environmental projects ("SEPs"), which operate as "good works" performed by companies in lieu of a certain percentage of penalties to be assessed as part of the cooperative settlement of enforcement action.[3]

MASSDEP-INITIATED ADMINISTRATIVE ACTIONS AND PENALTIES

Most MassDEP-initiated enforcement efforts wind their way through the administrative, rather than judicial system. Not surprisingly, therefore, the administrative procedure for enforcement is standardized, involving a phased progression from MassDEP's discovery of alleged non-compliance, through the process of notice and opportunity to respond to allegations of violations, to the assessment of penalties and the resolution of the action either by a consensual or a unilaterally issued administrative consent order. Each of these phases is discussed below. It should be noted that in some circumstances, however, discrete phases are compounded.

Discovery of Non-Compliance

MassDEP may discover non-compliance through routine or targeted file reviews. MassDEP also may conduct unannounced or arranged field inspections or facility audits. In such cases, an assembled "team" of MassDEP inspectors (each with an expertise in a certain media) and often EPA personnel conduct a "walk through" of facility operations, as well as a review of facility files, identifying alleged non-compliance with environmental laws. MassDEP further may respond to neighborhood complaints or inquiries and, in the process, identify non-compliance. Finally, as discussed below, a regulated entity may itself discover non-compliance and voluntarily disclose what it has found to MassDEP.

This facility-specific, factual information forms the basis for MassDEP's subsequent notice to the facility owner and the subsequent enforcement process. This initial information also may be supplemented, including by responses to MassDEP requests for information or during discovery, at MassDEP's option.

Notices of Alleged Non-Compliance

MassDEP's written communication of alleged non-compliance, the usual "first step" in environmental enforcement, may include either a Notice of Non-Compliance ("NON") or a field notice of non-compliance ("FNON"). In addition, in certain circumstances, the notice may be subsumed in a penalty assessment notice ("PAN"), an administrative order ("AO"), or an administrative consent order ("ACO"), all of which are discussed below. Absent notice to the regulated entity, MassDEP typically cannot assess an administrative penalty.[4]

NONs are limited-use, non-appealable written notices which document a facility's alleged non-compliance with environmental laws, and which do not contain a penalty.[5] An FNON is a sort of NON which may be issued in the field, provided it immediately follows an inspection and relates to six or fewer violation of the sort identified as qualifying for FNONs; *i.e.*, low-level non-compliance. Under normal circumstances, a NON or FNON is a precondition to issuance of a penalty or PAN.[6]

While, typically, MassDEP is not authorized to issue a PAN unless it first has issued a NON or FNON, MassDEP may issue a PAN immediately to an alleged violator for serious environmental violations. These include circumstances where: (a) there is a pattern of non-compliance by the alleged violator; (b) the alleged violator's failure to comply is willful and not the result of error; (c) the alleged violator's failure to comply results in a significant impact on public health, safety, or welfare or the environment; or (d) the alleged violator fails to report an unauthorized release or disposal of a hazardous substance or hazardous material.[7] PANs are subject to administrative appeal, when issued unilaterally.[8]

AOs are unilaterally issued, appealable written demands for compliance (typically, within a fixed deadline), and can include demands for the cessation of activities and penalties. AOs address circumstances considered more severe than those addressed in NONs, particularly those which warrant continued DEP oversight. AOs also are used as requests for submission by the regulated entity of information in response to MassDEP's inquiry.

ACOs are consensual administrative orders, and likewise can include a penalty. Because ACOs are consensual, however, they are not subject to appeal, even where a penalty is included.

Penalty Assessment

Under the Massachusetts Administrative Penalties Act, M.G.L. c. 21A, §16 (the "APA"), MassDEP can assess a monetary penalty for violation of any state environmental law that it administers or any regulation, order, license, or approval under such a law. DEP has issued regulations to implement the APA at 310 C.M.R. 5.01 to 5.37.

The penalty amounts authorized under the APA for each instance of non-compliance range from a "floor" of $100 to $25,000. Each day during which non-compliance occurs or continues may constitute a separate violation and, therefore, can be subject to a separate penalty.[9] As a result, a single substantive violation that continues for several weeks or months, theoretically, can accrue many thousands of dollars in potential penalties.

MassDEP may consider a number of factors in determining the amount of an administrative penalty.[10] These factors are as follows: (a) the actual or potential impact of the non-compliance on public health, safety, and welfare and the environment; (b) actual or potential costs incurred or damages suffered by the Commonwealth or others as a result of the non-compliance; (c) whether the violator took steps to prevent a failure to comply; (d) whether the violator took steps to come into compliance promptly; (e) whether the violator took any action to mitigate or remedy any harm caused by the non-compliance; (t) whether there are prior instances of non-compliance by the violator; (g) any economic benefit resulting from a failure to comply; (h) deterrence of future non-compliance by the violator and by others; (i) the financial condition of the violator; (j) the public interest; and (k) any other factor specifically referenced in the PAN.[11]

It is MassDEP's stated policy to refrain from reducing an assessed penalty or withdrawing a PAN, except in limited circumstances, such as where MassDEP was unaware of material facts at the time the penalty was assessed. However, while the penalty may not be eliminated, penalties often are negotiated and, in the negotiation process, reduced.[12] Conversely, if MassDEP determines that the assessment of a monetary penalty in the administrative context would not be an adequate enforcement response, it may refer the matter to the Attorney General's ("AG") office, which may decide to institute civil or criminal proceedings.[13]

As discussed above, whenever MassDEP seeks to assess a civil administrative penalty, except in the context of a non-consensual settlement, the person has a right to an administrative hearing.[14] Appeal of a PAN must occur within twenty-one days of its receipt by the regulated entity.[15]

MassDEP Policies Impacting Penalties

MassDEP's audit and SEP policies inform the enforcement process, ultimately by reducing penalty assessments, although at different stages in the enforcement process. Both policies are discussed below.

Where a regulated entity voluntarily discloses alleged non-compliance discovered within the context of a voluntarily performed environmental audit, MassDEP, as a matter of enforcement discretion, may agree to eliminate or reduce a certain portion of penalties (that otherwise could be assessed in the administrative context).[16]

To come within the MassDEP's Audit Policy, a regulated entity must make an oral or written disclosure to DEP within twenty-one days of its discovery (or a shorter period, if so required by law), with a written disclosure to follow within five (5) days of any oral disclosure, and correct the violation within sixty days of discovery. (Extensions to these time periods may be granted by MassDEP in appropriate circumstances, including where the violation is complex, or the appropriate remedy is unclear.) The regulated entity also must commit in writing to take steps to prevent recurrence of the violation in question.

The Audit Policy does not apply in all cases, however. For instance, to fall within the protections afforded by the Audit Policy, violations that are the subject of a voluntary disclosure cannot relate to a pending enforcement or third-party action. Likewise, violations that are the subject of voluntary disclosure cannot have been the subject of action taken by MassDEP against the regulated entity during the preceding five-year period, if that action related to the type of violation at issue or to a more serious, but similar, violation.

Where the MassDEP's Audit Policy applies, MassDEP may exercise its enforcement discretion by declining to issue an NON that otherwise could be issued, and/or by waiving or reducing the punitive or economic components of a penalty that otherwise could be assessed. This waiver of or reduction in the penalty is a primary incentive for voluntary disclosure.

MassDEP's SEP Policy[17] operates in the final stages of the enforcement process, in conjunction with the resolution of the amount of the penalty to be assessed. At essence, the SEP Policy allows a regulated entity facing enforcement to offset penalties by performing environmental projects which it otherwise would not be obligated to perform, all as part of the consensual settlement of the action.

From the perspective of a regulated entity, the SEP Policy may help to mitigate the effects of adverse publicity associated with major environmental enforcement action (and often measured by the size of the penalty assessed).

Administrative Appeals

Appeals of penalty assessments or MassDEP enforcement mandates, where taken, are to MassDEP's Office of Administrative Appeals ("OAA"). The OAA functions as an administrative judiciary, with administrative law judges ("ALJs") which oversee and conduct each proceeding, including discovery, motions and plenary evidentiary hearings, if not waived.[18] The ALJ need not observe the rules of evidence observed by other courts, although the rules of privilege do apply.[19] If the alleged violator denies that a violation occurred, MassDEP must prove the violation by a preponderance of the evidence.[20]

OAA decisions are considered final when signed by the Commissioner and, under the APA, may be appealed to Superior Court, where review is limited to the record of the hearing except in cases of alleged irregularities in procedure not shown in the record.[21] The AG's office defends DEP's actions in any such appeal.

CIVIL ACTIONS AND PENALTIES

The AG's office represents all Massachusetts agencies that are responsible for enforcing environmental laws, including MassDEP, in Massachusetts courts.[22] Moreover, many environmental laws administered by state agencies contain specific provisions expressly authorizing the AG to bring suits for enforcement,[23] although the AG rarely brings cases independently (apparently preferring to act in response to investigations and referrals of environmental cases from such agencies).

The AG's Environmental Protection Division institutes civil litigation in a variety of situations. Such litigation includes suits: (a) to obtain injunctive relief and civil penalties for violations of environmental laws and regulations and agency orders; (b) to require remedial action and reimbursement for government cleanup costs; (c) to recover natural resources damages; (d) to collect administrative penalties; and (e) for contempt. The AG also may settle an action. Any such resolution is memorialized in a judicial consent decree, which functions much as an ACO, by memorializing the non-compliance, any remedy or continued obligation by the alleged violator, and any penalty. In its capacity as the DEP-representative in Commonwealth courts, the AG has broad authority to develop its case against an alleged violator and to resolve an action.[24]

CRIMINAL ACTIONS AND PENALTIES

The AG's Criminal Bureau brings criminal prosecutions seeking fines and imprisonment against violators of the Commonwealth's environmental laws. Further, the Bureau may bring criminal enforcement proceedings, where not precluded by law, against a violator when it deems such action to be appropriate, even if the violator has reached a settlement with DEP or the EPA. Once a matter is assigned to an assistant attorney general in the Criminal Bureau further investigations may include undercover activities, execution of a criminal search warrant, or a grand jury investigation.

To screen the most series violations of the Commonwealth's environmental laws, the Massachusetts Environmental Strike Force was established (in the late 1980s). The Strike Force consists of civil and criminal prosecutors in the AG's office and personnel from MassDEP, the State Police, and the Environmental Police. MassDEP contributes legal, technical, and field staff to the Strike Force, and the Strike Force may share its resources with EPA. The Strike Force obtains cases through referrals from MassDEP and other government entities, private citizen complaints (including complaints by neighbors and employees), and the Strike For e's own efforts.

One of the Strike Force's priorities is the identification of unpermitted discharges of pollutants into the air, water, and soil and other activities that may pose an immediate threat to the environment. Although the Strike Force's top priority is prosecution of criminal actions, it has authority to consider all enforcement mechanisms. Because criminal enforcement of environmental laws has occurred infrequently in the Commonwealth, the Strike Force may look to decisions of various courts in different jurisdictions for relevant enforcement precedents, including decisions of the First Circuit Court of Appeals (interpreting the criminal enforcement provisions associated with federal environmental laws) and of courts in other states.

CITIZENS SUITS

Certain Massachusetts statutes allow persons aggrieved by issuance of a permit or other approval or authorization to appeal that permit, approval, or authorization. Thus, for example, an aggrieved party may appeal a tidelands license under M.G.L. c. 91 to MassDEP and subsequently to the Superior Court.[25] Similarly, the Wetlands Protection Act empowers a number of parties to appeal an order of conditions to MassDEP and subsequently to the Superior Court.[26] The issuance by a local board of health of a site assignment for a solid waste or hazardous waste facility may be appealed by an aggrieved party to MassDEP and then to the Superior Court.[27] Aggrieved persons, abutting landowners, as well as others who may be impacted by a MassDEP authorization or permit, also may have this ability to bring suit, referred to as judicial standing.

Apart from specific grounds of standing discussed above, M.G.L. c. 214, §7A (the "Statute") generally provides for citizen suits to restrain actions causing or about to cause damage to the environment, where such damage constitutes a violation of any state or local statute, ordinance, by-law, or regulation directed toward the prevention or minimization of environmental damage. For purposes of the Statute, "damage to the environment" does not include insignificant destruction, damage, or impairment to natural resources. The Statute confers standing on any group of ten persons domiciled in the Commonwealth.

While the Statute provides for citizen enforcement, there are obstacles and hurdles to a successful effort. No suit can be brought where governmental authorities have already instituted enforcement action. Further, at least twenty-one days before commencement of action, the citizens must give notice to the agency responsible for enforcing the pertinent law, as well as to the AG and the alleged violator. Only injunctive and declaratory relief are available under the Ten Citizens Suit Statute, subject to the *proviso* that costs and expert witness fees, but not attorney's fees, are recoverable.[28]

Pursuant to Section 10A of the APA, ten persons also may intervene in an adjudicatory proceeding to the extent that damage to the environment, or elimination or reduction of such damage, are at issue. Section 10A references the provisions of the Ten Citizens Suit Statute with respect to the definition of environmental damage, and thus insignificant damage would not be actionable.[29]

On a related note, the Massachusetts Superfund law, also known as Chapter 21E, authorizes a private party to bring a civil action for recovery of damages to that party's real or personal property caused by a release or threat of release of oil or hazardous materials, as well as for recovery of costs incurred in investigation or cleanup of a contaminated site. Chapter 21E includes a mandatory pre-litigation claims procedure, which is a prerequisite to filing a contribution or cost recovery suit to recover investigation or cleanup costs from other potentially responsible parties.[30] In any such suit brought by a Massachusetts resident, the court may award costs, including reasonable attorneys and expert witness fees, if the suit advances the purposes of the statute.[31]

EPA OVER-FILING AND MUNICIPAL ENFORCEMENT

Much state environmental law, including Massachusetts law, implements federal environmental requirements. Thus, for instance, the Massachusetts State Implementation Plan ("SIP") is promulgated to implement federal Clean Air Act mandates.[32] Under these so-called "delegated" programs, EPA may retain a right of enforcement and, on that basis, may decide to bring its own enforcement action for alleged violations of what may be perceived of as state-law requirements.[33] In other circumstances, MassDEP actually may request that EPA "take the lead" in an enforcement action, effectively referring the matter to the federal agency.

The scope and tenor of EPA and MassDEP enforcement often differ. EPA enforcement tends to increase the costs to regulated entities of environmental enforcement, as the penalties associated with EPA-initiated enforcement actions typically exceed those associated with MassDEP-initiated enforcement efforts, although the maximum penalty able to be assessed by EPA under federal environmental laws may be more than MassDEP's maximum under Massachusetts environmental laws.[34] Further, resolution of civil (as opposed to administrative) enforcement necessitates a consent decree negotiated by EPA and the U.S. Department of Justice (acting in a capacity analogous to the AG's office) and subject to public notice and comment, as well as judicial approval.

Likewise, municipalities may retain independent enforcement responsibilities under local ordinances or by-laws, particularly in the case of wetlands and air regulation.[35]

NOTES

1. *See* MassDEP's April 26, 1997 *Enforcement Response Guidance* (Policy ENF-97.001) (the "ERG") (revised 6/18/2008, https:// perma.cc/.2QD6–6LSL

2. *See* ERG, pp. 22, 16.

3. *See* DEP's *Interim Policy on Supplemental Environmental Projects* (Policy ENF-97.005) (supplementing the ERG) (the "SEP Policy").

4. *See* ERG, §C(l), p. 23. Exceptions include circumstances where there is a pattern of non-compliance or willful non-compliance.

5. 310 C.M.R. 5.05 and 5.12.

6. 310 C.M.R. 5.18(2)(a).

7. *See, e.g.*, 310 C.M.R. 5.10(2)(a).

8. *See* ERG, §B, p. 10.

9. M.G.L. c. 21A, §16; see also 310 C.M.R. 5.23 and 5.24.

10. 310 C.M.R. 5.20–5.29.

11. 310 C.M.R. 5.25.

12. *See* ERG, §C(3), pp. 25–27 (discussion of factors for penalty reductions).

13. M.G.L. c. 12, §11D.

14. M.G.L. c. 21A, §lb; *see also* M.G.L. c. 30A.

15. 310 C.M.R. 5.35.

16. *See* MassDEP's *Policy on Incentives for Self-Policing, Environmental Auditing Policy* (Policy ENF-07.002) (July 16, 2014) (the "Audit Policy")., available at https: //perma.cc/8MJL-KKZW.

17. Available at https://perma.cc/MH4S-S76B.

18. *See* 310 C.M.R. 1.01–1.03.

19. 310 C.M.R. 1.01(13)(h).

20. 310 C.M.R. 5.36(3).

21. M.G.L. c. 30A, §14(5); *see also* 310 C.M.R. 1.01(14)(f).

22. M.G.L. c. 12, §3.

23. *See, e.g.*, M.G.L. c. 111F, § 3(c) (Right-to-Know Act), M.G.L. c. 131, § 40 (Wetlands Protection Act), M.G.L. c. 21E (State Superfund law), and M.G.L. c. 91, §23 (Tidelands law).

24. M.G.L. c. 12, § 11D.

25. M.G.L. c. 91, § 18.

26. *See* M.G.L. c. 131, § 40.

27. M.G.L. c. 111, §§ 150A and 150B.

28. M.G.L. c. 214, § 7A.

29. M.G.L. c. 30A, § lOA. While Section lOA references the definition of "damage to the environment" in the Statute, it does not reference that Statute's requirement that the ten persons initiating legal action be *domiciled in the Commonwealth.* The Legislature's failure to include this limitation appears to be inadvertent, and thus it is likely that only persons *domiciled* in the Commonwealth were intended to be covered by Section lOA.

30. M.G.L. c. 21E, § 4A.

31. M.G.L. c. 21E, §§ 4, 5(a)(iii), and 15.

32. *See* 310 C.M.R. 7.00-7.60 (and Appendices A-C).

33. *See, e.g.,* 42 U.S.C. § 7413 (Clean Air Act enforcement provision).

34. In 2009 EPA adjusted its maximum to $32,500 and may add additional amounts to reflect inflation. 40 C.F.R. §19.4.

35. *See, e.g.,* M.G.L. c. 111 (giving local boards of health the power to limit outdoor air pollution).

Chapter 3

MEPA Review

The Massachusetts Environmental Policy Act ("MEPA"), M.G.L. c. 30, §§61–62I, and its implementing regulations at 301 C.M.R. §11.00 *et seq.* provide a substantive standard for environmental protection by state agencies and establishes a process for reviewing certain development projects in which one or more state agencies participate either as the project proponent or by granting a permit, providing financial assistance or closing a land transfer to a private proponent.[1]

MEPA and its regulations have two principal purposes. The purpose of the MEPA review process is to provide meaningful opportunities for public review of the potential environmental impacts of certain development projects for which certain actions by state agencies are required.[2] The purpose of MEPA's substantive standard is to ensure that each agency uses (in addition to applying any other applicable statutory and regulatory standards and requirements) all feasible means to avoid damage to the environment or, to the extent damage to the environment cannot be avoided, to minimize and mitigate damage to the environment to the maximum extent practicable.[3] Unlike the National Environmental Policy Act and other state environmental protection acts, however, MEPA review must occur within a relatively short period of time.

MEPA review is an administrative process that is intended to involve any interested party as well as the project proponent and each state agency that may act on the project. The Secretary of Energy and Environmental Affairs conducts MEPA review in response to one or more review documents prepared and filed by a project proponent, after which the Secretary (after public comment as appropriate) determines whether the review document is adequate. The Secretary's decision that a review document is adequate or that there has been other due compliance with MEPA and its regulations means that the proponent has adequately described the project and its alternatives and assessed its potential environmental impacts and mitigation measures. A state agency retains authority to fulfill its statutory and regulatory obligations in permitting or reviewing a project that is subject to MEPA review, which does not itself result in any formal adjudicative decision approving or disapproving a project.[4]

The staff of the Secretary that carries out day-to-day administration of MEPA is organized as the MEPA Office, under the direction of the Assistant Secretary of Energy and Environmental Affairs, who is also known as the MEPA Director.[5] The Secretary may delegate to the Assistant Secretary any of the Secretary's authority in accordance with MEPA and the regulations that the Secretary deems appropriate.[6] Under the direction of the Assistant Secretary, the MEPA Office exercises wide-ranging responsibilities from responding to inquiries and reviewing documents to conducting site visits and public consultation sessions and preparing drafts of certificates, public benefit determinations, advisory opinions, and other documents for the Secretary.[7]

MEPA review of a project is required only if there is jurisdiction over the project and if the project meets or exceeds one or more of the review thresholds specified in the MEPA regulations[8] or if the Secretary requires fail-safe review.[9] The regulations establish review thresholds for categories of projects or aspects thereof of a nature, size, or location that are likely, directly or indirectly, to cause damage to the environment.[10] Projects with significant environmental impacts will require two or more steps in the MEPA review including a mandatory Environmental Impact Report ("EIR"). Projects with a lesser potential impacts will require at least one step in MEPA review but the Secretary retains discretionary authority to require an EIR on an individual case basis.

Also relevant to the applicability of MEPA review requirements, the segmentation rule requires consideration of the entirety of the project, including any likely future expansion, with the regulations listing factors to be evaluated and providing specific examples that constitute one project for MEPA purposes.[11]

The proponent begins MEPA review by preparing and filing an Environmental Notification Form ("ENF") with the Secretary. The Secretary publishes the appropriate pages of the ENF in the next *Environmental Monitor*. A 30-day review period follows, during the first 20 days of· which any interested party, the MEPA Office (which ordinarily conducts a site visit and public consultation session), and the Secretary review and comment on the ENF. At the close of the review period for an ENF, the Secretary decides whether to require an EIR. If the Secretary does not require an EIR, an agency may act on the project by beginning the project (if it is the proponent) or by granting a permit, providing financial assistance, or closing a land transfer (for a project by a private proponent).[12]

If the Secretary requires an EIR, the proponent prepares and files it with the Secretary. The Secretary shall ordinarily require a draft and final EIR but may allow a single EIR. The Secretary publishes notice of the availability of the EIR in the next *Environmental Monitor.* A 37-day review period follows, during the first 30 days of which any interested party, the MEPA Office, and the Secretary review and comment on the EIR. At the close of the review period, the Secretary decides whether the EIR is adequate. An agency may act on the project, provided that the Secretary has determined that the single or final EIR is adequate, and 60 days have elapsed following publication of notice of the availability of the single or final EIR in the *Environmental Monitor.*[13]

An agency that acts on a project for which the Secretary required an EIR must: (a) issue Section 61 Findings that specify, based on the EIR, all feasible means to be used to avoid damage to the environment, or, to the extent damage to the environment cannot be avoided, to minimize and mitigate damage to the environment to the maximum extent practicable; (b) make its Section 61 Findings part of the permit or other document allowing or approving its action on the project; and (c) file a copy of its Section 61 Findings with the MEPA Office.[14]

REVIEW THRESHOLDS

The review thresholds ordinarily determine whether and how MEPA review is to be conducted.[15] The review thresholds consist of two types of performance standards. The first type includes high thresholds so that projects with particularly significant environmental impacts will require two (and perhaps more) steps in MEPA review, including a mandatory EIR. The second type includes comparatively lower thresholds so that projects with the potential for lesser but still significant environmental impacts will require at least one step in MEPA review, with the potential for the Secretary of Environmental Affairs to exercise discretionary authority and require an EIR on a case-by-case basis.

The analysis of whether a threshold has been met or exceeded (and thereby requires MEPA review) requires several factual inquiries about the nature, size and location of a project. First, there is a qualitative inquiry into the types of environmental impacts or infrastructure demands asking, for example, whether a project alters wetlands or discharges wastewater to a sewer system.[16] Second, there is a related quantitative inquiry into the amount of impact or demand asking, for example, how many gallons per day of water a project will withdraw or vehicle trips the project will generate.[17] Third, there is a conceptual inquiry into the relation of the threshold met or exceed to the basis for MEPA jurisdiction asking, for example, whether a private project meeting or exceeding a wetlands threshold requires a Superseding Order of Conditions or Water Quality Certification from the Department of Environmental Protection discussed in chapters 7 and 9 respectively of this

Handbook.[18] Each of these inquiries must be undertaken when determining whether MEPA review is required as a result of the application of a review threshold to the project.

A critical aspect of applying the review thresholds to a privately funded private project is relating the review thresholds to subject matter jurisdiction. The review thresholds apply to these projects only if there is a permit covering the same or a similar topic as the issue governed by the review threshold (or if an issue arising in an area subject to a land transfer from a state agency is the same as or similar to the issue governed by the review threshold). The environmental impact topics addressed by the review thresholds are typically reflected in the review threshold subsection headings (e.g., "wetlands, waterways, and tidelands" or "water"),[19] but even here there may be exceptions, such as in the "transportation" context, which covers roadways, transit, airports and traffic-generating land uses.[20] Any permit of any subject matter is deemed related to the review thresholds for alterations and conversions of land and for projects within Areas of Critical Environmental Concern, although subject matter jurisdiction limitations on the scope of review remain.[21]

There are certain exclusions from the review thresholds, and thus generally from MEPA review. One exclusion covers any lawfully existing structure, facility, or activity. Another is keyed to the Special Review Procedure mechanism, with an exclusion for projects that are consistent with a programmatic or area-wide review. The terms for determining consistency are ordinarily to be spelled out in the Secretary's Certificates on the Special Review Procedure. Finally, there are exclusions for "routine maintenance" and a "replacement project," each of which is defined in the regulations.[22] A proponent may seek an advisory opinion of the Secretary before relying on an exclusion.[23]

FAIL-SAFE REVIEW

There is another mechanism for requiring MEPA review beyond the review thresholds. An agency or a group of ten individuals may request that the Secretary (or the Secretary may on her own initiative) require a proponent to file an ENF or undergo other MEPA review for a project that does not meet or exceed any review thresholds so long as there remain some agency actions to be taken (e.g., a permit to be granted) on the project.[24] In order to grant this fail-safe review, the Secretary must find that: (a) the project is subject to MEPA jurisdiction and has the potential to cause damage to the environment; (b) the potential damage to the environment. either was not reasonably foreseeable or would be caused by an extraordinary set of circumstances; and (c) invoking fail-safe review is essential to avoid or minimize damage to the environment and will not result in an undue hardship for the proponent.[25] The regulations specify the steps to be taken (and timeframe within which they must be taken) to petition for and receive a decision concerning fail-safe review.[26]

THE ENVIRONMENTAL NOTIFICATION FORM

The Environmental Notification Form, commonly known as the ENF, is available from the MEPA Office or from the MEPA website.[27] The proponent shall complete the ENF in accordance with the regulations and any instructions provided on or with the ENF.[28] The proponent shall attach to the ENF an original United States Geologic Survey Map or other location map expressly approved by the Secretary that includes and indicates the project site, a site plan at an appropriate scale and level of detail, and a list of all those to whom the proponent circulated the ENF.[29] The regulations specify (in addition to certain absolute rules regarding the timing of filing) that the proponent may consult with the Secretary (typically, the consultation is with the MEPA Director) for specific advice as to when to file the ENF.[30]

The ENF shall: (a) include a concise but accurate description of the project and its alternatives; (b) identify any review thresholds the project may meet or exceed and any agency action it may require; (c) present the proponent's initial assessment of potential environmental impacts; and (d) propose mitigation measures. The ENF may include a proposed scope.[31]

In addition to filing a completed ENF and the required attachments, the proponent may file an expanded ENF containing more extensive and detailed information describing the project and its alternatives and assessing its potential environmental impacts and mitigation measures. Although the proponent may provide such additional information whenever it is available, it must provide it when requesting a single EIR, a Special Review Procedure, or a waiver. The Secretary shall duly consider such additional information in the ENF, although it shall not limit the Secretary's discretion to determine the scope.[32]

Upon receiving and accepting the ENF, the Secretary shall circulate it to agencies and relevant municipalities and shall publish the appropriate pages of the ENF in the next *Environmental Monitor,* which begins the review period for an ENF. The review period for an ENF lasts for thirty days (thirty-seven for an expanded ENF), unless extended by the Secretary on account of the proponent's failure to meet circulation or public notice requirements or with the consent of the proponent.[33] After receiving and accepting an ENF, the Secretary shall review the ENF and receive into the record written comments from anyone.[34] The Secretary may review relevant information from any source to determine whether to require an EIR, and, if so, what to require in the scope.[35] The Secretary shall ordinarily schedule with the proponent a site visit and public consultation session.[36]

Comments shall be filed with the Secretary within twenty days (thirty days for an expanded ENF) following publication of the ENF in the *Environmental Monitor* unless the comment period is extended (ordinarily for not more than thirty days). The Secretary may accept a late comment provided it is received prior to the Secretary's decision on the ENF.[37]

An agency shall review an ENF circulated to it by the proponent.[38] If it appears that the agency will act on the project, the agency shall participate in the consultation session and file comments with the Secretary.[39] Its comments shall specify any action required to be taken by the agency for the project; any aspect of the project or issue requiring additional description or analysis in an BIR; and any opportunity to maximize consistency and facilitate coordination between the agency action and MEPA review or any other agency actions.[40]

After the close of the public comment period and on or prior to the last day of the ENF review period, the Secretary shall issue a written certificate stating whether or not an EIR is required and, if so, what to require in the scope.[41] When issuing a scope, the Secretary shall ordinarily require a draft and final EIR but may allow only a single EIR ("one-pass review") if the Secretary makes specific findings based on the expanded ENF.[42] In all cases, the Secretary shall limit the scope of the EIR to those aspects of the project that are likely, directly or indirectly, to cause damage to the environment.[43] In the case of a privately funded private project, the scope shall be limited to the direct and indirect potential environmental impacts from those aspects of the project that are within the subject matter of any required permit or within the area subject to a land transfer.[44] The Secretary shall determine the form, content, level of detail, and alternatives required for the EIR and may establish guidelines as to page length and time necessary for preparation.[45] The Secretary may direct the proponent to consult with any agency and describe in the EIR any opportunity to maximize consistency and facilitate coordination between any agency action and MEPA review or any other agency action.[46]

THE ENVIRONMENTAL IMPACT REPORT

If the Secretary requires an EIR, the proponent shall prepare the EIR as soon thereafter as reasonably possible given the status of project planning and design, the type and size of the project, and the scope.[47] The proponent shall file the EIR with the Secretary and circulate copies of the EIR.[48] The proponent's failure to circulate the EIR properly shall allow the Secretary to require an extension or repetition of the EIR review.[49]

If the Secretary requires an EIR, the proponent shall first prepare a draft EIR, unless otherwise indicated in the scope.[50] The draft EIR shall present a reasonably complete and stand-alone description of the project and its alternatives, and an assessment of its potential environmental impacts and mitigation measures.[51] If the Secretary determines that the draft EIR is adequate, the proponent shall prepare a final EIR, the scope of which the Secretary may limit to aspects of the project or issues that require further description or analysis and a response to comments, instead of requiring a stand-alone document that meets all of the form and content requirements for an EIR.[52] If the Secretary has allowed a single EIR, the single EIR shall build on the information in the expanded ENF and shall present a complete, stand-alone and definitive description of the project and its alternatives, and assessment of its potential environmental impacts and mitigation measures sufficient to allow a participating agency to fulfill its Section 61 obligations.[53]

Unless the Secretary has indicated otherwise in the scope or as part of a Special Review Procedure, the depth and level of description and assessment in the EIR shall reflect the status of project planning and design, the type and size of the project, the requirements of any agency action, the availability of reasonable alternatives and methods to avoid or minimize potential environmental impacts, and the opportunity to assess environmental impacts and to identify appropriate mitigation measures.[54] The regulations prescribe the sections ordinarily to be contained in the EIR, unless the Secretary indicates in the scope or as a part of a Special Review Procedure that specific issues shall be described or analyzed in additional sections in the EIR or that any of the ordinary sections shall not be included in the EIR.[55]

Upon receiving the EIR, the Secretary shall publish notice of the availability of the EIR in the next *Environmental Monitor,* which begins the EIR review period.[56] The EIR review period lasts for 37 days, unless extended by the Secretary on account of the proponent's failure to meet circulation or public notice requirements, with the consent of the proponent for a draft EIR, or as part of a Special Review Procedure.[57]

An agency undertaking a project may hold public hearings, informal workshops, or public meetings at appropriate times prior to and during preparation of an EIR. The Secretary may hold an informational meeting prior to or during review of the EIR, and may, in the scope, require the proponent to hold an informational meeting.[58]

Comments on the EIR shall be filed with the Secretary within thirty days of the publication of the notice of filing of the EIR in the *Environmental Monitor* unless the public comment period is extended (ordinarily for not more than thirtydays). The Secretary may accept a late comment, provided that it is received prior to the Secretary's decision on the EIR.[59]

With the consent of the Secretary, the proponent may withdraw a single or final EIR prior to the Secretary's decision on the single or final EIR to provide further opportunity for public review (an extension of the review period for a single or final BIR, as opposed to withdrawal and resubmittal, would inappropriately intrude upon applicable legal challenge periods). After such withdrawal, the proponent may refile the single or final EIR, with or without changes, additions, or deletions, which shall be clearly identified in the refiled single or final EIR. The Secretary shall publish notice of the availability of the refiled single or final BIR in the next *Environmental Monitor.* A refiled single or final EIR restarts the review, comment and legal challenge periods.[60]

An agency shall review an EIR circulated to it by the proponent.[61] If it appears that the agency may have to act on the project, the agency shall file comments with the Secretary and specify in its comments: any required agency action; any aspect of the project or issue requiring additional description or analysis; and any opportunity to maximize consistency and facilitate coordination between the agency action and MEPA review or any other agency actions.[62]

Within seven days after the close of the comment period, the Secretary shall issue a written certificate stating whether or not the EIR adequately and properly complies with MEPA and the regulations.[63]

Upon review of a draft EIR, the Secretary shall: (a) determine that the draft EIR is adequate and require preparation of a final EIR; (b) determine that no substantive issues remain to be addressed-and publish notice in the next *Environmental Monitor* that the draft EIR shall be reviewed as a final EIR (a "roll-over EIR"); (c) or require the proponent to file responses to comments on the draft EIR and Proposed Section 61 Findings and publish notice in the next *Environmental Monitor* that such responses and findings shall be filed, circulated, and reviewed as a final EIR; or (d) determine that the draft EIR is inadequate and require the proponent to file a supplemental draft EIR.[64]

Upon review of a final EIR, the Secretary shall: (a) determine that a final EIR is adequate; or (b) determine that the final EIR is inadequate and require the proponent to file a supplemental final EIR.[65]

Upon review of a single EIR, the Secretary shall: (a) determine that the single EIR is adequate; (b) determine that substantive issues remain to be addressed and require the proponent to file a final EIR; or (c) determine that the single EIR is inadequate and require the proponent to file a supplemental single EIR.[66]

SPECIAL REVIEW PROCEDURES

With the consent of the proponent, and after consulting with any agency expected to act on a project, the Secretary may establish a Special Review Procedure for a project, notwithstanding the other provisions of the regulations, provided that the Special Review Procedure is consistent with the statutory requirements of MEPA. Among other things, a Special Review Procedure may provide for: review documents other than ENFs and EIRs and other periodic reports to be filed and reviewed; shortened or extended review periods; review of a project in phases, and establishment of a Citizens Advisory Committee.[67]

The proponent shall ordinarily request a Special Review Procedure prior to or when filing the ENF. The Secretary makes specific findings in the certificate establishing the Special Review Procedure. The Secretary shall publish notice in the *Environmental Monitor* of various significant steps in the Special Review Procedure.[68]

When establishing or modifying a Special Review Procedure, the Secretary shall ordinarily (in the case of a public project) or may (in the case of a private project) establish a Citizens Advisory Committee ("CAC") to assist in reviewing the project.[69] The CAC shall ordinarily consist of at least ten persons (including at least one representing the proponent).[70] The membership of the CAC shall be diverse in affiliation and experience and fairly represent a range of viewpoints.[71] The CAC shall ordinarily participate in the Special Review Procedure by advising in the Secretary's establishment of the Special Review Procedure and review of documents called for in the Special Review Procedure, and in the Proponent's review of detailed scopes of service for the consultant and preliminary review of the consultant work product.[72]

The regulations describe three types of Special Review Procedures. Programmatic Review shall be designed to assist an agency in fulfilling its obligations in accordance with Section 61 to review periodically, to evaluate, and to determine the potential significant environmental impacts of its implementation of its programs, regulations, and policies.[73] Area-Wide Review shall be designed to assist a proponent in establishing a future baseline in relation to which a project and its alternatives can be described and analyzed and its potential environmental impacts and mitigation measures can be assessed.[74] Coordinated Review shall be designed to assist the Secretary in adopting scoping decisions by another agency or other governmental entity, deferring to its scoping decisions, issuing joint scoping decisions or accepting a review document prepared in accordance with the statutes and regulations of the agency or entity as the full or partial equivalent of an ENF, BIR, or other review document.[75]

The regulations specify timeframes for the proponent's obligations under a Special Review Procedure.[76] The regulations also describe the potential effect of a Special Review Procedure on an individual agency action taken in accordance with its terms.[77]

PROJECT CHANGES AND LAPSES OF TIME

Unless the Secretary has indicated otherwise in the certificate on a review document or as part of a Special Review Procedure, the proponent shall (and anyone else may) file a Notice of Project Change with the Secretary if there is any material change in a project prior to the taking of all agency actions for the project. Although there is no definition of a "material change," the regulations do specify certain circumstances under which such a change certainly does not occur.[78] Unless the Secretary has indicated otherwise in the scope or as part of a Special Review Procedure, the proponent shall (and anyone else may) file a Notice of Project Change with the Secretary if more than three years have elapsed between the publication of the ENF and the publication of the notice of the availability of the single or final EIR or between (a) the publication of the notice of the availability of the single or final EIR and (b) the earlier of: (1) notification of commencement of construction (provided that the proponent has not thereafter suspended or abandoned construction for more than three years); and (2) commencement of non-construction related work or activity, including expenditure of funds for final design, property acquisition, or marketing, provided that the proponent has at all times continued to take major steps in a continuous sequence to advance the project.[79]

Unless the Secretary has indicated otherwise in e scope or as part of a Special Review Procedure, the Secretary shall deem MEPA review of a project closed if more than five years have elapsed between (a) the publication of the notice of the availability of the single or final EIR and (b) the earlier of notification of: (1) commencement of construction, (provided that the proponent has not thereafter suspended or abandoned construction for more than three years); or (2) commencement of non-construction related work or activity, including expenditure of funds for final design, property acquisition, or marketing, provided that the proponent has at all times continued to take major steps in a continuous sequence to advance the project. The proponent shall file a new ENF to open a new MEPA review, provided that the new project meets or exceeds one or more review thresholds. In the certificate on the new ENF, the Secretary shall make specific findings regarding segmentation.[80]

In determining whether a change in a project or the lapse of time might significantly increase environmental consequences, the Secretary shall consider various factors listed in the regulations (with certain carve-outs also noted), including: expansion of the project; generation of further impacts; change in expected date for commencement of the project, commencement of construction, completion date for the project, or schedule of work on the project; change of the project site; new application for a permit or new request for financial assistance or a land transfer.[81]

A proponent filing a Notice of Project Change shall circulate copies to anyone who received e ENF or commented on the ENF or any EIR. Anyone else filing a Notice of Project Change shall send a copy to the proponent prior to or when filing the Notice of Project Change with the Secretary.[82]

If the Secretary determines that a change in a project or a lapse of time may have significant environmental consequences, the Secretary shall: consult as appropriate with the proponent and others; publish notice of the Notice of Project Change in the next issue of the *Environmental Monitor;* receive into the record written comments concerning the need for and the nature of any further MEPA review, within twenty days following the publication of the notice of the Notice of Project Change; and determine within 10 days after the close of the public comment period whether the change or the lapse of time significantly increases the environmental consequences of the project such that it warrants further MEPA review by submission of a new ENF or a supplemental EIR, or changes, additions, or deletions to the scope.[83] The Secretary shall publish notice of any decision on whether to require further MEPA review as a result of a Notice of Project Change in the next *Environmental Monitor*.[84]

Any further MEPA review as a result of a Notice of Project Change shall be subject to the legal challenge periods. The Secretary's decision to require further MEPA review as a result of a Notice of Project Change shall not in itself invalidate any agency action previously taken by an agency or any conditions thereof.[85]

WAIVERS

The Secretary may waive any provision or requirement in the regulations not specifically required by MEPA itself and may impose appropriate and relevant conditions or restrictions, provided that the Secretary finds that strict compliance with the provision or requirement would result in an undue hardship for the proponent (unless based on delay in compliance by the proponent) and not serve to avoid or minimize damage to the environment.[86]

The EIR review thresholds identify projects or aspects thereof that are presumed to have particularly significant environmental impacts, and for which an EIR is presumed to benefit the project and the environment. Consequently, a waiver of an EIR review threshold shall follow the review of an expanded ENF and shall be based on a rebuttal of these presumptions.[87]

For a full EIR waiver, the Secretary shall at a minimum determine that the project is likely to cause no damage to the environment and ample and unconstrained infrastructure facilities and services exist to support the project or the aspects within subject matter jurisdiction. In support of a request for a full waiver, the proponent may provide evidence satisfactory to the Secretary that the agency action on the project will contain terms such as a condition or restriction that will cause benefits to environmental resources or quality or infrastructure facilities or services in excess of those that would result in the absence of the waiver.[88]

In the case of a partial waiver of an EIR review threshold that will allow the proponent to proceed with phase one of the project prior to preparing an EIR (a "phase one waiver"), the Secretary shall determine that: the potential environmental impacts of phase one, taken alone, are insignificant; ample and unconstrained infrastructure facilities and services exist to support phase one; the project is severable (into phase one and the rest); and the agency action on phase one will contain terms such as a condition or restriction in a permit, contract or other relevant document approving or allowing the agency action (or other evidence satisfactory to the Secretary) so as to ensure due compliance with MEPA and the regulations prior to commencement of any other phase of the project.[89]

A proponent shall request a waiver in writing and shall address with particularity any findings that the Secretary is required to make. The proponent who requests a waiver shall be deemed to consent to an extension of the review period. The Secretary shall publish notice of this request in the next *Environmental Monitor*.[90]

If the Secretary decides that a waiver request has merit, the Secretary shall prepare a record of decision that describes the project, the nature and extent of MEPA jurisdiction, and the potential environmental impacts from the project and mitigation measures, and sets forth the reasons for the waiver, including any required findings. The Secretary shall issue a draft record of decision for each full or phase one waiver of an EIR review threshold and publish the draft record of decision in the next *Environmental Monitor,* which begins the public comment period. The public comment period lasts for fourteen days, unless extended by the Secretary (ordinarily for not more than fourteen days) with the consent of the proponent. During the public comment period, the Secretary shall receive written comments into the record from anyone concerning the draft record of decision. The Secretary shall issue a final record of decision or a scope within seven days after the close of the public comment period. The Secretary shall publish notice of a decision on a waiver request in the next *Environmental Monitor* whether or not preceded by a draft record of decision.[91]

SECTION 61 FINDINGS

In accordance with Section 61 of MEPA itself, any agency that takes agency action on a project for which the Secretary required an EIR shall determine whether the project is likely, directly or indirectly, to cause any damage to the environment and make a finding describing the damage to the environment and confirming that all feasible measures have been taken to avoid or minimize the damage to the environment.[92] In 2008, Section 61 was amended by the Global Warming Solutions Act to include " reasonably foreseeable climate change impacts . . . and effects" in an EIR. In 2021, "An Act Creating a Next-Generation Roadmap for Massachusetts Climate Policy" builds on the Global Warming Solutions Act by setting as-yet-unspecified emissions limits with an ultimate goal of at least net zero statewide greenhouse gas emissions but in no event shall 2050 emissions be higher than a level 85 percent below the 1990 level. In the short term, 2030 emissions shall be 50 percent below the 1990 level, and 75 percent below the 1990 level for 2040. Mass DEP has the lead on engaging stakeholders, conducting public hearing, and proposing emission limits in five-year increments between 2025 and 2050.

The agency shall base its Section 61 Findings on the EIR and shall specify in detail: all feasible measures to be taken by the proponent or anyone else to avoid damage to the environment or, to the extent damage to the environment cannot be avoided, to minimize and mitigate damage to the environment to the maximum extent practicable; anyone responsible for funding and implementing mitigation measures, if not the proponent; and the anticipated implementation schedule that will ensure that mitigation measures shall be implemented prior to or when warranted by environmental impacts.[93]

Provided that mitigation measures are specified as conditions to or restrictions on the agency action, the agency shall: make its Section 61 Findings part of the permit, contract or other document allowing or approving the agency action, which may include additional conditions to or restrictions on the project in accordance with other applicable statutes and regulations, or refer in its Section 61 Findings to applicable sections of the relevant permit, contract or other document approving or allowing the agency action.[94]

In the case of a private project, any participating agency shall limit its Section 61 Findings or any mitigation measures specified as conditions to or restrictions on the agency action, to those aspects of the project that are within the subject matter of any required permit or within the area subject to a land transfer.[95] Proposed Section 61 Findings prepared by a proponent as part of an EIR are intended to assist a participating agency in fulfilling its Section 61 obligations but shall not mean thata participating agency has made its own Section 61 Findings.[96] The proponent and a participating agency shall each file a copy of the Section 61 Findings with the Secretary, who shall publish notice of the availability of the Section 61 Findings in the next *Environmental Monitor*, and shall each circulate copies of the Section 61 Findings to anyone upon request.[97]

LEGAL CHALLENGES

There are three noteworthy things about legal challenges under MEPA: they are difficult to file successfully (relating to cause of action constraints); they require detailed attention to procedure (reflecting pre-filing notice of intent and statute of limitations requirements); and they may ordinarily address only issues raised during MEPA review.

MEPA itself does not create a cause of action but merely establishes a statute of limitations.[98] Consequently, potential causes of action arise only out of other remedial statutes, such as the ten-citizen environmental standing statute (M.G.L. c. 214, §7A), declaratory judgment statute (M.G.L. c. 231A), or Administrative Procedures Act (M.G.L. c. 30A). Certiorari review is not available.[99]

The ten-citizen environmental standing statute allows any ten persons (individuals or entities) domiciled in the Commonwealth to bring a civil action: (1) for "equitable or declaratory relief . . . [from] damaging the environment [that] is occurring or is about to occur"; (2) when such damage "constitutes a violation of a statute, ordinance, by-law or regulation, the major purpose of which is to prevent or minimize damage to the environment."[100] It is necessary to allege damage to specific environmental resources in order to maintain a suit under this cause of action.[101] The Supreme Judicial Court has expressly held that MEPA's procedural requirements can be enforced under this statute, although no reported case addresses its application to MEPA's substantive directive.[102] The proper defendant—as the potential damages to the environment—is only the project proponent and not the Secretary as MEPA administrator (nor, presumably, other regulators issuing Section 61 Findings).[103]

Declaratory judgment may be an appropriate remedial mechanism as well. Declaratory relief from an allegedly improper administrative action is available when: (1) there is an actual controversy; (2) the plaintiff has standing; (3) necessary parties have been joined; and (4) available administrative remedies have been exhausted.[104] Necessary parties for a declaratory action relating to a MEPA decision are the project proponent and the Secretary of Environmental

Affairs.[105] However, it may be appropriate to join the head of any state agency taking action after MEPA review if the declaratory relief charges failure to meet obligations under Section 61 of MEPA.[106] On the merits, a declaratory judgment action may be useful to challenge an agency's Section 61 Findings after they are issued, as the adequacy of Section 61 Findings is judged against the results of the BIR process, presumably including both the EIRs and the Secretary's Certificates.[107]

A final cause of action which may have some utility for administrative decisions made after the completion of MEPA review arises under the Administrative Procedures Act (APA). Judicial review under the APA exists to remedy improper decisions rendered after an adjudicatory proceeding, which occurs only when a hearing has been held in accordance with constitutional or statutory requirements.[108] The Supreme Judicial Court has suggested the APA does not apply to the Secretary's MEPA decisions.[109] It is an open question whether a subsequent permit decision. informed by Section 61 Findings is reviewable under the APA by reference to MEPA' s substantive standard as well as any other applicable requirements.

Finally, it is clear that certiorari review is not available for a MEPA decision because it is not quasi-judicial as it is "discretionary and require[s] no hearing.[110]

Anyone alleging that the Secretary improperly decided that a project requires an EIR shall provide notice of intent to commence an action or proceeding within 60 days of the publication of the notice of the Secretary's decision in the *Environmental Monitor.* Anyone alleging that the Secretary improperly decided that a single or final EIR complies with MEP A and the regulations shall provide notice of intent to commence an action or proceeding within 60 days of the publication of the notice of the availability of the single or final EIR in the *Environmental Monitor.* This notice shall be provided on the form available from the MEPA Office to the Secretary, the proponent, and the Attorney General. This notice shall include the EOEA file number and shall identify with particularity the reasons why the decision is believed to be improper, and the point during MEPA review at which the matter complained of was raised. The notice procedures shall substitute for the notice and waiting period required in accordance with the ten-citizen environmental statute.[111]

An action or proceeding alleging that the Secretary improperly decided that a project requires an EIR shall commence no later than the later of: 30 days following the first issuance of a permit, a grant of financial assistance, or closing of a land transfer; or 60 days after the publication of the notice of the Secretary's decision in the *Environmental Monitor.* An action or proceeding alleging that a single or final EIR for a private project fails to comply with MEPA and the regulations shall commence no later than 30 days following the first issuance of a permit, grant of financial assistance, or closing of a land transfer.[112]

An action or proceeding alleging that the Secretary improperly decided that a public project requires an EIR shall commence no later than 120 days after the publication of the notice of the Secretary's decision in the *Environmental* Monitor.[113] An action or proceeding alleging that a single or final EIR for a public project fails to comply with the requirements of MEPA and the regulations shall commence no later than 120 days after publication of the notice of the availability of the single or final EIR in the *Environmental Monitor*.[114]

No allegation shall be made in any action or proceeding challenging a decision by the Secretary unless the matter complained of was raised previously at the appropriate point during _ MEPA review, provided that a matter may be raised upon a showing that it is material and that it was not reasonably possible with due diligence to raise it during MEPA review or that the matter sought raises critically important issues regarding the potential environmental impacts of the project.[115]

PUBLIC NOTICE, THE ENVIRONMENTAL MONITOR, FILING AND CIRCULATION

The regulations detail numerous public notices, filing and circulation requirements. First, no sooner than thirty days prior to and no later than the date of publication of an ENF in the *Environmental Monitor* the proponent shall publish notice of the filing of the ENF in a newspaper of local circulation in each municipality affected by the project, or in a newspaper of statewide circulation if an affected municipality is not served by a local publication.[116]Second, the Secretary shall publish in the *Environmental Monitor* the appropriate pages of the ENF and a draft record of decision on a waiver request.[117] Third, the Secretary shall publish notice of the following filings and decisions in the *Environmental Monitor:* a request for an advisory opinion; a fail-safe decision; a decision whether an EIR is required; the availability of an EIR; a decision on an EIR; matters regarding a Special Review Procedure; the filing of a Notice of Project Change; a decision regarding a Notice of Project Change; a decision on a waiver request; and the filing of Section 61 Findings.[118] Fourth, the Secretary may publish in the *Environmental Monitor* notice of: extensions of review periods and deadlines; hearings, workshops, and meetings; and such other matters as the Secretary deems appropriate.[119] Fifth, the regulations specify to whom ENFs, EIR.s and other review documents shall be sent and direct the proponent to promptly send a copy, free of charge, to anyone requesting it during the review period.[120]

NOTES

1. M.G.L. c. 30, §62A
2. 301 C.M.R. 11.0l(l)(a).
3. *Id.; see also* M.G.L. c.30, § 61.
4. *See* 301 C.M.R. 11.0l(l)(b).
5. 301 C.M.R. 11.01(5)(a).
6. Id.
7. 301 C.M.R. 11.01(5)(b), (6)(a).
8. 301 C.M.R. 11.03.
9. 301 C.M.R. 11.01(2)(a), (b).
10. *See* 301 C.M.R. 11.03.
11. 301 C.M.R. 11.01(2)(c).
12. 301 C.M.R. 1 l.01(4)(a).
13. 301 C.M.R. 1 1 .01(4)(b). The *Environmental Monitor* published two times per month, provides public notice of the filing including environmental notification forms, environmental impact reports and notices of project changes. It is available from the MEPA office, or in abbreviated form on the MEPA website at http://www.magnet.state.ma.us/mepa.
14. 301 C.M.R. ll.01(4)(c).
15. *See* 301 C.M.R. 11.03.
16. *See, e.g.,* 301 C.M.R. ll.03(3)(a)l, (b)l; 301 C.M.R. ll.03(S)(b)4.a.
17. *See, e.g.,* 301 C.M.R. ll.03(4)(b)l; 301 C.M.R. ll.03(6)(a)6, (b)13, (b)l4.
18. *See, e.g.,* 301 C.M.R. ll.03(3)(a)l, (b)l.
19. *See* 301 C.M.R. 11.03(3), (4).
20. *See* 301 C.M.R. 11.03(6).
21. 301 C.M.R. 11.01(2)(b)2; 301 C.M.R. 11.03 (preamble); 301 C.M.R. ll.01(2)(a)2.
22. 301 C.M.R. 11.01(2)(b)3; 301 C.M.R. 11.03 (preamble).
23. 301 C.M.R. 11.01(2)(b)3; 301 C.M.R. 11.03 (preamble).
24. 301 C.M.R. 11.04(1).
25. 301 C.M.R. 11.04(1) (a)-(c).
26. *See* 301 C.M.R. 11.04(2)-(4).
27. 301 C.M.R. 11.05(5).
28. Id.
29. 301 C.M.R. 1l.05(b).
30. *See* 301 C.M.R. 11.05(2).
31. 301 C.M.R. 11.05(4).
32. 301 C.M.R. 11.05(7).
33. 301 C.M.R. 11.06(1).
34. 301 C.M.R. 11.06(2).
35. Id.
36. Id.
37. 301 C.M.R. 11.06(3).
38. 301 C.M.R. 11.06(4).

39. 301 C.M.R. 11.06(4)(a), (b).
40. 301 C.M.R. 11.06(4).
41. 301 C.M.R. 11.06(7).
42. 301 C.M.R. 11.06(8).
43. 301 C.M.R. 11.06(9)(a).
44. 301 C.M.R. 11.06(9)(b).
45. 301 C.M.R. 11.06(9)(c).
46. Id.
47. 301 C.M.R. 11.07(2).
48. 301 C.M.R. 11.07(1).
49. Id.
50. 301 C.M.R. 11.07(3).
51. Id.
52. 301 C.M.R. 11.04(4)
53. 301 C.M.R. 11.07(5).
54. 301 C.M.R. 11.07(6) (preamble).
55. *See* 301 C.M.R. 11.07(6).
56. 301 C.M.R. 11.08(1).
57. 301 C.M.R. 11.08(1).
58. 301 C.M.R. 11.08(3).
59. 301 C.M.R. 11.08(4).
60. 301 C.M.R. 11.08(5).
61. 301 C.M.R. 11.08(7).
62. 301 C.M.R. ll.08(7)(a), (b).
63. 301 C.M.R. ll.08(8)(a).
64. 301 C.M.R. 11.08(8)(b).
65. 301 C.M.R. 11.08(8)(c).
66. 301 C.M.R. 11.08(8)(d).
67. 301 C.M.R. 11.09(1).
68. 301 C.M.R. 11.09(2).
69. 301 C.M.R. 11.09(3).
70. 301 C.M.R. 11.09(3)(a).
71. Id.
72. 301 C.M.R. 11.09(3)(b).
73. 301 C.M.R. 11.09(4)(a).
74. 301 C.M.R. 11.09(4)(b).
75. 301 C.M.R. 11.09(4)(c).
76. 301 C.M.R. 11.09(5).
77. 301 C.M.R. 11.09(b).
78. 301 C.M.R. 11.10(1).
79. 301 C.M.R. 11.10(2).
80. 301 C.M.R. 11.10(3).
81. 301 C.M.R. 11.10(6).
82. 301 C.M.R. 11.10(7).
83. 301 C.M.R. 11.10(8).

84. 301 C.M.R. 11.10(9).
85. 301 C.M.R. 11.10(10).
86. 301 C.M.R. 11.11(1).
87. 301 C.M.R. 11.11(2).
88. 301 C.M.R. 11.11(3).
89. 301 C.M.R. 11.11(4).
90. 301 C.M.R. 11.11(5).
91. 301 C.M.R. 11.11(6).
92. 301 C.M.R. 11.12(5).
93. 301 C.M.R. 11.12(5)(a).
94. 301 C.M.R. 11.12(5)(b).
95. 301 C.M.R. 11.12(5)(c).
96. 301 C.M.R. 11.12(5)(d).
97. 301 C.M.R. 11.12(5){e).
98. *Cummings v. Secretary of Environmental Affairs* 402 Mass. 611, 618 (1988).
99. *Town of Walpole v. Secretary of Environmental Affairs* 405 Mass. 67, 73 (1989).
100. M.G.L. c.214, §7A.
101. *Boston Investments Ltd. v. Secretary of Environmental Affairs* 35 Mass. App. Ct. 391, 395–96 (1993) (air and noise from a loading dock); *see also Walpole* 405 Mass. at 71 (complaint dismissed with alleged harm resulted only from tests performed on potential waste sites by environmental consultants).
102. *City of Boston v. Massachusetts Port Authority* 364 Mass. 639, 646–47 (1974).
103. *Cummings* 402 Mass. at 616; *see also Warren v. Hazardous Waste Facility Site Safety Council* 392 Mass. 107, 118 (1984) (holding that no action lay against the regulatory body allegedly violating another statute as it was not the potential damages of the environment).
104. *Villages* 410 Mass. at 106.
105. *Id.* at 106.
106. *See generally Williams v. Secretary of Human Services* 414 Mass. 551 (1993).
107. *See City of Boston v. Massachusetts Port Authority* 364 Mass. at 660 (interpreting earlier version of MEPA); *see also Secretary of the Environmental Affairs v. Massachusetts Port Authority* 366 Mass. 755, 778 (1975) (declining to assess Section 61 Findings in absence of required EIR).
108. M.G.L. c.30A, §§1, 14.
109. *City of Boston v. Massachusetts Port Authority* 364 Mass. at 662 n. 40.
110. *Walpole* 405 Mass. at 773.
111. 301 C.M.R. 11.14(1).
112. 301 C.M.R. 11.14(2)(a).
113. 301 C.M.R. 11.14(2)(b).
114. Id.
115. 301 C.M.R. 11.14(3).
116. 301 C.M.R. 11.15(1).
117. 301 C.M.R. 11.15(2)(a).

118. Id.
119. Id.
120. 301 C.M.R. 11.16(2), (3).

Chapter 4

Air Pollution Control

This chapter discusses the statutory and regulatory provisions which impose air pollution controls in Massachusetts, focusing on the Massachusetts Clean Air Act, M.G.L. c. 111, §§142A through 142K, and its implementing regulations (the "Massachusetts air program"),[1] which have been adopted by the Massachusetts Department of Environmental Protection ("MassDEP"), the environmental agency primarily responsible for controlling air pollution and enforcing the requirements of the Massachusetts air program. Because of the interrelationship between the federal Clean Air Act (the "CAA") and the Massachusetts air program, various CAA requirements, as promulgated and enforced by the U.S. Environmental Protection Agency ("EPA"), also figure in this chapter.

OVERVIEW OF THE FEDERAL-STATE RELATIONSHIP

To achieve the CAA mission of protecting national air quality and public health (including, by improving air quality currently considered impaired), the CAA controls targeted or "criteria" pollutants in geographic areas which are categorized based upon their status relative to each pollutant. The targeted "criteria" pollutants are sulfur dioxide ("SO_2"), nitrogen dioxide ("NOx"), lead ("Pb"), ground-level ozone, carbon monoxide ("CO") and particulate matter ("PM") of varying sizes (measured in microns).[2] The national ambient air quality standards ("NAAQS"), the cornerstone of the CAA, establish "benchmarks" and increasingly stringent air-quality milestones for each of these pollutants in geographic areas, variously characterized as in "severe non-attainment," "serious non-attainment," "non-attainment," "attainment" or "unclassified," depending on whether the ambient air in each area meets or exceeds NAAQS for the pollutant in question.[3] In addition, EPA has set "primary" and "secondary" standards to protect public health and public welfare interests, respectively. The standards must be reviewed and updated every five years.

Described as an "experiment in cooperative federalism,"[4] the CAA requires states to assume primary responsibility for meeting NAAQS within a set timeframe by regulating air-emission sources in a manner that brings non-attainment areas into attainment. This state-promulgated program to implement federal requirements is referred to as a State Implementation Plan ("SIP").[5] Each SIP must be approved by EPA.Among its several SIP responsibilities, for instance, each state must specify how it will comply with federal goals,[6] including by permitting stationary air-emissions sources and requiring emission-control measures designed to further reduce emissions. These permitting requirements are a centerpiece of the federal CAA and therefore the Massachusetts program. The control of emissions associated with motor vehicles or mobile air sources also (and increasingly) figure in the SIP. In short, the Massachusetts air program is shaped by the SIP, which includes most, but not all, of the air-related provisions adopted by MassDEP.[7]

MASSACHUSETTS AMBIENT AIR QUALITY AND ATTAINMENT STATUS

As of 2018 no part of Massachusetts was designated as a nonattainment area for any of the above-mentioned criteria pollutants. MassDEP has identified air-quality control regions within (or partially within) Massachusetts based upon each region's NAAQS status[8] and promulgated emissions limitations and standards which apply to stationary sources within those regions. These designations change periodically as a result of measured changes in ambient air quality, and MassDEP should be contacted for changes or updates in a region's NAAQS status, particularly since the classification may determine permitting and other applicable requirements. In addition, MassDEP regulations provide for transportation control measures to ensure compliance with the NAAQS.

STATIONARY SOURCE REQUIREMENTS

To meet NAAQS, the Massachusetts air program targets stationary and mobile sources, with the goal of reducing total annual emissions state-wide. Stationary sources, mainly electricity generating plants and manufacturing facilities, bear the brunt of that burden. In particular (and in response to its CAA mandates), the Massachusetts air program requires MassDEP review and approval[9] for the preconstruction, as well as for substantial reconstruction, of significant air-emissions sources (so-call "major" sources), *as well as* a MassDEP-issued operating permit (or, alternatively, an emissions "cap") for facilities capable of emitting significant quantities of air pollutants, including Greenhouse Gases ("GHGs").[10] The preconstruction and operating permitting programs also contain corresponding emission-control requirements, referred to by an "alphabet soup" of acronyms, including Reasonable Available Control Technology ("RACT"), Best Available Control Technology ("BACT"), and Lowest Achievable Emissions Rate ("LAER"), each of which essentially reflects the level of control technology and house-keeping procedures a facility must undertake to meet CAA requirements.[11]

While MassDEP excludes *de minimis* emissions (classified variously, but largely as sources capable of emitting less than one ton per year ("tpy")), as well as equipment operating under certain "permit by rule" provisions (for which no MassDEP approval is necessary), the majority of sizeable Massachusetts facilities with air emissions of any consequence require some sort of air permit.[12] Regulated entities also should be aware that permitting processes can be lengthy, taking from several months to in excess of a year to complete.

Major Source Preconstruction Approvals

Federal preconstruction-permitting requirements, which apply in both attainment and non-attainment areas (respectively, known as the prevention of significant deterioration ["PSD"] and New Source Review ["NSR"] programs), require certain sources to obtain permits and comply with certain emissions controls; *e.g.*, BACT for facilities receiving PSD permits, and LAER for facilities receiving NSR permits.

Prevention of Significant Deterioration Permit

The PSD program covers states, including Massachusetts, where NAAQS are now being attained. Under the PSD program, a permit must be obtained prior to the construction or major modifications[13] of a major source of air pollutants in a priority industry (known as PSD-source categories). MassDEP has not issued PSD requirements but relies upon EPA regulations.[14] A "major stationary source" is defined in EPA regulations to include a priority industry facility which emits, or has the potential to emit, at least 100 tpy of a regulated air pollutant, or any other type of stationary source which emits, or has the potential to emit, at least 250 tons per year of a regulated pollutant.[15] Priority industry categories include chemical process plants, fossil-fuel boilers, petroleum storage and transfer facilities, and various other categories.[16]

An applicant for a PSD permit may have to compile ambient air-monitoring data and to conduct mathematical modeling of the source's emission impacts to demonstrate that emissions from the source will not cause a violation of the PSD increments and NAAQS. An analysis of the source's impacts on vegetation and visibility, a demonstration of the source's compliance with new source performance standards and "air toxics" program, and its utilization of BACT for all pollutants emitted in significant quantities, also may be required.[17]

Hazardous Air Pollutants

Hazardous air pollutants ("HAPs") are those known or suspected to cause cancer or other serious health problems or adverse environmental effects. EPA is required to regulate them[18] and has, accordingly, has promulgated technology-based national emission standards for 187 HAPs ("NESHAPs") for categories of industrial sources including maximum available control technology ("MACT") and health-based standards.[19] These standards must be reviewed and updated, if necessary, every eight years.

OPERATING PERMITS AND "CAPS"

Title V Permits

Title V of the CAA established a program of operating permits for certain stationary sources of air emissions.[20] MassDEP has promulgated regulations to implement the operating permit program in Massachusetts.[21] At essence, a Title V or an operating permit is intended to contain all the emission limits, operational restrictions, monitoring and reporting requirements, and other air-pollution control provisions that apply to the permitted source under federal and Commonwealth law. All sources emitting over 50 tpy of NO_x or VOCs, 100 tpy of other criteria pollutants, 10 tpy of any Hazardous Air Pollutant ("HAP"), or 25 tpy of any combination of HAPs must obtain an operating permit from MassDEP.

Complete operating permit applications are comprehensive, often several-hundred pages long, and must contain detailed information, including information identifying the source and characterizing its emissions, as well as alternative operating scenarios which the applicant may propose to ensure operational flexibility. The application must identify all applicable air-pollution control requirements (in the Massachusetts air program) and contain a plan which documents compliance and sets forth a schedule for compliance with any requirements that have not yet been met. This compliance statement, in conjunction with the company-"certification" requirement in the permit application, can be a trap for the unwary facility operator by disclosing existing non-compliance at the facility and triggering enforcement action by MassDEP (or EPA).

MassDEP regulations call for preparation of a draft permit, public notice and opportunity to comment on the draft, opportunity for a public hearing, and submission of the proposed permit to EPA. If EPA objects to the proposed permit, MassDEP may revise the permit or, if MassDEP does not revise the permit, EPA may issue or deny the permit under the federal Title V operating permit program. Thus, EPA has veto power over the content and requirements of a facility's Title V permit.

Finally, an operating permit typically will contain monitoring and reporting obligations, as well as federal and state air-pollution control requirements, applicable to the facility. As such, Title V permits can, provided EPA, DEP and citizens groups with a "check list" by which to measure a facility's compliance and to initiate enforcement.[22]

Monitoring, Recordkeeping, and Registration Requirements

As a corollary to the permitting program, MassDEP regulations impose record-keeping and monitoring requirements upon certain sources of air emissions,[23] including the registration of smaller stationary sources not subject to the permitting requirements for "major" sources.[24] Thus, for instance, fossil-fuel combustion facilities with a rated input capacity of more than three or ten million Btu per hour ("MMBtu"), depending upon the type of fuel, are covered by the registration requirement. Similarly, subject to the registration requirements are hazardous-waste incinerators, other incinerators capable of burning in excess of 50 pounds per hour of waste, any facility emitting a pollutant covered by certain NESHAPs, and industrial facilities with a federal potential to emit at least 2.0 tpy of PM, 2.5 tpy of $SO_{s,}$ 10 tpy of organic material, or 4.4 tpy of NO_x.[25]

Incinerators and Municipal Waste Combusters

While not directly related to the PSD, NSR or operating permit requirements, MassDEP must approve the design and standard operating procedure for any new incinerator and for any substantial reconstruction or alteration of an existing incinerator.[26] In addition, the regulations call for MassDEP site location approval for "special" incinerators,[27] as well as for municipal, commercial, and industrial incinerators.

EPA issued emissions guidelines for Municipal Waste Combusters ("MWCs"), requiring states to provide appropriate SIP measures. MassDEP's regulations, applicable to several MWCs in Massachusetts, limit ambient air emissions from MWCs and require a plan to reduce toxic air emissions by separating material slated for combustion, as well as establishing timelines and fees for MassDEP's review of emissions-control plans.[28]

EMISSIONS STANDARDS AND LIMITATIONS

New Source Performance Standards

Section 111(b) of the CAA[29] directs EPA to publish a list of stationary source "categories" which EPA has concluded significantly contribute to air pollution and to establish federal, technology-based emission limitations and standards covering newly constructed sources in these categories. At essence, NSPS amount to uniform, national air-emission standards that limit the amount of pollution such sources emit, and which operate independent of the permitting requirements.

EPA has promulgated. its NSPSs[30] for many types of industrial and commercial facilities, and delegated implementation and enforcement of NSPSs in Massachusetts to MassDEP.[31]

Regulation of Sulfur and Sulfur Dioxide

MassDEP regulations contain provisions which are intended to reduce SO_2 emissions, including limitations on the sulfur content of fossil fuel burned at any facility, and a prohibition against the burning of residual fuel oil by a facility with an energy input capacity of less than three MMBtu.[32] In addition, the regulations establish a "cap" on statewide SO_2 emissions and require DEP to prepare an annual report identifying these emissions and a schedule and plan for meeting the "cap."[33]

Requirements for Miscellaneous Sources

MassDEP regulations impose limitations on the emission of some NAAQS "criteria" pollutants, as well as on certain other emissions, from various types of facilities. The categories of facilities and the pollutants covered by these limitations include the following: fossil- or wood-fuel utilization facilities with energy input capacities of at least three MMBtu per hour (PM and NO_x), ferrous cupola foundries (PM), asphalt-batching plants (PM), industrial facilities in general (PM), contact sulfuric acid plants (SO_2, acid mist, and opacity), and incinerators (PM).[34]

The MassDEP regulations also impose operating requirements on certain types of facilities. Facilities that store, handle, or distribute organic materials or motor-vehicle fuels are subject to tank design and construction, equipment usage, pressure limitation, emissions capture, and record keeping requirements while tank trucks carrying motor vehicle fuel to and from such facilities must comply with testing, washing; and vapor recovery requirements.[35] Fossil-fuel utilization facilities are also subject to certain equipment usage and monitoring requirements, as well as to inspection and testing requirements.[36]

MassDEP regulations also impose various limitations on the burning of fossil fuels by stationary sources, including limitations on the sale, distribution, and burning of used oil fuel; ceilings on the sulfur content of fuel; prohibitions on the burning of residual fuel oil or used oil fuel in furnaces that exceed certain energy input capacities; and limitations on the burning of solid fuel in hand-fired furnaces above a specified energy input capacity. MassDEP also limits the ash content of fossil fuel and the use of fuel additives, unless approved by MassDEP, the concentration of polychlorinated biphenyls ("PCBs") and other pollutants in used oil fuel, and the methods for burning such fuel. Finally, MassDEP imposes registration and record keeping requirements on fuel suppliers.[37]

Regulation of Asbestos

MassDEP regulations impose notification, work-practice, and disposal requirements applicable to the demolition and renovation of facilities containing friable asbestos or any material containing one percent or more of asbestos by weight. In most cases, the facility owner or operator must notify MassDEP in writing of such work (on a MassDEP-approved form) at least 10 working days before commencement of the work, subject to the *proviso* that such notification may be made orally within one working day of emergency demolition or renovation operations.

Regulation of Visible Emissions, Dust, Odor and Noise

MassDEP regulations impose opacity limitations on emissions of air pollutants from stationary sources. In addition, the regulations specify limitations on such visible emissions from marine vessels, aircraft, and certain kinds of engines.[38]

MassDEP also bas identified certain industrial and commercial operations and activities that can produce dust and odor, and prohibits emissions from such operations and activities which would "cause or contribute to a condition of air pollution."[39] The regulations also require written notice to MassDEP at least ten working days before initiation of construction or demolition of an industrial, commercial, or institutional building or of a residential building with twenty or more dwelling units.[40]

Under the MassDEP regulations, persons owning, leasing, or controlling "a source of sound" also must take the necessary steps to preclude "unnecessary emissions" from the source which "may cause noise."[41] The regulations provide examples of unnecessary sound emissions, such as prolonged and unattended sounding of burglar alarms, construction and demolition equipment noise that could be suppressed by the use of proper equipment, and suppressible and preventable industrial and commercial noise. The regulations also set forth certain exemptions from the noise restrictions.[42]

MOBILE SOURCE REQUIREMENTS

MassDEP regulations require inspection of vehicles registered in Massachusetts to determine their CO-and hydrocarbon-exhaust emissions, using DEP-approved emission analyzers.[43] A vehicle that fails to pass an emission test and a subsequent retest cannot be driven unless the vehicle's air pollution control devices are shown to be in working order or the estimated cost of ensuring compliance with the exhaust emission limits exceeds certain stated amounts.[44]

In 1990, the Massachusetts Legislature called for MassDEP adoption of the California vehicle-emission standards, which are more stringent than the federal standards, unless the California standards will not produce greater reductions in vehicle emissions than the federal standards.[45] MassDEP has promulgated regulations covering low emission vehicles ("LEVs"), ultra-low emission vehicles ("ULEVs"), and zero emission vehicles ("ZEVs").[46]

GREENHOUSE GASES AND CLIMATE CHANGE

Federal Regulation of Greenhouse Gases

In 2007 the U.S. Supreme Court held that CO_2 and other greenhouse gases ("GHGs") are "pollutants" and thus could be regulated by EPA under the CAA.[47] EPA then published its findings that current and projected concentrations of CO_2, methane, nitrous oxide, hydrofluorocarbons, perfluorocarbons, and sulfur hexafluoride in the atmosphere endanger public health and welfare, thus identifying these gases as "subject to regulation."[48] Earlier that year EPA published its Greenhouse Gas Reporting Rule requiring facilities that emit more than 25,000 metric tons of carbon dioxide equivalent ("CO_2e") greenhouse gases to report their emissions to EPA. EPA's enforcement of GHG emission particularly from electric power plants is in flux as three presidential administrations change the rules.

Massachusetts Regulations of Greenhouse Gases

M.G.L. c. 111, §§142A–142N, originally enacted as part of the health code, is the principal Massachusetts law regulating air pollution. Under Chapter 111, MassDEP is authorized to regulate air pollution sources, order cessation of violations, and enforce against violators with criminal penalties up to $25,000 or one year in jail or both, and civil penalties up to $25,000 per day per offense. The regulation are found at 310 C.M.R. 6.00 (codifying NAAQS), 7.00, 8.00 (authorizing MassDEP to declare and deal with air pollution episodes and emergencies), and 60.00 (authorizing the vehicle emission inspection program and limiting CO_2 emissions from state-owned vehicles). Part 7.00 regulates stationary (industrial facilities, fossil-fuel-fired power plants, dry cleaners, and more) and mobile sources (automobiles) and is broad in its coverage.

MassDEP requires submission of plan approvals (with some exemptions) by any owner or operator intending to construct, substantially reconstruct, or alter its facility.[49] Depending on the size or emission potential of a facility, plan approvals may be comprehensive or limited.[50] Regardless whether the facility requires a comprehensive or limited plan approval, all facilities requiring a plan approval must demonstrate the inclusion of Best Available Control Technology, that other facilities owned by the owner-operator are in compliance with 310 C.M.R. 7.00 and any permits, and that the proposed new emission would not cause Massachusetts to violate applicable NAAQS.[51]

Major new sources[52] must comply with the lowest achievable emission rate ("LAER") and, the source must use emission offsets at a greater than 1:1 ration to ensure a net air quality benefit. Federal regulations define "major" as the source having the potential to emit at least 250 tpy of a regulated pollutant or 100 tpy if the source falls within a listed source category. Federal PSDF regulations apply to major new stationary sources and modifications to existing sources that significantly increase the source's potential to emit criteria pollutants for which the area is in "attainment."

All sources with the potential to emit more than 50 tpy of NO_x or VOCs, 10 tpy of one HAP or 25 tpy of any combination of HAPs, or 100 tpy of any other regulated pollutant must have a Title V operating permit. A facility does not need an operating permit for solely GHG emissions, but it is required to report those emissions to MassDEP.[53] Many facilities must register their emissions on an annual or triennial basis depending on the size of the facility.[54] Owners and operators may be required by MassDEP to conduct emission tests.[55]

In 2008 the Massachusetts legislature enacted the Global Warming Solutions Act ("GWSA")[56] requiring the state to set GHG emission reduction goals. The GWSA also included a reporting requirement for large GHG emitters. The legislature also enacted the Green Communities Act ("GCA") which focused on increasing the availability of renewable and alternative energy and All Massachusetts regulations may be enforced by MassDEP, any local health department, building inspector, or police or fire department.[57]

Regional Greenhouse Gas Initiative

Massachusetts is a participant in the Regional Greenhouse Gas Initiative ("RGGI"), a multistate program to reduce emissions of carbon dioxide. RGGI is implemented by regulations.[58] The regulations establish a cap-and-trade program covering CO_2 from fossil-fired units that serve as an electricity generator with a capacity of at least 25 megawatts. The CO_2 allowances issued by Massachusetts may be sold in a joint auction with other RGGI member states.

Massachusetts also regulates the CO_2 emissions from fossil fuel-fired power plants through the Massachusetts Carbon Allowance Registry under which generators may register their facilities, receive distributed allowances using an auction system, and use, bank, or trade their allowances. Retail electricity sales are also required to include increasing amounts of clean energy, starting at 16 percent in 2018 and increasing by 2 percent every year until it reaches 80 percent in 2050.

ENFORCEMENT ISSUES

All Massachusetts regulations may be enforced by MassDEP, any local health department, building inspector, or police or fire department.[59]

Violation of a MassDEP air pollution control regulation, after due notice, constitutes a misdemeanor and is punishable by a fine of up to $25,000 for each day of violation, as well as by imprisonment for as much as one year. In addition, EPA can enforce violations of the Massachusetts SIP under the provisions of the CAA.

Violations of rules or regulations adopted by a municipal board of health or other local authority with jurisdiction over atmospheric pollution are punishable by a fine of $50 to $100 per day of violation for the first offense and $200 to $500 per day of violation for subsequent offenses. As noted earlier, atmospheric pollution is specifically defined to include industrial odors and dust. The Superior Court is given equity jurisdiction to enforce the aforementioned rules and regulations adopted by a local authority and to issue injunctions to restrain violations.[60]

NOTES

1. *See* 310 C.M.R. 6.01 to 6.04, 7.00 to 7.60 (and appendices)., and 8.01 to 8.31.

2. While DEP adopted federal NAAQS (except for PM_{10}), in some instances EPA has determined that the Massachusetts SIP is inadequate to ensure compliance with the NAAQS and issued supplemental regulations.

3. *See* 42 U.S.C. §§7501 to 7515.

4. *See, e.g., Connecticut* v. *EPA* 696 F.2d 147, 151 (2nd Cir. 1982).

5. 42 U.S.C. §§7401 to 7671q.

6. 42 U.S.C. §7409.

7. 40 C.F.R. Part 52, Subpart W; the specific MassDEP regulations which have been approved by EPA are identified at 40 C.F.R. §52.1120. *See also* 310 C.M.R. §7.00.

8. *See* 310 C.M.R. §§7.00 to 7.60. The air quality control districts are comprised of all of the intrastate air quality regions and the Massachusetts portions of the interstate air quality regions which are set forth at 40 C.F.R. § 52.1121 and in the Legend, description found at the beginning of 310 C.M.R. §7.00. The districts are identified as the Metropolitan Boston District, the Merrimack Valley District, the Southeastern Massachusetts District, the Central Massachusetts District, the Pioneer Valley District, and the Berkshire District.

9. MassDEP uses the term "plans approval," as a synonym for permit. *See* 310 C.M.R. §7.02.

10. *See* 310 C.M.R. 7.02(2) and (4). In certain circumstances, a streamlined approval process is applicable.

11. For instance, BACT is defined as an emission limitation based on the maximum degree of reduction of a regulated air contaminant which DEP determines is achievable on a case-by-case basis, taking into account energy, environmental, and economic impacts and other costs. *See* 310 C.M.R. 7.00. Although DEP has not yet promulgated substantive BACT regulations for implementing the requirement, available policies have informed DEP's BACT decisions to date. Similarly, LAER is defined as the rate of emissions which reflects the most stringent emission limitation io the SIP of any state or which has been achieved in practice by comparable sources. 310 C.M.R. 7.00, Appendix A.

12. *See, e.g.,* 310 C.M.R. 7.02(4)(a)(l) and (10). This is in part because DEP uses a hypothetical calculation, known as the "potential to emit" ("PTE") calculation, to define a source's emissions. To determine its PTE, a source must calculate its ability to release pollutants to the ambient air under the assumption that each piece of equipment in the facility io question is operating twenty-four hours a day, 365 days per year (or "8760" hours). While there are some mechanisms for limiting or off-setting PTE, PTE calculations often grossly overstate a source's emissions, with the result that seemingly small emissions sources nonetheless trigger permitting thresholds.

13. PSD requirements are similar to non-attainment review requirements (discussed below), although there are differences in the definition of major source which impact pollution control measures and applicable pollutants. A "major modification" is defined in EPA's regulations as a physical change in a major source or in its method of operation that would result in a significant net increase in the emission of a regulated air pollutant. 40 C.F.R. § 52.2l(b)(2). A significant net increase is in tum identified in the regulations for several pollutants, including CO (100 tons per year), NOx (40 tons per year), PM (25 tons per year in general or 15 tons per year of PM10 emissions), ozone (40 tons per year of volatile organic compounds ("VOCs")), and lead (0.6 tons per year). 40 C.F.R. § 52.2l(b)(23).

14. *See* 310 C.M.R. 7.02(2)(a) (referencing 40 C.F.R. § 52.21).

15. 40 C.F.R. § 52.2l(b)(l). Because to require a PSD permit, a source must both meet the 100-tpy emissions limit and be a regulated source category, PSD permits are not as commonplace as NSR or operating permits.

16. 40 C.F.R. §52.21.

17. 40 C.F.R. §52.21(i).

18. 42 U.S.C. §7412.

19. 40 C.F.R. pts. 61 and 63.

20. 42 U.S.C.§§ 7661 to 7661f.

21. *See* 310 C.M.R. 7.00, Appendix C.

22. The regulations also contain an "application shield" which protects a party that has submitted a timely and complete permit application from enforcement for operating without a permit.

23. 310 C.M.R. 7.12, 7.13, and 7.14.

24.Annual registration is required for any facility with actual emissions greater than or equal to 25 tons pe year of VOCs or NO_x or 100 tons per year of any other pollutant regulated under the federal Clean Air Act. 310 C.M.R. 7.12(1)(a) and (b).

25. 310 C.M.R. 7.12(4) to (6).

26. *See* 310 C.M.R. 7.08.

27. A "special incinerator" is defined as one designed for a special purpose, such as the burning of biological, pathological, or toxicological refuse, or an incinerator for a specific facility. 310 C.M.R. 7.00 (Definitions).

28. *See* 310 C.M.R. 7.08(2); 310 C.M.R. 4.10.

29. 42 U.S.C. §7411(b).

30. *See* 40 C.F.R. Part 60.

31. 40 C.F.R. § 60.4(b){W).

32. 310 C.M.R. 7.05(1) and (2).

33. 310 C.M.R. 7.21 and 7.22.

34. 310 C.M.R. 7.02(8)–(11).

35. 310 C.M.R. 7.24.

36. 310 C.M.R. 7.04.

37. 310 C.M.R. 7.04 and 7.05.

38. 310 C.M.R. 7.06.

39. 310 C.M.R. 7.09.

40. 310 C.M.R. 7.09(2).

41. 310 C.M.R. 7.10(1).

42. 310 C.M.R. 7.10(2) and (3).

43. Under Section209(a) of the CAA, states (except California) may not promulgate individual motor-vehicle emissions standards to attain NAAQS. *See* 42 U.S.C. § 7543. Thus, states merely duplicate the federal and certain California requirements.

44. 310 C.M.R. 7.16.

45. M.G.L. c. 111 § 142K..

46. 310 C.M.R. 7.40.

47. *Massachusetts v. EPA*, 549 U.S. 497 (2007).

48. 74 Fed. Reg. 66,496 (Dec. 15, 2009)

49. 310 C.M.R. 7.02.

50. 310 C.M.R. 7.02(5), 7.02(4), respectively.

51. 310 C.M.R. 7.02(3)(j).

52. pollutant, or major modifications must satisfy additional requirements. 310 C.M.R. 7.02 and 310 C.M.R. 7.00, App. A.

53. 310 C.M.R. 7.71.

54. 310 C.M.R. 7.12 (l)..

55. 310 C.M.R. 7.13, 7.14.

56. M.G.L. c. 21N.

57. 310 C.M.R. 7.52

58. M.G.L. c. 21A, §22;

59. 310 C.M.R. 7.52

60. M.G.L. c. 111, §31C.

Chapter 5

Water Pollution Control

The primary water pollution control statute is the Massachusetts Clean Waters Act, M.G.L. c. 21, §§26–53. This statute directs MassDEP to take all actions necessary to secure the benefits of the federal Clean Water Act,[1] adopt water quality standards, prescribe effluent limitations and permit programs for the discharge of pollutants to Massachusetts waters, and adopt regulations for the operation and maintenance of wastewater treatment facilities. The regulations that implement the Clean Waters Act are set forth at 314 C.M.R. 2.01 to 12.10.

"Pollutant" is broadly defined to include "any element or property of sewage, agricultural, industrial or commercial waste, runoff, leachate, heated effluent, or other matter in whatever form and whether originating at a point or major nonpoint source, which is or may be discharged, drained, or otherwise introduced into any sewage system, treatment works, or waters of the commonwealth."[2] "Waters of the commonwealth" are defined to include surface and groundwaters.[3] MassDEP also includes disposal of wastes on land that may leach into groundwater. By contrast, the federal Clean Water Act covers surface waters and only discharges from a point source.

WATER QUALITY STANDARDS

Surface Waters

The Massachusetts Clean Waters Act requires MassDEP to adopt minimum water quality standards,[4] which MassDEP has promulgated for Massachusetts surface waters at 314 C.M.R. 4.00, and for groundwaters at 314 C.M.R. 5.00. These standards establish ambient concentration and other limits for various physical, chemical, biological, and aesthetic surface water parameters, including concentrations of specified pollutants.[5] In all cases, however, all surface water "shall be free from pollutants in concentrations or combinations that are toxic to humans, aquatic life, or wildlife."[6] In general, the standards include a designation of uses for particular surface waters, minimum criteria to sustain those uses, and a classification system under which all segments of surface waters are assigned to a class of uses. Class A surface waters are primarily a source of public water supply. Class B surface waters are habitat for fish and wildlife, primary and secondary contact recreation, and, where designated, public water supply with appropriate treatment. In applying these standards, MassDEP may allow a "mixing zone" in the receiving waterbody for dilution purposes provided the mixing zone does not interfere with the migration or free movement of aquatic life. The regulations also contain antidegradation provisions, which are designed to protect existing beneficial uses of all surface waters and the quality of certain high-value or especially vulnerable surface waters.[7]

Groundwaters are classified as Class I or Class II—both a source of potable fresh or mineral water supply.[8] Class III groundwaters are used for other than a potable water supply. Except for groundwaters classified as Class III prior to March 20, 2009, all state groundwater is designated as a source of potable water supply consequently it must meet the effluent limitations in 314 C.M.R. 5.10(3)(a) and (b).[9] The sole exception is for groundwaters which MassDEP has determined is not a source of drinking water.[10]

DISCHARGES TO SURFACE WATERS

Although the U.S. Environmental Protection Agency ("EPA") can authorize a state environmental agency to implement its own permit program in place of the National Pollutant Discharge Elimination System ("NPDES") permit program under the federal Clean Water Act, EPA has not yet done so in Massachusetts. Consequently, the federal and state programs operate concurrently in the Commonwealth. MassDEP reviews NPDES permit applications and may add conditions to the permit beyond those prescribed by EPA.

Unless an exemption applies, MassDEP regulations require a permit for the discharge of pollutants to surface waters of the Commonwealth, as well as for the construction, installation, modification, operation, or maintenance of an outlet for such a discharge or a treatment works required to treat such a discharge, and for any other activity that may reasonably result, either directly or indirectly, in such a discharge.

Among the discharges subject to the permit requirement are point source discharges of pollutants to surface waters from publicly and privately owned treatment works, including any bypasses or overflows from such works, and from manufacturing, commercial, and mining activities and processes, whether treated or untreated.[11] MassDEP regulations contain a list of discharges that are exempt from the permit requirement. These discharges include: (a) certain discharges from waterborne vessels; (b) discharges of dredged or fill material that are regulated under Section 404 of the federal Clean Water Act[12] and are exempted from the need for a permit pursuant to the state water quality certification regulations; and (c) certain non-point discharges of pollutants from agricultural and silvicultural activities.[13]

In addition to the surface water discharge regulations, EPA has issued stormwater management standards geared toward controlling water quality problems due to urban runoff and discharges from stormwater outfalls. The projects to which these standards apply include industrial, commercial, institutional, and residential subdivision projects of various sizes but not single-family residence projects or residential subdivisions of four or fewer lots. For new development, the standards are implemented during routine project review by local conservation commissions or MassDEP under-the Wetlands Protection Act, and any restrictions on stormwater discharges are incorporated into the order of conditions. For existing sources of stormwater discharge, the standards are implemented by relying on MassDEP's authority under the Massachusetts Clean Waters Act for assessment and remediation of such discharges; however, existing discharges that meet the management standards do not require a surface water discharge permit.

Surface water discharge permits contain two types of conditions—general conditions and special conditions. General conditions apply to every permit issued under the surface water discharge permit regulations, whether or not they are specified in the permit itself.[14] The general conditions are set forth in the regulations and cover numerous matters, including requirements for reporting specified types of non-compliance.[15]

Special conditions are incorporated in surface water discharge permits on a case-by-case basis. Among the types of special conditions are effluent limitations and standards; limits on permit duration, which may not exceed five years; monitoring, recordkeeping, and reporting requirements; and schedules of compliance.[16]

The effluent limitations imposed in surface water discharge permits restrict the discharge of specified pollutants to Massachusetts waters, and the permit must incorporate the more stringent of: (a) water quality-based effluent limitations; and (b) technology-based effluent limitations. A water quality-based limitation is intended to ensure that water quality standards applicable to the receiving waters will be attained and maintained. A technology-based limitation is a numerical limit that reflects the use of a specified type or level of technology.[17]

The MassDEP regulations set many technology-based effluent limitations at levels equivalent to those imposed by EPA's effluent limitations and standards under the federal Clean Water Act.[18] The federal statute typically requires EPA to base such limitations on a generically 4escribed technology that, by definition, mandates more stringent numerical limits as more effective pollution control technologies are developed.[19] Because discharge permits must be renewed periodically, such technology-based limits may become more stringent over time. The DWPC regulations also provide for variances from technology-based effluent limitations.[20]

DISCHARGES TO GROUND WATERS

Permits

The Massachusetts Clean Waters Act requires a permit for the discharge of pollutants from a point or major non-point source to waters of the Commonwealth, including ground waters, and for an outlet for such a discharge or a treatment works, as well as for any other activity that may reasonably be expected to result in the discharge of pollutants to such waters.[21] MassDEP has promulgated regulations for discharges of pollutants to ground waters at 314 C.M.R. 5.01 to 5.19, and these regulations are similar to the surface water discharge regulations.

Unless an exemption applies, the MassDEP regulations require a permit for the discharge of pollutants to ground waters of the Commonwealth, as well as for the construction, installation, modification, operation, or maintenance of an outlet for such a discharge or a treatment works required to treat such a discharge, and for any other activity that may reasonably result, either directly or indirectly, in such a discharge.[22] These discharges and activities include: (a) discharges of liquid effluent onto or below the land surface; (b) discharges of liquid effluent to percolation pits, ponds, or lagoons; (c) discharges of liquid effluent via subsurface leaching facilities such as pits, galleries, chambers, trenches, fields, and pipes; (d) discharges of liquid effluent into Class V injection wells, which are discussed in below; and (e) the collection, storage, treatment, or disposal of wastewaters or sludges in unlined pits, ponds, lagoons, or surface impoundments from which liquids seep into the ground.[23] It should be noted that the MassDEP ground water discharge regulations prohibit the issuance of a permit under certain circumstances, including the situation where a sewer system is reasonably accessible and permission to enter the sewer system can be obtained from the appropriate authorities.[24]

The MassDEP regulations contain a list of discharges that are exempt from the ground water discharge permit requirement. These include: (a) discharges of liquid effluent from sewage treatment works that are designed to receive and do receive no more than 15,000 gallons of sewage per day and comply with the MassDEP regulations applicable to subsurface disposal of sewage;

(b) discharges of not more than 2,000 gallons per day of non-contact cooling water with a temperature not exceeding 40 degrees Celsius; and discharges from a conveyance or system of conveyances operated primarily for the purpose of collecting and conveying stormwater runoff which does not constitute a "stormwater discharge." In addition, MassDEP's stormwater management standards apply to discharges to ground waters as well.[25]

The general and special conditions imposed in ground water discharge permits are similar to those found in surface water discharge permits.[26] Accordingly, ground water discharge permits generally contain the more stringent of: (a) water quality-based effluent limitations; and (b) technology-based effluent limitations.[27] Although the MassDEP regulations do not include variance provisions, they allow for the imposition of less stringent effluent limitations in certain permits covering treatment works that employ land application techniques and land utilization practices, treatment works designed and used for restoring contaminated ground water, and discharges to waters with high natural background levels of pollutants.[28] It should be noted that a ground water discharge permit or an exemption from the permit requirement does not relieve the discharger of its responsibilities under the Massachusetts underground injection control program.

Injection Wells

The federal Safe Drinking Water Act[29] provides for EPA approval of state programs to implement the federal underground injection control requirements.[30] The Massachusetts underground injection control program was developed pursuant to the Massachusetts Clean Waters Act and M.G.L. c. 111, §160, which provides for protection of water supplies and is referred to in Section 6.2 of this Handbook. The program received EPA approval in 1982.[31] The DEP regulations that implement the underground injection control program are set forth at 310 C.M.R. 27.01 to 27.11.

The Massachusetts underground injection control program covers underground injection of fluids into wells. "Fluids" are broadly defined to include any material or substance that is capable of movement, whether it is a sludge or is in a semisolid, liquid, gaseous, or any other physical state. A "well" is defined as a bored, drilled, or driven shaft, or a dug hole, whose depth is greater than its largest surface dimension.[32]

The MassDEP regulations divide underground injection wells into five classes designated as Classes I through V, and they prohibit any person from constructing, installing, or maintaining wells in Classes I, II, III, or IV.[33] These four classes include wells used by hazardous waste facilities and certain other facilities to inject fluids beneath the lowermost formation containing an underground source of drinking water, wells used to inject certain fluids associated with oil or natural gas operations or to inject fluids for storage of liquid hydrocarbons, wells used to inject fluids for extraction of minerals, and wells used by hazardous waste or radioactive waste facilities to dispose of such wastes into or above an aquifer.[34]

The MassDEP regulations generally allow for construction, installation, and maintenance of Class V wells. Such wells include: (a) cooling water return flow wells; (b) drainage wells used to drain surface storm runoff into soil or bedrock; and (c) recharge wells used to replenish the water in an aquifer.[35] The regulations, however, prohibit underground injection through a Class V well that causes pollution of underground sources of drinking water in violation of Massachusetts drinking water regulations or that has an actual or potential adverse effect on public health.[36]

Under the MassDEP regulations, owners and operators of all Class V wells other than domestic sewage septic systems below 15,000 gallons per day capacity must notify MassDEP of the existence of such wells. Although the MassDEP regulations do not appear to contain any ongoing notification requirement that would apply to newly installed Class V wells, MassDEP takes the position that registration of all Class V wells is required.[37]

Class V wells also must comply with other applicable regulations and statutes. These may include the ground water discharge permit regulations discussed below, as well as the regulations covering subsurface disposal of sanitary sewage that are discussed below. If injection fluids or fluids that occur naturally in a given rock formation move from a Class V well into any underground source of drinking water, DEP may require corrective action to prevent such movement, including closure of the well.[38]

WASTEWATER DISCHARGES FROM HAZARDOUS WASTE MANAGEMENT FACILITIES

Under the authority of the Clean Waters Act, MassDEP has promulgated supplementary water pollution control regulations for hazardous waste management facilities at 314 C.M.R. 8.01 to 8.20. These regulations impose a variety of requirements, including permit requirements, on certain wastewater treatment works that treat, store, or dispose of hazardous waste generated onsite and that have a MassDEP permit for a discharge to surface waters or ground waters.[39]

DISCHARGES TO PUBLIC SEWER SYSTEMS

Sewer Extension and Connection Permits

The Massachusetts Clean Waters Act provides that no person shall construct, maintain, modify, or use a sewer extension or connection without a MassDEP permit, unless covered by an exemption contained in the regulations.[40] MassDEP has promulgated regulations for sewer extensions and connections at 314 C.M.R. 7.01 to 7.20. These regulations define the term "sewer connection" as the sewer pipes and appurtenant works necessary to connect a building or estate to a sewer system, and they define the term "sewer extension" as the addition to a sewer system of a sewer pipe, together with appurtenant works, which when connected to the sewer system. becomes the property of, and is operated and maintained by, the person owning the sewer system.[41]

The MassDEP regulations exempt certain sewer extensions and connections from the permit requirements. These exemptions cover certain existing sewer extensions and connections and also generally cover any new connection that will contribute less than 15,000 gallons of sanitary sewage per day to the sewer system. In addition, the MassDEP regulations specify the circumstances in which alterations and modifications of, increases in flow through, and changes in use of existing sewer extensions and connections require permits or other MassDEP review.[42]

Sewer extension and connection permits contain both general conditions and special conditions. The general conditions are listed in the permit application.[43] Special conditions are established on a case-by-case basis and may include effluent limitations and standards; pretreatment requirements; limits on permit duration, which may not exceed five years; monitoring, recordkeeping, and reporting requirements; and schedules of compliance.[44]

The MassDEP regulations allow a public entity that controls a publicly owned treatment works ("POTW") to apply to MassDEP for approval to administer the system of sewer extension and connection permits for discharges of industrial waste within the POTW system.[45] However, the public entity may not administer the sewer connection permit system for discharges of industrial waste from the public entity itself,[46] MassDEP approval of an application from a public entity will be based on several criteria; and these include: (a) the adequacy of the public entity's permit program; (b) whether the public entity has EPA approval of its pretreatment program, if required; whether the public entity possesses adequate resources and has an appropriate fee program; and whether the public entity has or proposes to have a pollutant reduction program.[47]

Pretreatment Requirements

In general, discharging pollutants that interfere with the operation of a POTW or pass through the POTW without adequate treatment. Under the authority of the Clean Waters Act, MassDEP has promulgated regulations to govern the pretreatment of wastewater discharged by facilities to POTWs. In addition, pretreatment is required for industrial users of sewer systems under federal law.[48]

Categorical pretreatment standards are numerical limits for certain parameters that are established by EPA on an industry-by-industry basis and are set forth at 40 C.F.R. Chapter I, Subchapter N. The MassDEP regulations incorporate these standards, as well as other EPA regulations related to the federal categorical standards, but they qualify and elaborate on the EPA provisions.[49]

State-imposed standards are discharge limits established by MassDEP on a case-by-case basis where such limits are necessary to enforce the general and specific prohibitions described above. Such limits may be established as a condition of an individual sewer connection permit or may be incorporated in an administrative order.[50] Where a number of pretreatment prohibitions, limits, or standards cover an indirect discharge to a POTW, the most stringent requirement applies.[51]

Sewer System Requirements

The MassDEP regulations impose a variety of detailed requirements on private and public sewer systems and treatment works. The requirements address such issues as operation and maintenance, safety, wastewater sampling and analysis, recordkeeping, and reporting.

DISCHARGES TO ON-SITE SEWAGE DISPOSAL SYSTEMS AND WASTEWATER TREATMENT FACILITIES AND EQUIPMENT

On-Site Sewage Disposal Systems

MassDEP has promulgated regulations at 310 C.M.R. 15.001 to 15.505 to govern the siting, construction, and upgrading of on-site septic systems under M.G.L. c. 21A, § 13. These regulations are known as Title 5 of the State Environmental Code. MassDEP has also promulgated regulations at 310 C.M.R. 11.01 to 11.13 which consist primarily of procedural provisions applicable to Title 5.

Title *5* requires a permit from the local board of health for the construction, upgrade, or expansion of an on-site subsurface sewage disposal system, as well as a certificate of compliance from the board of health after completion of such work and prior to discharge of sewage to that system.[52] A new system, or the upgrade or expansion of an existing system, may not be approved unless it: (a) receives or is designed to receive only sanitary sewage from a facility where the total design flow is less than 10,000 gallons per day; (b) serves a facility with a total design flow of 10,000 gallons per day or greater but less than 15,000 gallons per day, provided that it complies with special requirements for systems designed for such flows and with Title *5* transition provisions applicable to certain systems for which permit applications had previously been filed or approvals had previously been granted; or (c) serves a previously approved subdivision consisting of dwellings with an aggregate design flow of 10,000 gallons per day or greater and certain conditions are met.[53] "Sanitary sewage" is defined under Title *5* as greywater and blackwater from domestic, commercial, and other non-industrial sources.[54] In addition, no system may be constructed, upgraded, or expanded if it is feasible to connect the building to a sanitary sewer, unless the system is an approved alternative system or the owner has obtained a variance pursuant to the regulations.[55]

Title *5* applies only to on-site collection, treatment, and disposal of sanitary sewage, and to the transport and disposal of associated septage and grease and does not apply to wastewater containing wastes from other activities, including but not limited to numerous industrial categories specified in the regulations. The discharge of wastes from any of the specified industries to a system regulated under Title 5 is prohibited, as is the discharge to such a system of any oil, hazardous material or waste, medical waste, radioactive waste, waste from backwash of water purification or filtration devices, and waste from certain other sources. A system that is designed for the disposal of only sanitary sewage from an industrial facility may be approved under Title 5.[56]

Title 5 includes specific design and construction standards for on-site sewage disposal systems and appurtenant equipment.[57] A system generally must consist of a septic tank discharging its effluent to a suitable subsurface sewage disposal area.[58] Title 5 also includes general criteria regarding the areas in which on-site sewage disposal systems may be located,[59] as well as various setback requirements, including setbacks from environmentally sensitive areas such as reservoirs and wetlands.[60]

Title 5 sets forth standards for determining whether an on-site sewage disposal system fails to protect public health, safety, and the environment, and requirements for upgrading a failed system. Failed systems include systems exhibiting hydraulic failures (*e.g.*, breakout or backup), and systems with cesspools or other components located within certain distances of public or private water supplies.[61] The regulations generally require inspections of systems at the time of property transfer, change of use, or expansion.[62]

Variances from the Title 5 requirements may be issued by the local board of health under certain conditions, except where expressly forbidden.[63] In addition, local boards of health may adopt and enforce their own more stringent requirements for on-site disposal of sanitary sewage.[64] The regulations also set forth procedures for obtaining approval for an implementing alternative system.[65]

Wastewater Treatment Facilities and Equipment

Under the Massachusetts Clean Waters Act, MassDEP has promulgated regulations at 314 C.M.R. 12.01 to 12.10 to govern the operation of wastewater treatment facilities. The MassDEP regulations require any person proposing to construct, install, operate, or maintain a wastewater treatment facility to obtain MassDEP approval in accordance with applicable provisions of the surface water and ground water discharge permit regulations, the supplemental requirements for wastewater discharges from hazardous waste management facilities, or the sewer extension and connection permit regulations,.[66] Although the wastewater treatment facility regulations do not specifically require a separate MassDEP approval for the construction of facilities or equipment to pretreat wastewater prior to its discharge to a sewer system, MassDEP requires such approval based on a number of statutory provisions.[67]

ENFORCEMENT

The Massachusetts Clean Waters Act includes both civil penalty and criminal penalty provisions that apply to any person who: (a) directly or indirectly discharges or allows the discharge of any pollutant into waters of the Commonwealth except in accordance with a permit issued under the Act; (b) violates any provision of the Act or any valid regulation, order, or permit promulgated or issued thereunder; (c) knowingly makes any false representation in an application, record, report, or plan required under the Act; or (d) falsifies, tampers with, or renders inaccurate a monitoring device or method required under the Act. Such a person can be subject to: (a) a civil penalty of up to $50,000 for each day of violation; or (b) imprisonment for up to one year and/or a fine of between $2,500 and $50,000 for each day of violation.[68] A person who violates the Massachusetts Clean Waters Act or a MassDEP regulation, order, or authorization issued thereunder may be subject to a penalty under the Massachusetts Administrative Penalties Act.

In addition to authorizing the imposition of civil and criminal penalties, the Massachusetts Clean Waters Act and its implementing regulations authorize MassDEP to modify, suspend, or revoke any permit for cause.[69] The Act also authorizes MassDEP personnel and certain other state agency personnel to investigate and inspect discharges and possible discharges of pollutants, monitoring equipment, and the actions taken by dischargers to comply with permit requirements.[70] MassDEP may also issue administrative orders in response to various types of unlawful behavior, including orders requiring a discharger to ·apply for a permit, to take other appropriate action under the MassDEP regulations, and to cease and desist discharging after a specified date until compliance with the order is fully achieved. The issuance of such an order does not prohibit DWPC from also seeking civil or criminal penalties.[71]

The Massachusetts Clean Waters Act also authorizes the Attorney General to seek injunctive or other equitable relief at MassDEP's request against any person violating a provision of the Act or of any permit, order, regulation, or determination issued thereunder. MassDEP must request the Attorney General to bring such a suit if MassDEP determines that a discharge or combination of discharges presents an imminent and substantial threat to the health, welfare, or livelihood of any persons.[72]

Additional enforcement provisions apply to the underground injection control program and the sewer extension and connection permit program. Under the federal Safe Drinking Water Act, any state with· a federally approved underground injection control program, such as the Massachusetts program, has primary enforcement responsibility with respect to underground injection.[73] The Commonwealth exercises its enforcement responsibility through the Massachusetts Clean Waters Act and the regulations implementing the Act, as well as under MassDEP's Title 5 requirements. Under the sewer extension and connection program, MassDEP may prohibit or otherwise restrict further extensions of or connections to a sewer system if there are violations of certain water pollution control requirements or such violations are likely to occur or if the system is or might become overloaded.[74]

NOTES

1. 33 U.S.C. §§1251 to 1387.
2. M.G.L. c. 21, §26A.
3. Id.
4. M.G.L. c. 21, § 27(5).
5. 314 C.M.R. 4.05(3) to (5).
6. 314 C.M.R. 4.05(5).
7. 314 C.M.R. 4.04.

8. 314 C.M.R. 5.11.
9. 314 C.M.R. 5.11.
10. 314 C.M.R. 5.10(9)(c).
11. 314 C.M.R. 3.03, 3.04(1).
12. 33 U.S.C. §1344.
13. 314 C.M.R. 3.04(2) to (4), 3.05.
14. 314 C.M.R. 3.10(1).
15. 314 C.M.R. 3.19.
16. 314 C.M.R. 3.10(2) to (11).
17. 314 C.M.R. 3.10(2) to (6).
18. 314 C.M.R. 3.10(5), (6).
19. *See, e.g.*, 33 U.S.C. §1316(a)(l), (b)(l)(B), (e).
20. 314 C.M.R. 3.10(12), 3.11.
21. M.G.L. c. 21, §§26A, 43(2).
22. 314 C.M.R. 5.00.
23. 314 C.M.R. 5.03, 5.04(1). *See also* 310 C.M.R. 15.000 regarding septic tanks.
24. 314 C.M.R. 5.06.
25. 314 C.M.R. 5.04(2) to (4), 5.05.
26. 314 C.M.R. 5.10(1) to (8), 5.19.
27. 314 C.M.R. 5.10(2)(b).
28. 314 C.M.R. 5.10(9).
29. 42 U.S.C. §§ 300ftO 3QOj-26.
30. 42 U.S.C. § 300h-1.
31. *See 41* Fed. Reg. 52,705 (Nov. 23, 1982).
32. 310 C.M.R. 27.02.
33. 310 C.M.R. 27.03, 27.04(1).
34. 310 C.M.R. 27.03.
35. 310 C.M.R. 27.05.
36. 310 C.M.R. 27.04(2).
37. 310 C.M.R. 27.08. However, DEP has also taken the position that a Class V well authorized under a currently valid ground water discharge permit does not require notice under the underground injection well regulations.
38. 310 C.M.R. 27.10.
39. 314 C.M.R. 8.03 to 8.09.
40. M.G.L. c. 21, § 43(2).
41. 314 C.M.R. 7.02.
42. 314 C.M.R. 7.05.
43. 314 C.M.R. 7.10(1), 7.20(21).
44. 314 C.M.R. 7.10(2) to (6).
45. 314 C.M.R. 7.16.
46. 314 C.M.R. 7.16(1).
47. 314 C.M.R. 7.16(1)(a) to (h).
48. 40 C.F.R. 403.
49. 314 C.M.R. 12.08(4)(a) to (g).
50. 314 C.M.R. 12.08(5).

51. 314 C.M.R. 12.08(6).
52. 310 C.M.R. 15.003(2), 15.020, 15.021.
53. 310 C.M.R. 15.004(2). *See* 310 C.M.R. 15.004(3).
54. 310 C.M.R. 15.002.
55. 310 C.M.R. 15.004(4).
56. 310 C.M.R. 15.004(5) to (9).
57. 310 C.M.R. 15.201 to 15.293.
58. 310 C.M.R. 15.201.
59. 310 C.M.R. 15.100 to 15.107.
60. 310 C.M.R. 15.211.
61. 310 C.M.R. 15.303 to 15.305.
62. 310 C.M.R. 15.301.
63. 310 C.M.R. 15.410 to 15.422. *See also* 310 C.M.R. 11.11, 11.12.
64. 310 C.M.R. 15.003(3), (5).
65. 310 C.M.R. 15.280 to 15 289.
66. 314 C.M.R. 12.03(4).
67. *See* M.G.L. c. 21, §§27(13), 34, 43(2),43(8); M.G.L. c. 111, §17.
68. M.G.L. c. 21, § 42.
69. M.G.L. c. 21, § 43(10); 314 C.M.R. 2.10, 3.12(1), 5.12(1), 7.12(1). *See* M.G.L. c. 21, § 45.
70. M.G.L. c. 21, § 40.
71. M.G.L. c. 21, § 44(1), (3). *See* M.G.L. c. 21, § 46A.
72. M.G.L. c. 21, § 46.
73. 42 U.S.C. §§ 300h-l(b)(3), 300h-4(c)(l), (2).
74. 314 C.M.R. 7.04.

Chapter 6

Protection and Regulation of Water Supplies

Under M.G.L. c. 111, §§159 and 160, MassDEP is charged with "general oversight and care" of all surface waters and ground waters used as sources of ice or water supply and of all springs, streams, and watercourses tributary thereto and is authorized to adopt rules and regulations and issue orders necessary to protect such waters. To implement these provisions, MassDEP has issued drinking water regulations at 310 C.M.R. 22.01 to 22.2.

SCOPE OF COVERAGE

MassDEP's drinking water regulations apply to any "public water system," which is defined as a system that provides the public with piped water for human consumption and: (a) has at least 15 service connections; or (b) regularly serves an average of at least 25 individuals daily at least 60 days of the year.[1] A public water system falls within one of two categories: (a) a "community water system," which is a system serving at least 15 service connections used by year-round residents or regularly serving at least 25 year-round residents; or (b) a "non-community water system," which is any public water system that is not a community water system.[2] Non-community water systems are either non-transient or transient. A "non-transient non-community water system" is a non-community public water system that regularly serves at least 25 people for approximately four or more hours per day, at least four days per week, and at least six months or 180 days per year, such as a workplace providing water to its employees. A "transient noncommunity water system" is a non-community public water system that serves water to 25 different people at least 60 days per year, such as restaurants, motels, campgrounds, parks, golf courses, ski areas, and community centers.[3] The classification of a public water system is important because it can affect which of MassDEP's requirements apply to the system.

The regulations do not apply to a public water system that: (a) consists only of distribution and storage facilities and does not have any collection and treatment facilities; (b) obtains all of its water from but is not owned or operated by a public water system to which the regulations apply; (c) does not sell water to any person; and (d) is not a carrier which conveys passengers in commerce.[4]

APPROVAL, LOCATION, AND CONSTRUCTION REQUIREMENTS

MassDEP's drinking water regulations prohibit any person from constructing, substantially modifying, or operating a public water system without obtaining MassDEP approval of the system, and MassDEP will not grant such approval unless: (a) the source of supply will meet criteria set forth in the MassDEP regulations; (b) the storage, treatment, and distribution facilities for the system will be designed and constructed in accordance with the MassDEP regulations and guidelines DEP's guidelines; and (c) the owner and operator of the system demonstrates to MassDEP's satisfaction that they have the technical, managerial, and financial resources to operate and maintain the system in a reliable manner and provide continuous adequate service to consumers.[5]

MassDEP's regulations specify types of land areas that should be avoided in locating a new or substantially modified public water system, including certain areas subject to a significant risk from earthquakes, floods, fires, or other disasters.[6] In addition, MassDEP's regulations contain construction standards applicable to distribution systems for public water supplies,[7] and MassDEP's public water system guidelines contain specifications, design criteria, and construction standards for public water systems.[8]

SYSTEMS UTILIZING GROUND WATER SOURCES

MassDEP's regulations provide that no public water supply well or wellfield may be constructed, expanded, replaced, or brought on-line unless: (a) the proponent has complied with MassDEP's guidelines; (b) the water supply will achieve applicable water quality standards specified in the regulations; (c) the proponent has properly determined and obtained ownership or control over land within a specified protective radius around the well or wellfield (Zone I); (d) current and future land uses within Zone I are limited and will have no significant adverse impact on water quality; and (e) the proponent has obtained written approval from MassDEP.[9] The regulations further provide that suppliers of water shall acquire sufficient land around wells, infiltration galleries, springs, and other sources of ground water used for drinking water to protect the water from contamination.[10] Criteria for determining the necessary amount of land to be acquired or controlled under the aforementioned provisions are set forth in MassDEP's regulations and public water system guidelines.[11] In addition, a community water system that relies on ground water sources must have a back-up water source or storage capacity meeting certain requirements.[12]

Prior to construction, expansion, or replacement of a well or wellfield designed to pump 100,000 gallons of water per day or more, a proponent must also: (a) properly determine the area of an aquifer which contributes water to a well under the most severe pumping and recharge conditions that can be realistically anticipated (i.e., Zone II and the area beyond Zone II from which surface water and ground water drain into Zone II (i.e., Zone III);[13] (b) submit to MassDEP for approval a ground water monitoring well program designed to evaluate water quality impacts of land uses within Zone II (or, under certain conditions, Zone III);[14] and (c) prepare wellhead protection zoning or non-zoning controls that prohibit certain activities and the siting of certain land uses within Zone II (or, under certain conditions, Zone III).[15] MassDEP may waive the requirement that the proponent delineate Zone II provided that: (a) the proponent has properly delineated Zone II; (b) wellhead protection zoning or non-zoning controls are in effect within Zone II; (c) the proponent has submitted to MassDEP a ground water monitoring well program plan designed to evaluate water quality impacts of land uses within Zone II; and (d) the waiver may be granted without substantial detriment to the public good.[16]

Wellhead protection zoning and non-zoning controls submitted to MassDEP must prohibit certain activities and land uses, including the following: (a) landfills and open dumps; (b) the landfills receiving only wastewater residuals and/or septage; (c) automobiles graveyards and junkyard; (d) the stockpiling and disposal of snow or ice containing certain chemic used for snow or ice removal; (e) petroleum, fuel oil, and heating oil bulk stations and terminals; individual sewage disposal systems exceeding a specified size and certain wastewater treatment works; (g) certain facilities that generate, treat, store, or dispose of hazardous waste; and (h) any floor drainage systems in certain existing facilities that discharge to the ground without MassDEP authorization.[17] Wellhead protection zoning and non-zoning controls must also prohibit certain activities and land uses unless they meet specified performance standards.[18] These activities and land uses include the following: (a) the storage of sludge and septage; (b) the storage of chemicals used for snow or ice removal; (c) the storage of commercial fertilizers; (d) the storage of animal manures; (e) the storage of liquid hazardous materials and/or liquid petroleum products; (f) the removal of soil, loam, sand, gravel, or other mineral substances within four feet of the historical high ground water level; and (g) the covering of more than 15 percent or 2,500 square feet, whichever is greater, of any lot with an impervious surface, unless a system for artificial recharge of precipitation is provided.[19] MassDEP may grant a variance from the requirements for wellhead protection zoning and non-zoning controls if a municipality is unable, despite its best efforts, to adopt one or more of such controls and the Department finds, based on consideration of certain factors, that strict compliance with the requirements would result in an undue hardship and would not serve to further the intent of MassDEP's regulations.[20]

A well or wellfield designed to pump 100,000 gallons of water per day or more may not commence operation until: (a) the ground water monitoring plan has been approved by MassDEP and fully implemented; and (b) the municipalities in which Zone II of the well or wellfield is located have imposed wellhead protection controls conforming to MassDEP's regulations or, if an entity other than a municipality owns or controls the public water system, the proponent of the well or wellfield has demonstrated to MassDEP's satisfaction that it has used best efforts to have such controls established.[21] A municipal well or wellfield to be owned and operated by the municipality in which it is located may not be placed into operation unless the municipality has such wellhead protection controls in effect.[22]

OPERATING, MONITORING, AND REPORTING REQUIREMENTS

Every public water system must be operated under the direct supervision of a certified operator and in accordance with staffing requirements set forth in MassDEP's regulations.[23] MassDEP's drinking water regulations set forth maximum contaminant levels ("MCLs") for coliform bacteria and for various inorganic and organic chemicals and action levels for lead and copper, and they specify limitations for turbidity and radionuclides. The regulations also contain provisions governing treatment of water and other measures to achieve compliance with applicable standards. In addition, the regulations require the owner or operator of a public water system to monitor the system for various constituents at specified frequencies in accordance with prescribed methods, and they require public water system owners and operators and certified laboratories conducting analyses of drinking water to retain certain records for specified periods of time.[24] The applicability of monitoring requirements and the parameters and frequency of monitoring depend upon the classification of the public water system. In general, community water systems are subject to more requirements or more stringent standards than non-community water systems.

MassDEP may grant a variance from a maximum contaminant level if it determines that the variance will not result in an unreasonable risk to health and may grant a variance from a treatment requirement if it determines that such requirement is not necessary to protect public health because of the nature of the water source.[25] MassDEP also may grant an exemption from a maximum contaminant level or treatment requirement for a public water system in operation on the effective date of such provision if it determines that the system is unable to comply due to compelling circumstances and the exemption will not result in an unreasonable risk to health.[26] MassDEP must impose a compliance schedule in connection with any such variance or exemption.[27]

The owner or operator of a public water system must notify the users of the system, and in some instances DEP, when it fails to comply with an applicable limitation or treatment requirement or with certain other provisions of the regulations, or when it fails to comply with a variance[28] or exemption[29] from those requirements. Detailed requirements regarding the method for providing notice and the content of the notice are set forth in the regulations.[30] In addition, the owner or operator of a public water system must provide MassDEP, and in some cases other agencies, with specified information and documents. These include the following: (a) notification that a maximum contaminant level has been exceeded or that certain other contaminant levels have been found; (b) information regarding non-compliance with MassDEP's regulations; (c) the results of all required tests, measurements, and analyses; (d) information regarding chemicals added to the water supply; (e) annual reports of the amount of water that passes through the distribution system; and (t) public notices required under MassDEP's regulations.

The owner or operator of a public water system using a surface water source or a ground water source under the direct influence of surface water must, by specified deadlines, either: treat the water using both disinfection and filtration; or (b) meet certain conditions necessary to avoid filtration, unless notified in writing by MassDEP that filtration is required.[31] Among these conditions are the following: (a) compliance with certain standards regarding contaminant levels and other parameters; (b) performance of disinfection meeting certain requirements; and (c) implementation of a watershed protection/control program conforming to MassDEP requirements and determined adequate by MassDEP.[32] The regulations specify standards which must be achieved by systems required to provide filtration, and they mandate certain analytical,. monitoring, recordkeeping, and reporting requirements to demonstrate compliance with the requirements for filtration or avoiding filtration.[33]

PROTECTION OF WATER SUPPLIES

Surface Water Supplies

In order to protect surface water supplies, MassDEP's drinking water regulations prohibit numerous facilities and activities on or in certain lands, waterways, and water bodies used as or tributary to public water systems. Among the prohibited facilities and activities are: cesspools, septic tanks, dry wells, leaching fields, filters, and other facilities for human waste; the direct or indirect discharge of various waste materials and pollutants; (c) sewers and other wastewater disposal works, unless constructed in accordance with MassDEP requirements and the State Plumbing Code; (d) burial or cemeteries, except with written permission of the Board of Water Commissioners or the body with jurisdiction; (e) hospitals and places for treating contagious or infectious diseases, unless MassDEP has approved the location; (f) manufacturing or processing plants producing toxic or injurious wastes, unless DEP has approved the location; (g) fishing or boating without authorization, or bathing; and (h) the application of herbicides without a permit from MassDEP.[34]

The owner or operator of a public water system using a surface water supply must make "regular and thorough inspections" of the watershed to ensure compliance with the prohibitions outlined above, must inform any violator of the prohibitions, and must "take appropriate action" to enjoin any violation if it is not corrected immediately.[35]

Ground Water Supplies

New wells and well fields are subject to various requirements intended to protect ground water quality. In addition, an existing public water supply well or wellfield for which MassDEP has not approved a specific Zone II is subject to an interim wellhead protection area ("IWPA). The IWPA for a source with a pumping rate of at least 100,000 gallons per day is an area with a radius of one-half mile measured from the well or wellfield, and the radius of the IWPA for a source with a lower pumping rate is determined pursuant to a specified formula.[36]

The owner or operator of a public water system using a ground water supply must conduct an annual survey of the land uses within Zones I, II, and III or the IWPA for each well serving the system and must report annually to MassDEP concerning new land uses within such areas that could adversely affect water quality.[37] The owner or operator must notify the local board of health or health department within forty-eight hours of detecting any statutory or regulatory violation and must notify the person responsible for enforcing local zoning or non-zoning controls within the same time period after detecting any violation of a local land use control that may adversely affect the water supply or distribution system.[38] The owner or operator must also notify MassDEP's Office of Water Supply at the relevant MassDEP regional office.[39] In addition, the water system owner or operator must "take appropriate action" to determine whether the violation has been removed or remedied and must notify the Office of Water Supply at the MassDEP regional office once this has occurred.[40]

All Water Supplies

MassDEP's regulations prohibit the sale, lease, assignment, or other disposition or the change of use of lands used for water supply purposes without MassDEP's written approval, and they prohibit the abandonment of a source of water supply without MassDEP approval.[41] In addition, the regulations prohibit the removal of a water supply source from service unless the supplier first demonstrates to MassDEP's satisfaction that such removal will not have a significant adverse impact on its ability to meet the demands of consumers, and a supplier must maintain each source removed from service as an emergency source of supply unless MassDEP approval to sell or abandon the supply is obtained.[42]

Cross Connections

M.G.L. c. 111, § 160A and its implementing regulations at 310 C.M.R. 22.22 prohibit a physical cross connection between the distribution system of a public water supply used for drinking, domestic, or culinary purposes and the distribution system of any water supply not approved by MassDEP as being of safe sanitary quality for human consumption, unless specified review and permitting requirements have been satisfied.[43] Under these provisions, such a cross connection must be reviewed by MassDEP, or by the owner or operator of a public water system or the local plumbing inspector who is authorized to conduct such review, and certain approvals and permits must be obtained from these parties.[44] In addition, MassDEP's regulations require installation of devices to prevent backflow of water or other materials not approved for human consumption into the public water system,[45] and the regulations specify requirements regarding the acceptable types of backflow prevention devices, and the location and installation of such devices.[46] The regulations also contain requirements regarding the certification of testers for backflow prevention devices and the inspection, testing, and overhauling of such devices.[47] Finally, the regulations impose requirements regarding cross connections on suppliers of water, including requirements to survey industrial, commercial, and institutional premises to identify cross connections, report the results of such surveys to MassDEP, and report violations of the cross-connection regulations to MassDEP.[48]

Enforcement

MassDEP is authorized to determine the quality of public water supplies and may, upon request, investigate the granting or withholding of any permit or approval required by the regulations.[49] MassDEP also is empowered to issue orders as it deems necessary to protect public health, to restrain the use of waters to the extent that such use could adversely affect the public health,[50] and to require the cessation of discharges of pollution to drinking waters and the removal of sources of such pollution.[51] In addition, the Department of Public Health is authorized to issue orders requiring the cessation or correction of violations of MassDEP's drinking water standards and regulations.[52]

A person who violates any of MassDEP's drinking water regulations or a MassDEP order issued pursuant to the authority described above or who maintains a cross connection without a MassDEP permit can be subject to: (a) a civil penalty of up to $25,000 for each day of violation; or imprisonment for up to one year and/or a fine of up to $25,000 for each day of violation.[53] In addition, a person who violates any of the statutory or regulatory provisions discussed above, or a DEP order, permit, or approval issued thereunder, can be subject to an administrative penalty under the Massachusetts Administrative Penalties Act, which is discussed in Section 2.2 of this Handbook.

MASSACHUSETTS WATER MANAGEMENT ACT

The Massachusetts Water Management Act (the "MWMA"), M.G.L. c. 21G, §§1 to 19, requires MassDEP and the Water Resources Commission (the "Commission") of the Executive Office of Energy and Environment. al Affairs to cooperate in planning, establishing, and managing programs to assess water uses in the Commonwealth and to plan for future water needs.[54] The Commission is charged with adopting principles, policies, and guidelines for effective planning and management of water use and conservation and for administering the MWMA to ensure water supplies of adequate volume and quality.[55] MassDEP is required to adopt regulations to manage ground waters and surface waters in the Commonwealth as a single hydrological system and to ensure, where necessary, a balance among competing water withdrawals and uses.[56] MassDEP has adopted such regulations at 310 C.M.R. 36.01 to 36.44.

Permits and Registrations for Water Withdrawals

The MWMA provides that no person may make a new withdrawal of water in excess of the "threshold volume" from any water source, or construct any building or structure that may require such a new withdrawal of water, unless a permit for the withdrawal has been obtained from MassDEP.[57] In addition, any person making an existing withdrawal of water is required to file a registration statement in accordance with MassDEP's regulations, and each registrant is required to file an annual statement of withdrawal in accordance with the regulations.[58]

Under the MWMA and MassDEP's water management regulations, the withdrawal threshold volume is an average daily volume of 100,000 gallons, although MassDEP is authorized to raise or lower the threshold volume by regulation if it finds that a different threshold is "necessary and adequate to protect the public health, safety and welfare."[59] In addition, for any particular water source, MassDEP may establish in its regulations a lower threshold volume than that volume generally applicable in the Commonwealth if it finds that such water source requires special protection because of the nature or volume of demands made on it.[60] For purposes of determining whether a withdrawal is in excess of the threshold volume, any "non-consumptive use" of water, which is defined as any use of water that results in its being discharged back into the same water source at or near the withdrawal point in substantially unimpaired quality and quantity, is not to be counted in the volume of water withdrawn.[61] However, notice of such non-consumptive use must be provided to MassDEP.[62]

MassDEP's regulations establish a water withdrawal permit application deadline for facilities in each river basin of the Commonwealth.[63] The regulations contain detailed. provisions concerning the permit application and issuance process and the process for registering existing withdrawals of water and renewing such registrations.[64] In reviewing a permit application, MassDEP must consider numerous factors specified. in the regulations, including environmental and economic impacts of the proposed water withdrawal, effects on other water uses, and water conservation measures.[65] MassDEP must deny an application for a water withdrawal if it finds that the combined volume of existing, permitted, and proposed withdrawals from the water source exceeds the safe yield of the source or that existing, permitted, or proposed water withdrawals are otherwise in conflict.[66] When issuing a permit, MassDEP may impose conditions, including limitations on the use of the water and implementation of water conservation measures.[67] MassDEP may also impose conditions, such as requirements to obtain and maintain information on past and present water use, in connection with the registration of an existing water withdrawal.[68]

Water Emergencies

The MWMA authorizes MassDEP to declare a state of water emergency if it finds that a water supply shortage endangers or will endanger the public health, safety, or welfare.[69] During a state of water emergency, MassDEP may require the operator of the water system to prepare a plan for ending the water emergency, including restrictions on the use of water and a moratorium on the issuance of building permits.[70] In addition, the operator of the water system may take land by eminent domain or purchase water from another public water system, provided that specified conditions are met.[71] Furthermore, MassDEP may, subject to certain conditions, issue orders which establish priorities for water distribution and regulate and limit the use of water from a water source.[72]

Enforcement

MassDEP may issue orders as it deems necessary to aid in the enforcement of the MWMA and may request the Attorney General to bring an action to enjoin any conduct prohibited by the MWMA or to compel compliance with a MassDEP order.[73] A person who violates any provision of the MWMA, its implementing regulations, or an order or permit issued thereunder, or who attempts to obtain a permit by misrepresentation or failure to disclose all relevant facts, can be subject to: (a) a civil penalty of up to $25,000 for each day of violation; or (b) imprisonment for up to 180 days and/or a fine of from $1,000 to $10,000 for each day of violation.[74] Finally, it should be noted that a person who violates the MWMA or a MassDEP order or permit issued thereunder can be subject to an administrative penalty under the Massachusetts Administrative Penalties Act.

WATERSHED PROTECTION FOR METROPOLITAN BOSTON WATER SUPPLY

Watershed protection statutes set forth at M.G.L. c. 92, §§ 104, 105, 107A, and 108 to 111 prohibit and restrict certain land uses and activities in specified portions of the watersheds of drinking water sources for the metropolitan Boston water supply system. The Division of Watershed Management ("DWM") of the Metropolitan District Commission ("MDC") is responsible for maintaining and operating this system of water sources to supply the Massachusetts Water Resources Authority ("MWRA") and for utilizing and conserving the water within the system to protect, preserve, and enhance the environment and assure the availability of pure water.[75] In addition, DWM is required to promulgate regulations for the protection of this system of water sources[76] and has promulgated watershed protection regulations at 350 C.M.R. 11.01 to 11.13.

Areas Subject to Regulation

The watershed protection statutes and regulations impose prohibitions and restrictions on activities in certain portions of the watersheds in central Massachusetts that encompass the natural basin from within which water drains, or in the natural course would drain, into the Quabbin Reservoir, the Wachusett Reservoir, or the Ware River upstream of the Ware River intake (collectively, the "Central Massachusetts Watersheds"). The areas of the Central Massachusetts Watersheds that are subject to the statutory and regulatory prohibitions and restrictions include the following: (a) land within a specified distance of the bank of one of the Reservoirs; (b) land within specified distances of the bank of a tributary to one of the Reservoirs or to the Ware River upstream of the Ware River intake or within specified distances of the bank of a surface water; (c) land within the floodplain of, or certain wetlands bordering on, a tributary or surface water or one of the Reservoirs; and (d) land that overlies aquifers in the Wachusett watershed that have certain potential well yields.[77]

The watershed protection statutes and regulations also impose prohibitions and restrictions regarding certain property in central and eastern Massachusetts associated with the metropolitan Boston water supply system. These provisions apply to real and personal property held immediately prior to August 18, 1992, the effective date of certain of the statutory provisions, by or on behalf of the Commonwealth in and for the MDC water system which is part of or appurtenant to the Quabbin watershed, Quabbin Reservoir. Ware River watershed, Wachusett watershed, Wachusett Reservoir, North and South Sudbury watersheds, Sudbury Reservoir, Framingham Reservoirs 1, 2, and 3, Blue Hills Reservoir, Bear Hill Reservoir, Spot Pond Reservoir, Fells Reservoir, Weston Reservoir, Norumbega Reservoir, and Chestnut Hill Reservoir, as well as any enlargements or additions to this water supply system acquired or constructed by DWM (the "MDC Property").[78]

Requirements for Central Massachusetts Watersheds

The watershed protection statutes and regulations prohibit a wide range of land alterations as well as the generation, storage, disposal, or discharge of pollutants within 200 feet of the bank of a tributary or surface water or within 400 feet of the bank of one of the Reservoirs.[79] The statutes and regulations also specify uses and activities that are prohibited within the following areas:

(a) the area between 200 and 400 feet from the bank of a tributary or surface water; (b) the floodplain of a tributary or surface water or of one of the Reservoirs; (c) certain wetlands bordering on a tributary or surface water or on one of the Reservoirs; (d) land that overlays an aquifer with a potential well yield of at least 100 gallons per minute; and (e) land that overlays an aquifer with a potential well yield of one or more but less than 100 gallons per minute, if DWM makes a finding regarding the need for regulation of such aquifer.[80] The land uses and activities prohibited within these areas include: (a) disposal of pollutants from a sewage treatment facility; (b) placement of the leaching field of a subsurface wastewater disposal system less than four feet above the maximum annual high water table level; (c) storage of liquid petroleum products, except for heating fuel storage by the end user of such fuel in accordance with certain conditions; (d) use, generation, treatment, storage, or disposal of hazardous material or hazardous waste, other than a reasonable volume incidental to normal residential use; (e) storage or disposal of solid waste, other than a reasonable volume incidental to normal residential use; (t) outdoor storage of road salt or other de-icing chemicals, except outdoor storage of sand, gravel, or materials used in road construction, provided they are not hazardous materials or waste; (g) outdoor storage of fertilizers; (h) use or storage of certain pesticides or herbicides which pose a threat or potential threat to ground water; (i) outdoor, uncovered storage of manure; (j) servicing, washing, or repairing of boats or motor vehicles other than as reasonably incidental to normal residential use; (k) operation of junk and salvage yards; (l) rendering impervious more than ten percent of any lot or 2,500 square feet, whichever is greater; (m) excavation of gravel and sand beyond a specified depth, except where incidental to construction of a permitted structure; (n) alteration of certain wetlands; (p) construction of a dwelling that exceeds a density of two bedrooms per acre; (q) any use that generates more than 220 gallons of sanitary sewage per acre per day; and (o) other activity that DWM determines could degrade water quality.[81] The statutes and regulations also limit the construction of dwellings in excess of certain densities and prohibit uses that generate more than specified amounts of sanitary sewage per day on land t overlays an aquifer with a potential well yield of 100 gallons per minute or greater or on other land that DWM determines is necessary for the protection of water quality.[82]

Exemptions and Variances

The watershed protection statutes and regulations exempt a number of land uses and activities from the prohibitions and restrictions including: (a) uses, structures, and facilities lawfully in existence or for which all applicable permits and approvals, other than building and septic system permits, were obtained prior to July 1, 1992; and (b) any reconstruction, extension, or structural change to a structure lawfully in existence on July 1, 1992, provided that the reconstruction, extension, or change does not constitute a substantial change to or enlargement of the structure and will not degrade water quality.[83] In addition, the construction of a single-family dwelling on a lot existing prior to July 1, 1992 and the subdivision of an owner-occupied lot existing on July 1, 1992 to provide one additional lot are exempt from the statutory and regulatory-prohibitions and restrictions, provided that, wherever possible, no alterations shall occur within 400 feet of a bank of one of the Reservoirs or 200 feet of the bank of a tributary or surface water.[84] Furthermore, the density and sanitary sewage generation limits do not apply to construction involving a direct connection to a sewer system in existence prior to July 1, 1992 if expansion of the sewer system capacity is not needed and the connection is used for all sanitary sewage of the dwelling or structure.[85] Finally, the prohibitions and restrictions do not apply to certain work of DWM or MWRA and to various activities regarding agriculture, existing or proposed public roadways and railroads, utility systems, and remediation of hazardous materials and wastes, provided that these activities satisfy certain standards regarding protection of water quality.[86]

DWM may grant a variance for a particular land use, structure, or activity and must grant a variance for a crossing of a tributary or wetlands when it finds that, because of soil conditions, slope, or topography of the land affected by the use, structure, or activity, relief can be granted without substantial detriment to the public good and without impairing water quality.[87] DWM may impose reasonable conditions, safeguards, and limitations on any variance if necessary to protect water quality, and a notice of the variance must be recorded and indexed at the registry of deeds or registered at the registry district of the land court for the county or district where the land is located.[88]

Requirements for Metropolitan District Commission Property

M.G.L. c. 92, § 109 prohibits the taking or diversion of any water of the metropolitan Boston water supply system, as well as any action that would "corrupt, render impure, waste, or improperly use any such water."[89] The MDC regulations contain various prohibitions and restrictions applicable to the lands and waters within the MDC Property. Among the prohibited activities are the following: (a) engaging in construction that involves filling, dredging, or land alterations, or constructing, establishing, or maintaining any agricultural facility where animal manure is or may be deposited or accumulated, without adequate measures to prevent erosion of materials into the waters of the water supply system and any other activity that could degrade the quality of such waters; (b) allowing a condition to exist on one's property that could result in a direct or indirect discharge of pollutants to the waters of the water supply system; and (c) various recreational activities within the waters of the water supply system or otherwise on the MDC Property, with the exception of certain activities that can be specifically authorized by MDC.[90] Special restrictions apply to the Quabbin Reservoir, the Wachusett Reservoir, the Ware River, and the Sudbury Reservoir and allow some recreational activities in accordance with specified conditions.[91]

Enforcement

Any person who violates MDC's watershed protection regulations, unlawfully takes or diverts any water from the water supply system or corrupts or defiles the water supply can be subject to a criminal fine of up to $50,000 or imprisonment for up to one year. In a case of continuing violation, however, the maximum fine may be $10,000 for each day of violation.[92] Upon written request of DWM, MassDEP has the authority to enforce the watershed protection statutes and regulations and to impose administrative penalties pursuant to the Massachusetts Administrative Penalties Act.[93]

NOTES

1. 310 C.M.R. 22.02. The definition of "public water system" includes collection, treatment, storage, and distribution facilities under the control of the operator of the system, as well as collection and pretreatment storage facilities not under such control but used primarily in connection with such system. 310 C.M.R. 22.02.
2. 310 C.M.R. 22.02.
3. 310 C.M.R. 22.02.
4. 310 C.M.R. 22.03(2).
5. 310 C.M.R. 22.04(1).
6. 310 C.M.R. 22.04(2).
7. 310 C.M.R. 22.19.
8. 310 C.M.R. 22.21(1)(b).
9. 310 C.M.R. 22.21(1)(a), (b). Zone I includes a protective area around a public water supply well or wellfield with a radius based on the well's pumping rate or yield. 310 C.M.R. 22.02 (definitions). Criteria for delineating Zones are set forth in MassDEP's guidelines.
10. 310 C.M.R. 22.21(3)(b).
11. 310 C.M.R. 22.21(1)(g), (3)(b).
12. 310 C.M.R. 22.21(3)(a).
13. 310 C.M.R. 22.21(1)(c)2; Zone II includes the area that contributes to a well under the most severe pumping and recharge conditions that can be anticipated. Zone

III includes the area beyond Zone II from which surface water and ground water drain into Zone II. 310 C.M.R. 22.02 (definitions).

14. 310 C.M.R. 22.21(1)(c)3, (f)3.

15. 310 C.M.R. 22.21(1)(c)4, (l)(f)2, and (k).

16. 310 C.M.R. 22.21(1)(f).

17. 310 C.M.R. 22.21(2)(a).

18. 310 C.M.R. 22.2l(l)(b).

19. 310 C.M.R. 22.21(2)(b).

20. 310 C.M.R. 22.21(5).

21. 310 C.M.R. 22.21(1)(d), (j). *See* 310 C.M.R. 22.21(1)(1), (m), (2)(c).

22. 310 C.M.R. 22.2l(l)(e). *See* 310 C.M.R. 22.21(1)(1).

23. 310 C.M.R. 22.1lB and 22.20A(l)(d).

24. 310 C.M.R. 22.05(1), (2), (3), (8), (9); 22.06(1)-(13), (15), (16); 22.06A(l), (2), (3), (6), (7); 22.06B(l)(a)-(t), (h), 0), (2)-(5), (7)-(10), (12); 22.06C(l); 22.07(1), (2); 22.07A(l)-(13), (15)-(17); 22.07B(l)-(8), (10)-(14); 2.07C(l)-(11); 22.08(1)-(4), 22.09(1), (2); 22.10; 22.13(7); 22.17; 22.19(4), (5), (7); 22.23(1), (2). *See* 310 C.M.R. 22.04(5), (6); 22.11A, and 22.12.

25. 310 C.M.R. 22.13(1)(a), (b).

26. 310 C.M.R. 22.14(1)(a), (b), (c).

27. 310 C.M.R. 22.13(1), (3); 22.14(2).

28. 310 C.M.R. 22.13(3)(e), (g).

29. 310 C.M.R. 22.14(4(d), (4)(t).

30. *See e.g.,* 310 C.M.R. 22.05(7); 22.06(5)(h), (i), (6)(g), (h), (9)(b), (12)(d), and (14).

31. *See* 310 C.M.R. 22.20A.

32. 310 C.M.R. 22.20A(l)-(4).

33. 310 C.M.R. 22.20A(5), (6).

34. 310 C.M.R. 22.20B(l)-(7), (10).

35. 310 C.M.R. 22.20B(9).

36. 310 C.M.R. 22.02, 22.21(1)(i).

37. 310 C.M.R. 22.21(4)(a), (b).

38. 310 C.M.R. 22.21(4){c).

39. 310 C.M.R. 22.21(4)(c).

40. 310 C.M.R. 22.21(4)(d).

41. 310 C.M.R. 22.24, 22.25.

42. 310 C.M.R. 22.25(1)-(2). *See* 310 C.M.R. 22.21(1)(1).

43. 310 C.M.R. 22.22(2). A "cross connection" is defined to include any by-pass arrangements, jumper connections, removal section, swivel or changeover connection, or other temporary or permanent connection through which backflow can or may occur. 310 C.M.R. 22.02. Note that the regulations state that DEP "strongly advocates the elimination of all cross connections." 310 C.M.R. 22.22(1).

44. 310 C.M.R. 22.22(1), (5), (8)(b).

45. 310 C.M.R. 22.22(3)(s).

46. 310 C.M.R. 22.22(8)-(12).

47. 310 C.M.R. 22.22(5), (6).

48. 310 C.M.R. 22.22(3).
49. M.G.L. c. 111, § 160.
50. M.G.L. c. 111, § 160.
51. M.G.L. c. 111, §§ 160, 162. *See* M.G.L c. 111, §§ 163, 164, 165; 310 C.M.R. 22.03(3), (4), (6); 22.04(9).
52. M.G.L. c. 111, § 160B. *See* 310 C.M.R. 22.03(3), (4).
53. M.G.L. c. 111, §§ 160, 160A, 162.
54. M.G.L. c. 21G, § 3.
55. M.G.L. c. 21G, § 3.
56. M.G.L. c. 21G, §3.
57. M.G.L. c. 21G, § 7; 310 C.M.R. 36.17, 36.18(2). *See* M.G.L. c. 210, §§ 2, 4.
58. M.G.L. c. 21G, § 5; 310 C.M.R. 36.04, 36.06, 36.11, 36.33(1). *See* M.G.L. c. 21G, §§ 2, 4; 310 C.M.R. 36.05. The MWMA also allowed any person making a withdrawal of water prior to January 1, 1986 below the threshold volume but in excess of 10,000 gallons per day to file a voluntary registration statement on or before July 1, 1991. M.G.L. c. 21G, § 5.
59. M.G.L. c. 21G, § 4.
60. M.G.L. c. 21G, §4.
61. M.G.L. c. 210, §§2, 4; 310 C.M.R. 36.03, 36.05, 36.17(1), 36.19(3), 36.38.
62. M.G.L. c. 210, §4; 310 C.M.R. 36.05, 36.38.
63. 310 C.M.R. 36.18(1), (7), and (8).
64. 310 C.M.R. 36.04 to 36.10; 36.17, 36.18(2)-(6), (9), (10); 36.19 to 36.32; 36.33(3), (4); 36.34 to 36.37; 36.39 to 36.41. *See* M.O.L. c. 210, §§ 5–12.
65. 310 C.M.R. 36.26(1), (2); 36.31. *See* M.O.L. c. 210, § 7.
66. M.G.L. c. 210, § 11; 310 C.M.R. 36.26(2)(c), 36.30(2), 36.31.
67. M.G.L. c. 210, § 11; 310 C.M.R. 36.25, 36.28.
68. 310 C.M.R. 36.08(3).
69. M.G.L. c. 210, § 15.
70. M.G.L. c. 210, § 15.
71. M.G.L. c. 210, § 16.
72. M.G.L. c. 210, § 17.
73. M.G.L. c. 210, § 14.
74. M.G.L. c. 21G, § 14; 310 C.M.R. 36.43. *See* M.G.L. c. 210, § 13; 310 C.M.R. 36.42.
75. M.G.L. c. 92, § 105. The commissioner is directed to establish the Quabbin and Ware River watershed advisory committees to advise the DWM on its policies and regulations regarding certain activities within the respective watersheds. *See* M.G.L. c. 92, §§ 114, 114A.
76. M.G.L. c. 92, § 108.
77. M.G.L. c. 92 §§ 104 and 107A(a) and (b)(l); 350 C.M.R. 11.03 and 11.04(1).
78. M.G.L. c. 92, §104; 350 C.M.R. 11.03 (definition of watershed system).
79. M.G.L. c. 92, §107A(a); 350 C.M.R. ll.04(3}(a).
80. M.G.L. c. 92, §107A(b)(l); 350 C.M.R. 11.04(3)(b).
81. M.G.L. c. 92, §107A(b)(2) and (d); 350 C.M.R. ll.04(3)(b)(2). *See* 350 C.M.R. 11.04(3)(e) and (f) (contiguous property). A landowner may request DWM to provide

an advisory ruling or a determination as to whether existing or proposed land uses, structures, or activities on such person's property are allowed under the watershed protection requirements. 350 C.M.R. 11.06(1) and (2).

82. M.G.L. c. 92, § 107A(e) and (f); 350 C.M.R. ll.04(3)(c) and (d).
83. M.G.L. c. 92, §107A(c); 350 C.M.R. 11.05(1) and (2).
84. M.G.L. c. 92, §107A(h); 350 C.M.R. 11.05(3).
85. M.G.L. c. 92, §107A(g); 350 C.M.R. 11.05(4).
86. M.G.L. c. 92, §§107A(n) and (r); 350 C.M.R. 11.05(6)–(16).
87. M.G.L. c. 92, §107A(l); 350 C.M.R. 11.06(3); *see* 350 C.M.R. 11.05(5).
88. M.G.L. c. 92, §107A(l); 350 C.M.R. 11.06(3)(h).
89. M.G.L. c. 92, §109.
90. 350 C.M.R. 11.09(1) and (2).
91. 350 C.M.R. 11.09(2)(b)-(e).
92. M.G.L. c. 92, §111; 350 C.M.R. 11.10. *See* M.G.L. c. 92, §§ 110 and 112.
93. M.G.L. c. 92, §107A(o); 350 C.M.R. 11.10.

Chapter 7

Regulation of Activities in and Affecting Wetlands, Riverfront Areas, Floodplains, Coastal Areas, Waterways, Water Bodies, and Tidelands

Several Massachusetts statutes regulate projects and other activities in and affecting wetlands, riverfront areas, floodplains, coastal areas, waterways, water bodies, and present and former tidelands. The Massachusetts Wetlands Protection Act[1] requires review and authorization of activities that will or could alter certain wetland, riverfront, and floodplain areas. The Massachusetts Coastal Zone Management program includes policies and review procedures for federal and state agency activities taking place in the coastal zone. Chapter 91 of the Massachusetts General Laws imposes restrictions and license and permit requirements on activities in tidewaters and on tilled tidelands, as well as activities in certain waterways and bodies of water.

MASSACHUSETTS WETLANDS PROTECTION ACT

The Massachusetts Wetlands Protection Act prohibits the removal, filling, dredging, or alteration[2] of specified wetland areas, riverfront areas and areas subject to flooding without authorization from the conservation commission for the municipality where the work is proposed. The Act authorizes the Massachusetts Department of Environmental Protection ("MassDEP") to hear appeals of conservation commission decisions and to adopt regulations to implement the Act. DEP has adopted such regulations at 310 C.M.R. 10.01 to 10.60.

Areas Subject to Protection

The Wetlands Protection Act and MassDEP's regulations define and describe in detail the types of land and water areas subject to protection. These areas are: (a) banks, freshwater wetlands, marshes, swamps, coastal wetlands, beaches, dunes, and flats bordering on the ocean or on any estuary, creek, river, stream, pond, or lake; (b) land under such a body of water or waterway; land subject to tidal action, coastal storm flowage, or flooding; and (d) riverfront areas.[3]

Orders of Conditions and Performance Standards

Under the Wetlands Protection Act and MassDEP's regulations, a person proposing work that will remove, fill, dredge, or alter any of the areas subject to protection, or any area within the 100-foot buffer zone must submit a Notice of Intent ("NOI") describing such work to the local conservation commission. The commission must publish in a local newspaper five days[4] prior notice of the public meeting on the NOI. The public meeting must be held within twenty-one days of the commission's receipt of the NOI.[5] The conservation commission must then hold a public hearing on the NOI and must determine whether the location of the proposed work is significant to any of eight interests identified in the Wetlands Protection Act. These interests are: (a) protection of public and private water supply; (b) protection of ground water supply; (c) flood control; (d) prevention of storm damage; (e) prevention of pollution; (t) protection of land containing shellfish; (g) protection of fisheries; and (h) protection of wildlife habitat. After the public hearing, the commission must issue an "order of conditions" for the proposed work which imposes conditions designed to achieve the aforementioned interests.[6]

MassDEP's regulations specify standards and presumptions to be used in determining whether an area subject to protection under the Wetlands Protection Act is significant to any of the interests identified in the WPA, and they specify performance standards applicable to work in such areas.[7] Among the performance standards are the following: (a) a prohibition on the destruction or impairment of any bordering vegetated wetland (wet meadow, marsh, swamp, or bog), except that the order of conditions may allow the loss of up to 5,000 square feet of bordering vegetated wetland if an equal area of replacement wetland that meets specified standards will be created;[8] (b) a requirement to provide a compensatory flood storage area meeting specified standards if a project within bordering land subject to flooding will cause or contribute incrementally to an increase in the horizontal extent and level of floodwaters during peak flows;[9] and (c) a prohibition on development in riverfront areas unless the applicant can prove by a preponderance of the evidence that such work will have no significant adverse impact on the area for the eight wetland interests identified above, and that there is no practicable and substantially equivalent economic alternative to the proposed project with less adverse effects.[10]

The order of conditions must impose such conditions as are necessary to meet the performance standards for protection of any area found to be significant to one or more of the interests identified in the WPA. If the proposed activity cannot be conditioned to meet the standards, the order must prohibit the activity.[11] However, projects falling within specified categories may be authorized under an order of conditions even though all of the relevant performance standards will not be satisfied. Among these project categories are assessment and remediation of oil and hazardous materials in accordance with specified requirements, certain agricultural activities, construction of utility lines in accordance with specified requirements, and construction of a roadway or driveway meeting certain standards where there is no alternative access from a public way to an upland portion of the property.[12]

No work authorized by an order of conditions can be undertaken until all administrative appeal periods have elapsed or, if an appeal has been taken, until all proceedings before MassDEP have been completed. In addition, no such work can be undertaken until the order has been recorded in the registry of deeds, or in the land court if the property is registered land, in accordance with requirements specified in the Wetlands Protection Act and MassDEP's regulations. An order of conditions is generally valid for three years from the date of its issuance, although extensions of the order may be granted. Upon written request of the applicant, a certificate of compliance for the work covered by an order of conditions may be issued.[13]

Determination of Applicability

Under the WPA and MassDEP's regulations, a person may request the conservation commission to determine whether the WPA applies to a particular area or to work that may affect an area subject to protection under the WPA (a "Request For Determination" or "RFD"). After such RFD is filed, the conservation commission must determine, at a public meeting, whether the WPA applies to all or part of the land or proposed activities in question. If the conservation commission determines that the WPA applies and the commission's determination is not reversed on appeal, an NOI must be filed, and an order of conditions issued for activities in the area to which the WPA applies. If the conservation commission determines that the WPA does not apply and the determination is appealed to MassDEP, the proposed work may proceed at the owner's risk, with notice to the conservation commission and MassDEP required in some cases.[14]

100-Foot Buffer Zone

A notice of intent or a request for a determination of applicability also must be submitted to the conservation commission for work proposed within the 100-foot zone lying horizontally outward from the boundary of a bank, freshwater wetland, coastal wetland, beach, dune, flat, marsh, or swamp bordering the ocean or an estuary, creek, river, stream, pond, or lake. The 100-foot buffer zone provision does not apply to land subject to flooding, coastal storm flowage, or tidal action, or to riverfront areas.[15]

No filing with the conservation commission is required prior to commencement of work located outside an area subject to protection under the Act and the 100-foot buffer zone. After such work has been conducted, however, the conservation commission or MassDEP may impose requirements as it deems necessary to accomplish the objectives of the Wetlands Protection Act if it determines that such work has in fact altered an area subject to protection under the WPA.[16]

Appeals

An order of conditions or a determination of applicability issued by a conservation commission, or the commission's failure to act on a NOI or an RFD of applicability within the required time period, may be appealed to MassDEP. The appeal must contain a detailed statement of reasons, including direct case evidence, within forty-five days of the prescreening conference which MassDEP will hold within thirty days of the appeal.[17] With one exception, the regulations require the filing of an appeal within ten business days of the commission's action or of the date when the commission was to have acted if it failed to do so. If the commission has failed to act on a notice of intent, the regulations require the filing of an appeal within seventy calendar days of the date when the commission was to have acted.[18] MassDEP will then issue a superseding order of conditions or a superseding determination of applicability. Such an appeal to MassDEP may be filed by: (a) the applicant; (b) the property owner, if not the applicant; (c) any person aggrieved by the order who may suffer an injury in fact which is different in kind or magnitude from that suffered by the general public, which is within the scope of the interests identified in the WPA, and who was a previous participant in the proceedings;[19] (d) an owner of land abutting the property on which the work is proposed; or (e) any ten residents of the municipality in which the land is located.[20]

A superseding order of conditions or superseding determination of applicability may be appealed within ten business days of its issuance by any of the aforementioned parties. MassDEP regulations state that a superseding order or determination may also be appealed by ten persons pursuant to a specified provision of the Massachusetts Administrative Procedure Act, although the provision referred to authorizes ten persons to intervene in, rather than to seek, an adjudicatory proceeding.[21] If a superseding order or determination is appealed, MassDEP will conduct an adjudicatory hearing,[22] and the decision reached after that hearing may in turn be appealed in accordance with the Massachusetts Administrative Procedure Act and MassDEP's regulations governing adjudicatory proceedings.

MassDEP has deadlines of thirty-five days on appeals of determinations and seventy days on appeals of orders of conditions to issue a superseding order or determination after the initial appeal, except in the case where MEPA requires an EIR.[23] MassDEP site inspections are optional.

Enforcement

MassDEP's regulations authorize the conservation commission, MassDEP, or the Environmental Strike Force to issue an enforcement order when such agency has determined that an activity is in violation of the WPA, MassDEP's wetlands regulations, or an order of conditions. The WPA empowers any court with equity jurisdiction to restrain a violation of the WPA and to enter orders as it deems necessary to remedy such violation. If a person acquires property on which work has been done in violation of the WPA or any order issued thereunder, such person must comply with the order or restore the property to its condition prior to the violation, provided that any enforcement action against such person must be brought within three years after the recording of the deed or the date of the death of the person from whom the property was acquired.[24]

The Wetlands Protection Act also provides that a person who violates the Act can be subject to: (a) a civil penalty of up to $25,000 for each day of violation; or (b) up to two years imprisonment and/or a fine of up to $25,000 for each day of violation.[25] In addition, a person who violates the WPA or MassDEP regulation, order, or authorization issued thereunder can be subject to a penalty under the Massachusetts Administrative Penalties Act.

Inland Wetlands Regulation

Inland wetlands are defined as freshwater wetlands (as defined by M.G.L. c. 131, §40) and that portion of any bank which touches any inland waters or any freshwater wetland, and any freshwater wetland subject to flooding.[26] Bordering vegetated wetlands, delineated pursuant to 310 C.M.R. 10.55, carry a rebuttable presumption of significance. An order of conditions is necessary unless the developer rebuts the presumption. Development is otherwise restricted except (1) where up to 5,000 square feet are eliminated but are also functionally replaced; or (2) where less than 500 square feet are eliminated provided the area extends in finger-like projections into adjacent uplands and it is unreasonable to redesign the work to avoid the loss. Beaches, banks, and dunes always require an NOI. The standard of performance is that there be no impairment of (1) a bank's physical stability, (2) water-carrying capacity, (3) ground water or surface water quality, and (4) breeding habitat, escape cover, and food for fisheries. Development in land subject to flooding (defined as located within FEMA's 100-year flood map or the highest flood record or observation) may not diminish flood storage capacity unless an equal amount of capacity in created on the same property at the same elevation. A special subset, isolated land subject to flooding, allows no adverse effect from development. Land under water is presumed significant but may be altered to maintain or improve boat channels so long as best practical measures are taken to minimize adverse effects.

Riverfront Area Regulations[27]

Development within 200 feet of rivers and streams must pass two tests: (1) no practicable[28] and substantially equivalent economic alternative is available; (2) the applicant must apply for all possible variances;[29] and (3) the proposed project must have no significant adverse effect. An alteration of up to 5,000 square feet or 10 percent of the riverfront area may be allowed providing a 100-foot-wide area of undisturbed vegetation is maintained. In densely developed areas the setback is reduced to 25 feet. There are two general performance standards: (1) there are no practicable and substantially equivalent economic alternatives; and (2) there can be no significant and adverse impacts on the riverfront area to protect public and private water supplies, wildlife habitat, fisheries, shellfish, groundwater, and to prevent flooding, storm damage, and pollution.

Coastal Wetlands Regulations

Coastal wetlands are presumed to be significant with each resource area defined in 310 C.M.R. 10.23–.35. The performance standards differ for each resource area. Existing structures are grandfathered in but maintenance of such structures may not have any adverse effect on specified habitat sites of rare vertebrate and invertebrate species.

COASTAL ZONE MANAGEMENT PROGRAM

As required by M.G.L. c. 21A, §4A, the Massachusetts Coastal Zone Management ("CZM") Office has been established within the Massachusetts Executive Office of Energy and Environmental Affairs ("EOEEA") and has adopted a CZM program to carry out the purposes of the federal CZM Act.[30] The EOEEA regulations implementing the CZM program are set forth at 301 C.M.R. 21.00.[31]

The "coastal zone" is defined under the CZM regulations as the area bounded by the outer limit of the United States territorial sea and the northern and southern lateral seaward boundaries of the Commonwealth and extending 100 feet inland of certain roads, rail lines, and rights-of-way listed in the CZM regulations, including all islands within this area but excluding federal lands. The coastal zone also includes certain intertidal areas, coastal wetlands and beaches, tidal rivers and adjacent uplands, anadromous/catadromous fish runs, and floodplains lying inland of the listed roads, rail lines, and rights-of-way.[32]

Coastal Zone Management (CZM) Program

The CZM management program includes: (a) program policies which embody coastal policy for the Commonwealth, upon which federal consistency review is based, and which are enforceable under state statutes and regulations; and (b) management principles which, while not based on existing state environmental statute or regulation and therefore not enforceable under existing state law, provide guidance to proponents of activities in the coastal zone and represent the preferred policy direction of the CZM Office.[33] The CZM program policies and management principles cover: (a) water quality in the coastal zone; (b) protection of habitats; (c) protection of areas of substantial concern, such as scenic rivers and historic sites; (d) coastal hazards, including storm damage prevention and flood control; (e) port and harbor infrastructure; (t) protection and improvement of public access; (g) siting of energy facilities and energy conservation; (h) protection of ocean resources; and (i) growth and development management.[34]

Coastal Zone Management Consistency Review Process

Under the federal CZM Act, a federal agency that conducts or supports activities directly affecting the coastal zone must do so in a manner which is, to the maximum extent practicable, consistent with the applicable federally approved state CZM program. In accordance with the CZM regulations

adopted by the National Oceanic and Atmospheric Administration, EOEEA's CZM regulations list federal agency activities or development projects and permit and license activities that are likely ·to affect the coastal zone and therefore require a determination of consistency with the state CZM program and review of such determination by the CZM Office.[35] In the case of a federal agency project, the agency must provide the CZM Office with the consistency determination. For a private project requiring a federal agency permit or license, the project proponent must submit a consistency certification. In addition, the CZM Office must monitor federal agency activities and applications for federal agency permits and licenses to determine whether any such activities not listed in the CZM regulations warrant consistency review.
CZM regulations set forth the process for CZM Office review of, and public comment on, a consistency determination or certification, CZM Office concurrence with or objection to the determination or certification, and resolution of disagreements between the CZM Office and the party submitting the determination or certification.[36]

The CZM regulations set forth a special consistency review process for federal license and permit activities described in Outer Continental Shelf plans which affect the coastal zone. The regulations also set forth a special consistency review process for state and local government activities supported by federal financial assistance that affect the coastal zone and for emergency situations.[37]

CHAPTER 91

Chapter 91 of the Massachusetts General Laws ("Chapter 91"), first enacted in 1866, provides the EOEEA with general authority over harbors, tidewaters, flats, lands over which tidewaters flow, waters and banks of the Connecticut River and of the nontidal portion of the Merrimack River, and certain other rivers and streams, as well as all structures therein, in order to prevent interference with navigation and encroachment in tidewaters and to protect the rights of the Commonwealth and its inhabitants in such waters, flats, and lands.[38] Chapter 91 codifies the common law public trust doctrine under which certain lands beneath tidewaters are considered to be held in trust by the sovereign for the benefit of all citizens.[39]

Chapter 91 provides for the issuance by MassDEP of licenses and permits for projects and activities in the areas described above and directs MassDEP to protect the interests of the Commonwealth and its inhabitants in issuing such. licenses and permits.[40] MassDEP has issued regulations implementing the licensing requirements at 310 C.M.R. 9.01 to 9.55.

License and Permit Requirements

Geographic Scope

The licensing and permitting requirements of Chapter 91 and MassDEP's implementing regulations cover projects and certain other activities in various waterways, water bodies, and tidelands. The areas subject to these requirements include: (a) flowed tidelands[41] and submerged lands below the high water mark of great ponds,[42] of the Connecticut River, of certain portions of the Merrimack and Westfield Rivers, and of the navigable portions of non-tidal rivers and streams on which public funds have been expended for stream clearance, channel improvement, or flood control or prevention; and (b) all filled tidelands,[43] except if they are landlocked, and all filled lands lying below the natural high water mark of great ponds.[44]

"Landlocked tidelands" are defined as those filled tidelands which were entirely separated by a public way from any flowed tidelands as of January 1, 1984, are at least 250 feet from the present high water mark, and are not located in a designated port area.[45] Large areas of the cities of Boston and Cambridge are covered by this definition. Some areas of filled tidelands do not constitute landlocked tidelands, however, even though they are not located on the waterfront, and such areas are therefore subject to the licensing and permitting requirements of Chapter 91.

Flowed and filled tidelands fall within one of two categories—private tidelands and Commonwealth tidelands. Private tidelands encompass the area landward of the historic low water mark or of a line 100 rods (1,650 feet) seaward of the historic high-water mark, whichever is farther landward. These tidelands can be privately owned, subject to an easement of the public for purposes of navigation, fishing, fowling, and passing over and through the water. Commonwealth tidelands encompass the area seaward of the historic low water mark or of a line 100 rods (1,650 feet) seaward of the historic high-water mark, whichever is farther landward. These tidelands are held by the Commonwealth or one of its political subdivisions or agencies in trust for the benefit of the public, or they are held by a private person by license or grant of the Commonwealth subject to an express or implied condition subsequent that they be used for a public purpose.[46]

Activities Requiring Licenses and Permits

Under Chapter 91 and MassDEP's regulations, a MassDEP license is required for projects and various other activities in or on the areas described above if such a project or activity is not authorized by a valid legislative grant or agency license. These projects and activities include: (a) construction, reconstruction, placement, demolition, or removal of a structure; (b) placement or excavation of fill; (c) use of a structure or fill; (d) structural alteration of a structure or fill from the specifications in a previous grant or license; and (e) change in use of a structure or fill from the use authorized in a previous grant or license or, if no use was specified, from that use determined by MassDEP to be implicit in the grant or license.[47]

Under Chapter 91 and MassDEP's regulations, a MassDEP permit is required for various activities not involving work on fill or structures, unless such activities are authorized by a valid grant or license. These activities include: (a) beach nourishment; (b) dredging; (c) disposal of unconsolidated material below the low water mark; (d) burning of rubbish or other material upon the water; and (e) lowering of the water level of a great pond, other than a water body used for agricultural, manufacturing, mercantile, irrigation, or insect control purposes, for flowing cranberry bogs, or for public water supply.[48]

Other activities are exempt from the Chapter 91 license and permit requirements. These include: (a) maintenance, repair, and minor modification of authorized fill or structures if specified conditions are met; (b) continuation of certain pre-1984 uses and structures and of certain public agency and infrastructure projects not authorized under Chapter 91; (c) continued use of an unauthorized water-dependent structure accessory to a single-family residence if authorization was sought under the amnesty provisions of MassDEP's regulations; (d) continued use of certain pre-1939 fill or structures on non-tidal rivers and streams; (e) placement of certain wires, pipes, cables, fish ladders, fishways, bulkheads, headwalls, storm drainage outfalls, or similar structures in non-tidal rivers and streams; (f) certain changes in configuration and use of licensed marina docking facilities; (g) removal of fill or structures in accordance with certain requirements; (h) emergency actions in accordance with certain requirements; and (i) installation of temporary moorings, floats, and rafts.[49]

Determination of Applicability

The Chapter 91 regulations establish a procedure for requesting and obtaining a MassDEP determination regarding the applicability of the regulations to a particular area of land or water or to a proposed activity.[50]

Licensing and Permitting Procedures

MassDEP's regulations establish procedures and schedules to govern application for and issuance of a license or permit under Chapter 91. In its review of a license or permit application, Mass DEP must determine whether a project or activity is a water-dependent use or a non-water-dependent use.

Water-dependent uses are those that require direct access to, or location in, tidal or inland waters. Such uses include: (a) marinas and boating facilities; (b) commercial fishing and fish processing facilities; (c) water-based recreational facilities; (d) parks and other waterfront pedestrian facilities to promote public use and enjoyment of the water; (e) waterborne passenger transportation facilities; (t) beach nourishment, dredging for certain purposes, and shore protection structures for certain purposes; (g) navigation aids; (h) discharge pipes and outfalls; (i) wildlife sanctuaries and habitats; (j) certain industrial uses dependent upon waterborne transportation or requiring the withdrawal or discharge of large volumes of water for cooling, process, or treatment purposes; (k) certain bridges, tunnels, pipelines, and similar infrastructure facilities crossing waterways; and (1) facilities determined by MassDEP to be accessory to a water-dependent use project. Non-water-dependent uses include restaurants, retail stores, parking facilities, office facilities, residential facilities, parks and other pedestrian facilities that are not for public use and enjoyment of the water, roads and other facilities for vehicular movement if not determined to be water-dependent, and disposal of material excavated from or originating on land.[51]

MassDEP's licensing and permitting procedures provide for notice and opportunity for comment on a license or permit application. Under the regulations, MassDEP must hold a public hearing for a proposed non-water-dependent use. For a proposed water-dependent use, MassDEP may hold a hearing and must do so if requested by certain municipal officials. A municipality, a ten-citizen group, or an aggrieved person that has submitted written comments may intervene in the license or permit proceeding.[52]

Licensing and Permitting Standards

Chapter 91 and MassDEP's regulations impose detailed and far-reaching licensing and permitting standards. The regulations identify certain types of fill and structures that do not meet the statutory requirements of Chapter 91 or are not consistent with the purposes of the agency's regulations and that, therefore, cannot be licensed or permitted. The regulations also specify broad categories of fill and structures that can satisfy the statutory and regulatory requirements and standards.[53]

No license or permit may be issued for a project or activity on tidelands or a great pond unless it either constitutes a water-dependent use in private tidelands or MassDEP determines that it serves a proper public purpose that provides greater benefit than detriment to the public's rights in such area. If the project or activity constitutes a water-dependent use, MassDEP must presume that the proper public purpose standard referred to above has been met. If the project or activity constitutes a non-water-dependent use, MassDEP is to presume that the proper public purpose standard has been met only if the project or activity complies with detailed standards set forth in the Chapter 91 regulations.[54]

Among the most significant of the standards set forth in MassDEP's regulations are provisions designed to: (a) preserve, protect, and enhance the exercise of the public's rights to use tidelands, great ponds, and waterways for fishing, fowling, navigating, and related activities;[55] (b) preserve the availability, suitability, and capacity of tidelands, great ponds, and waterways for water-dependent uses; (c) avoid interference with existing water-dependent uses; and (d) ensure that tidelands proposed for non-water-dependent uses also include water-dependent uses and public uses.[56] In addition, a non-water-dependent use in the coastal zone subject to Chapter 91 must be consistent with the state CZM policies.[57]

A project or activity subject to Chapter 91 must also comply with: (a) environmental regulatory programs of the Commonwealth;[58] (b) local zoning requirements and the municipal harbor plan, if such a plan has been adopted for the area where the project is located;[59] (c) design, engineering, and construction standards intended to prevent interference with navigation and promote safety and environmental protection;[60] (d) standards governing public access to and use of recreational boating facilities;[61] and (e) restrictions and standards governing dredging and dredged materials disposal intended to prevent interference with navigation and promote environmental and marine resources protection.[62] Finally, special requirements apply, in place of the other regulatory standards, to certain transportation and utility projects in tidelands and great ponds in order to minimize the adverse impacts of such projects on the public's water-related interests.[63]

License and Permit Provisions

Chapter 91 licenses are issued for a term of 30 years or less, except under certain conditions when MassDEP may issue a license for a longer term. For example, MassDEP may issue a license for up to 65 years for a project or activity located on flowed tidelands or a waterway, for up to 99 years for a project located on filled tidelands or a great pond, and for an unlimited term in the case of certain public projects. A permit under Chapter 91 is valid for a fixed term not to exceed five years, except that permits with terms of ten years may be issued for performance of maintenance dredging. In addition, a license or permit may be extended by MassDEP for a term not exceeding that originally authorized. All work authorized under a Chapter 91 license or permit must be completed within five years of issuance or within such other time period as may be specified therein, unless MassDEP grants an extension.

A license expires if the authorized fill or structure is abandoned and not used for its authorized purpose for five consecutive years or more.[64]

A license must be recorded in the appropriate registry of deeds, or in the land court if the property is registered land, within 60 days of its issuance, and notice of recording must be provided to MassDEP prior to commencement of the project authorized by the license.[65] In addition, the licensee must request MassDEP to issue a certificate of compliance within 60 days after completion of the licensed project. If such a request is not filed and a certificate is not issued, the license may be revoked.[66]

A person obtaining a license for a structure or fill that will displace tidewaters below the high water mark must, at MassDEP's direction, pay a tidewater displacement fee, excavate an area in the same harbor to compensate for such displacement, or implement harbor improvements. Under certain circumstances, a person obtaining a license for an existing and previously unlicensed fill or structure must pay any unpaid tidewater displacement fee. In addition, a person obtaining a license for any activity in, on, or over land to which the Commonwealth holds title must pay a tidelands occupation fee. These fee requirements do not apply to certain projects of municipalities, public agencies, and non-profit organizations or to a project for which a permit rather than a license is required.[67]

Moorings, Floats, and Rafts

MassDEP's regulations establish procedures to govern application for and issuance of permits for moorings, floats, and rafts. Such a permit is issued on an annual basis by the municipal harbormaster or by another municipal official if there is no harbormaster. The regulations require harbormasters to establish written permit procedures, and they specify restrictions on the location of moorings, floats, and rafts.[68]

Appeals

A number of parties are entitled to request an adjudicatory hearing pursuant to the Massachusetts Administrative Procedure Act[69] on a MassDEP decision to issue or deny a license or permit. These parties include the license or permit applicant who has demonstrated property rights in the lands in question or which is a public agency, as well as any of several other parties that have participated in specified ways during the public comment period for the license or permit application. Such parties include: (a) a person aggrieved by MassDEP's action who may suffer an injury in fact which is different in kind or magnitude from that suffered by the general public and which is within the scope of the interests protected by M.G.L. c. 91, and M.G.L. c. 21A; (b) ten residents of the Commonwealth pursuant to a specified provision of the Massachusetts Administrative Procedure Act, although the provision referred to authorizes ten persons to intervene in, rather than to seek, an adjudicatory proceeding;[70] (c) certain municipal officials; the CZM office, for any project in the coastal zone,; and (e) EOEEA for any project in an ocean sanctuary.[71] A request for an adjudicatory hearing must be filed with MassDEP within 21 days of the date of MassDEP's written determination, draft license, or draft permit, or of the date of issuance of the license or permit if a determination or draft is not required.[72]

Any of the persons and entities entitled to seek an adjudicatory hearing on a license or permit may also appeal the issuance of a MassDEP determination of the applicability of Chapter 91 and its implementing regulations.[73] In addition, any person aggrieved by denial of a permit for a mooring, float, or raft or a condition in such a permit may request a review by MassDEP within 30 days of the action being appealed, and MassDEP's decision on appeal constitutes the final administrative review of such action.[74]

Municipal Harbor Plans

EOEEA has adopted regulations at 301 C.M.R. 23.01 to 23.09. which govern the creation and implementation of harbor plans by municipalities. A municipal harbor plan is a document specifying community objectives, standards, and policies to guide public and private utilization of land and water within a defined harbor area or other waterway, as well as legal and institutional arrangements, financial strategies, and other measures to achieve the desired sequence, patterns; and characteristics of development and other activities in the area covered by the plan. Such a plan must be approved by the Secretary of EOEEA. The provisions of an approved plan for a particular harbor would substitute for some of the specific requirements of MassDEP's Chapter 91 regulations with respect to licensing and permitting of projects and activities in that harbor.[75]

Enforcement

MassDEP may revoke a license or permit for non-compliance with its provisions, including a change in use from that specified or from that determined to be implicit if none was specified. A license issued before January 1, 1984 is void if it was not recorded in the appropriate registry of deeds within one year of issuance or if there has been an unauthorized substantial change in use or substantial structural alteration, although such a change of use or alteration occurring before 1984 does not void a license for filled private tidelands. A license issued after January 1, 1984 is void if not recorded in the appropriate registry of deeds within 60 days of issuance or if there has been an unauthorized substantial change in use or substantial structural alteration.[76]

MassDEP may seek discontinuation of use, removal, or other remedial action with respect to fill or a structure that is determined to be a public nuisance. Such fill and structures include those not previously authorized by MassDEP or the Legislature, those for which a grant or license is not presently valid, and those not conforming to the terms and conditions of a grant or license. In addition, MassDEP must remove or have removed any fill or structure which is, in MassDEP's opinion, dilapidated, unsafe, a menace to navigation, or a source of floating debris constituting or likely to become a menace to navigation. MassDEP has authority to issue enforcement orders requiring compliance with the Chapter 91 regulations or with any license or permit condition and to revoke a license for non-compliance with the terms and conditions thereof.[77]

A person whose fill or structure constitutes a public nuisance because it is not properly authorized or in accordance with a license or grant can be subject to: (a) a civil penalty of up to $25,000 for each day the nuisance or violation continues; or (b) imprisonment for up to one year and/or a fine of up to $25,000 for each day the nuisance or violation continues. These penalties also apply to a person who violates the Chapter 91 provisions governing dredging in tidewaters or transportation or disposal of dredged material or a license or permit for such activities.[78] In addition, a person who violates Chapter 91 or a MassDEP regulation, order, or authorization issued thereunder can be subject to a penalty under the Massachusetts Administrative Penalties Act.

NOTES

1. M.G.L. c. 131, §40; 310 C.M.R. 10.01–.99.

2. "Alter" is defined under the Wetlands Protection Act regulations as changing the condition of any area subject to protection under the Act, including but not limited to: (a) changing of pre-existing drainage characteristics, flushing characteristics, salinity distribution, sedimentation patterns, flow patterns, and flood retention areas; (b) lowering of the water level or water table; (c) destruction of vegetation; and (d) changing of water temperature, biochemical oxygen demand, and other physical, biological, and chemical characteristics of the receiving water. 310 C.M.R. 10.04.

3. M.G L. c. 131, §40; 310 C.M.R. 10.02(1), 10.04, 10.27 to 10.35, 10.54 to 10.58.

4. For periods of ten days or less, "days" will be counted in business days. The commission's order of conditions will be the date of its mailing, not the date on the order.

5. The hearing may be continued but only with the applicant's consent.

6. M.G.L. c. 131, §40; 310 C.M.R. 10.01(2); 10.04, 10.05(4)(a), (6)(a).

7. 310 C.M.R. 10.05(6)(a), 10.21 to 10.37, 10.51 to 10.60.

8. 310 C.M.R. 10.55(4)(a), (b).
9. 310 C.M.R. 10.57(4)(a).
10. 310 C.M.R. 10.58(4)(c), (d).
11. 310 C.M.R. 10.05(6)(b).
12. 310 C.M.R. 10.24(7), 10.53(3).
13. M.G.L. c. 131, § 40; 310 C.M.R. 10.05(6)(b), (d), (g), (7)(k), (8), (9).
14. 310 C.M.R. 10.05(3)(a)l, (b), (d).
15. 310 C.M.R. 10.02(2)(b), 10.05(3)(a)2.
16. 310 C.M.R. 10.02(2)(c}, 10.05(4)(d), (6)(b).
17. 310 C.M.R. 10.05(j).
18. It should be noted that while DEP's regulations require that an appeal be filed within 70 days of the commission's failure to act, the WPA requires that the appeal be filed within ten days.
19. The "previous participant" must have submitted written information to the conservation commission prior to the close of the public hearing, requesting a Superseding Order or Determination, or providing written information to MassDEP prior to issuance of a Superseding Order or Determination. 310 C.M.R. 10.05(7)(j).
20. 310 C.M.R. 10.05(3)(c), (d), (7)(a)–(j); M.G.L. c. 131, §40. *See* 310 C.M.R. 10.05(1).
21. The provisions referred to is M.G.L. c. 30A, §10A, which provides for ten persons to intervene in an adjudicatory proceeding in which damage to the environment as defined under M.G.L. c. 214, §7A is or might be an issue. M.G.L. c. 214, § 7A.. Such intervention is limited to the issue of damage to the environment· and the elimination or reduction thereof so that any decision in the adjudicatory proceeding will include disposition of that issue. Such an intervenor has certain procedural rights, including the right of appeal. M.G.L. c. 30A, §10A.
22. 310 C.M.R. 10.05(7)0); M.G.L. c. 30A, §§10, 10A, 11, 12.
23. 310 C.M.R. 10.05(3)(c), 7(f).
24. 310 C.M.R. 10.08(1); M.G.L. c. 131, § 40.
25. M.G.L. c. 131, § 40.
26. 310 C.M.R. 13.02.
27. 310 C.M.R. 10.58.
28. "Practicable" means that costs, existing technology, proposed use and logistics can be satisfied. "Logistics" refers to the existence of legal or physical constraints on a proposed alternative.
29. The variance procedure may be found at 310 C.M.R. 10.05(10).
30. 16 U.S.C. §§1451 to 1465.
31. At the time of publication of this Handbook, the CZM regulations are in the process of being revised and will eventually be split into two separate chapters in 301 C.M.R. The revised regulations will remain substantially similar to those currently found at 301 C.M.R. 21.00, with added provisions establishing procedures for resolving conflicts between state agencies with respect to projects and activities in the coastal zone.
32. 301 C.M.R. 21.05, 21.99, Boundary Appendix.
33. 301 C.M.R. 21.02, 21.03, 21.05, 21.98.

34. 301 C.M.R. 21.98.

35. 301 C.M.R. 21.02 to 21.05. *See* 16 U.S.C.' § 1456(c)(l); 15 C.F.R. § 930.53(b).

36. 301 C.M.R. 21.02 to 21.08.

37. 301 C.M.R. 21.02 to 21.11.

38. M.G.L. c. 91, §§ 2, 10.

39. *See* Lahey, *Waterfront Development and the Public Trust Doctrine* 70 Mass. Law Rev. *55* (1985).

40. M.G.L. c. 91, §§ 2, 10, 14, 15, 18.

41. "Flowed tidelands" are defined as submerged lands and tidal flats subject to tidal action. 310 C.M.R. 9.02.

42. A "great pond" is a pond with an area, in its natural state, of more than ten acres. M.G.L. c. 91, §35; 310 C.M.R. 9.02.

43. Filled tidelands are those areas which are former submerged lands and tidal flats which are no longer subject to tidal action due to the presence of fill. Fill does not include material placed by natural processes, material placed on a beach for beach nourishment purposes, or dredged material placed below the low water mark for purposes of subaqueous disposal. 310 C.M.R. 9.02.

44. 310 C.M.R. 9.04(1), (2).

45. 310 C.M.R. 9.02.

46. 310 C.M.R. 9.02; M.G.L. c. 91, §1. The "historic" low and high-water marks are the water marks that existed prior to human alteration of the shoreline by filling, dredging, excavating, impounding, or other means. 310 C.M.R. 9.02.

47. 310 C.M.R. 9.05(1). *See* M.G.L. c. 91, §§12, 12A, 13, 14, 18, 19, 20.

48. 310 C.M.R. 9.05(2); M.G.L. c. 91, §§19A, 52, 53.

49. 310 C.M.R. 9.05(3). *See* 310 C.M.R. 9.07, 9.08, 9.10, 9.20, 9.22, 9.27, 9.39(1)(b); M.G.L. c. 91, § 1.

50. 310 C.M.R. 9.06.

51. 310 C.M.R. 9.12.

52. 310 C.M.R. 9.11, 9.13, 9.14.

53. 310 C.M.R. 9.32.

54. 310 C.M.R. 9.31(2); M.G.L. c. 91, §§ 14, 18.

55. 310 C.M.R. 9.35.

56. 310 C.M.R. 9.36, 9.51, 9.52, 9.53.

57. 310 C.M.R. 9.54; M.G.L. c. 91, § 18.

58. 310 C.M.R. 9.33.

59. 310 C.M.R. 9.34.

60. 310 C.M.R. 9.37, 9.39.

61. 310 C.M.R. 9.38

62. 310 C.M.R. 9.40.

63. 310 C.M.R. 9.55.

64. 310 C.M.R. 9.15, 9.25; M.G.L. c. 91, §15.

65. 310 C.M.R. 9.18. *See* M.G.L. c. 91, §18.

66. 310 C.M.R. 9.19.

67. 310 C.M.R. 9.16(2)-(4); M.G.L. c. 91, §§ 21, 22. *See* M.G.L. c. 91, §§ 18, 24.

68. 310 C.M.R. 9.07; M.G.L. c. 91, §10A.

69. M.G.L. c. 30A.

70. The provision referred to is M.G.L. c. 30A, §10A, which provides for ten persons to intervene in an adjudicatory proceeding in which damage to the environment as defined under M.G.L. c. 214, §7A is or might be an issue.

71. 310 C.M.R. 9.17(1)..

72. 310 C.M.R. 9.17; M.G.L. c. 91, § 18. *See* M.G.L. c. 30A.

73. 310 C.M.R. 9.06(6).

74. 310 C.M.R. 9.07(5); M.G.L. c. 91, § l0A.

75. 310 C.M.R. 9.02. *See* 301 C.M.R. 23.02.

76. 310 C.M.R. 9.26. *See* M.G.L. c. 91, § 18.

77. 310 C.M.R. 9.08; M.G.L. c. 91, §§15, 18, 23, 49B.

78. M.G.L. c. 91, §§23, *55;* 310 C.M.R. 9.08.

Chapter 8

Solid Waste Management and Facility Siting

The regulation of solid waste facilities under Massachusetts law is governed by Sections 150A and 150A½ of Chapter 111 of the Massachusetts General Laws and Chapter 21H of the Massachusetts General Laws. Under M.G.L. c. 111, §150A, a facility that treats, stores, or disposes of solid waste must obtain a site assignment from the local board of health, as well as a permit and approval of plans to construct and operate the facility from the Massachusetts Department of Environmental Protection ("MassDEP"). "Facility" is defined as "a sanitary landfill, a refuse transfer station, a refuse incinerator rated by [MassDEP] at more than one ton of refuse per hour, a resource recovery facility, a refuse composting plant, a dumping ground for refuse or any other works for treating, storing, or disposing of refuse." "Refuse" is defined as "all solid or liquid waste materials, including garbage and rubbish, and sludge, but not including sewage and those materials defined as hazardous wastes in section two of chapter twenty-one C and those materials defined as source, special nuclear or by-product material under the provisions of the Atomic Energy Act of 1954."

M.G.L. §150½ directs MassDEP to promulgate regulations governing the siting of facilities in which seventeen environmental considerations must be satisfied: (1) the location, nature and extent of any existing or potential sources of public or private drinking water supplies in relation to the site, including the recharge area of a sole source aquifer; (2) the relationship of the site to groundwater elevations; (3) the proximity of wetlands, as defined in section forty of chapter one hundred and thirty-one; (4) the proximity of surface water bodies; (5) the proximity of flood plains; (6) the nature and extent of residential areas in proximity to the site; (7) the availability and suitability of access roads to the site; (8) whether areas adjacent to the proposed site have been previously used for solid waste disposal; (9) the potential for adverse impact on air quality; (10) the potential for creation of a nuisance from noise, windblown litter, or the proliferation of rodents, flies or other vermin; (11) the potential for the adverse public health and safety impacts; (12) the potential impact on agricultural uses; (13) the potential adverse impact on wildlife or on wildlife habitat; (14) the potential impact of increased traffic volume on roads to the site; (15) the extent to which existing solid waste disposal facilities are located within a municipality. Site assignments for new facilities are preferred in municipalities without existing facilities; (16) the extent to which the solid waste disposal needs of the municipality in which the site is sought are met as a member of a regional refuse disposal district (Site assignments in municipalities not participating in regional refuse disposal districts are preferred); and (17) the potential adverse impacts on communities within one-half mile of the proposed site including the potential adverse impacts on the considerations stated within this section for which site suitability standards and criteria are established.

M.G.L. c. 21H directs MassDEP to identify and clean up pollution and threats of pollution from existing and closed solid waste management facilities. M.G.L. c. 21H also imposes liability for costs incurred by MassDEP in taking such action. Facility siting and operation is governed by 310 CMR 16.00. Solid waste management facilities are governed by 310 CMR 19.00.

Currently there are seven landfills in Massachusetts with closure scheduled for six of them. All of the current landfills are lined to prevent leachate from entering the groundwater. Closed landfills are in the process of being permitted for energy generation facilities, including solar panel arrays.

MassDEP issues a "Solid Waste Master Plan" every ten years, the most current of which at this writing is the Draft 2020–2030 Solid Waste Master Plan (the "Draft 2020–2030 Plan"). The Draft 2020–2030 Plan envisions a "zero waste future" by "encouraging and requiring any reusable, recyclable or compostable material to be diverted from disposal at an extremely high rate while eliminating the use of products or packaging that are not reusable, recyclable, or compostable." Until zero waste is accomplished, MassDEP lists seven "Major New and Expanded Initiatives" which include source reduction and reuse; organics waste reduction; residential waste reduction; commercial waste reduction; construction and demolition materials waste reduction; market development for reusable, recyclable, and compostable materials; and solid waste facility oversight and capacity management. In addition to its premise that the "three Rs" (waste reduction, reuse, and recycling) are preferable to disposal of solid waste, MassDEP has added the "rescue" of fresh and perishable foods.

FACILITY SITING

Under M.G.L. c. 111, §150A, a facility that treats, stores, or disposes of refuse cannot be maintained, operated, or expanded without a site assignment granted by the local board of health. MassDEP has promulgated regulations to implement the site assignment requirement at 310 C.M.R. 16.01 to 16.99.

MassDEP's site assignment regulations refer to "solid waste" instead of "refuse," and they define "solid waste" to encompass any useless, unwanted, or discarded solid, liquid, or contained gaseous material, with certain exceptions. These exceptions include hazardous wastes, septage and sewage, sludge from a regulated wastewater treatment plant, properly reused ash from coal combustion, solid or dissolved materials in irrigation return flows, certain nuclear materials as defined under the Atomic Energy Act of 1954, materials and by-products reused within the manufacturing process in which they are generated, and compostable or recyclable material when utilized in accordance with specified regulations.[1]

Chapter 111, § 150A generally applies to any place or site where solid waste or refuse has been or will be treated, stored, deposited, or disposed. However, MassDEP's site assignment regulations contain the following exemptions: (a) facilities that manage hazardous waste and are regulated under MassDEP's hazardous waste management regulations set forth at 310 C.M.R. 30.000; (b) facilities that manage wastewater treatment plant residuals, do not co-dispose of solid waste, and are regulated under MassDEP's water pollution control regulations set forth at 314 C.M.R. 12.00; (c) solid waste combustion facilities rated by MassDEP as being capable of burning no more than one ton of refuse per hour; (d) properly managed operations involving the collection, storage, and processing of beverage containers covered by the state's beverage container deposit law;[2] (e) dumpsters, roll offs, and other temporary storage containers used exclusively to collect solid waste at the site where it is generated, as well as those used exclusively by the Massachusetts Department of Public Works ("DPW") for properly managed solid waste generated and collected by DPW; (f) temporary storage by specified industries of presorted recyclable materials and utilization of such materials by those industries in a manufacturing or industrial process; (g) various types of properly managed recycling and composting operations; (h) various types of properly managed medical wastes collected or stored on-site, or off-site by the facility owner; (i) vehicle storage by a solid waste transporter during a transport layover; (j) residential disposal of wood waste; and (k) certain wood chipping and shredding operations.[3]

MassDEP's site assignment regulations set forth the requirements for review and issuance of a site assignment authorizing the siting of a new facility or a facility expansion. Such requirements include the following: (a) submission of a detailed site assignment application,[4] which must demonstrate compliance with the environmental impact review process under the Massachusetts Environmental Policy Act ("MEPA"); (b) issuance of a MassDEP written determination regarding the completeness of the application; (c) public notice of application to abutters to the site and publication in a newspaper of general circulation of notice of the application;[5] and (d) a public hearing held by the local board of health.[6]

PLANS APPROVAL AND PERMITTING

Chapter 111, § 150A requires MassDEP review and approve of the operating plans and design specifications of a facility for the treatment, storage, or disposal of refuse, as well as a MassDEP permit for such a facility. MassDEP has issued solid waste management regulations which implement these plan approvals and permit requirements at 310 C.M.R. 19.001 to 19.083. The MassDEP regulations combine the two requirements and provide for the issuance of a permit that incorporates MassDEP approval of plans and specifications.[7] These regulations provide exemptions from the permit requirement for the same categories of facilities as the solid waste facility site assignment regulations described below.[8]

Under MassDEP's regulations, any new or existing facility must have a site assignment as well as a Mass DEP permit that includes MassDEP approval of certain plans, MassDEP authorization to construct the facility, and MassDEP authorization to operate the facility.[9] A permit application for a new or existing facility must include: (a) a site plan; (b) a recycling and composting plan in the case of a landfill accepting municipal wastes or demolition debris or a solid waste combustion facility, other than an infectious waste incinerator; (c) a facility design plan; (d) an operation and maintenance plan; (e) a closure/post-closure plan; (f) a public health report prepared by DPH if such a report was prepared in response to MassDEP's site suitability report issued in connection with the site assignment process; (g) proof that a proposed facility will be located within the boundaries of a valid site assignment; and (h) information regarding the .applicability of MEPA requirements.[10]

The solid waste management regulations provide for public notice of a draft permit or a permit denial and distribution of the draft permit or denial to the local board of health.[11] MassDEP may hold a public hearing on the permit application and must do so if requested by the permit applicant.[12] The issuance or denial of a permit may be appealed to the Superior Court.[13] Section 150A requires that notice of a MassDEP solid waste facility permit be recorded in the appropriate registry of deeds, or the registry section of the land court if the site is registered land. MassDEP's regulations specify requirements for and restrictions on the transfer of a solid waste facility permit.[14]

MassDEP's regulations impose a tax on privately owned and operated resource recovery facilities[15] and landfills, other than those used solely for disposal of solid waste generated at the owner's premises. The amount of the tax is based on the tonnage of solid waste processed by such a facility. This tax is paid to the municipality in which the facility is located in lieu of all taxes, fees, charges, and assessments imposed by that municipality, other than the real estate tax covering the land on which the facility is located.[16]

FACILITY CLEANUP AND LIABILITY FOR CLEANUP

Chapter 21H directs MassDEP to identify and clean up pollution and threats of pollution from existing and closed facilities where solid waste is or has been treated, stored, or disposed.[17] Under the statute, the current facility owner and any party otherwise legally responsible for such pollution can be held jointly and severally liable for the costs of investigation and cleanup, except to the extent that a party establishes it is not responsible for such costs. Where the Commonwealth has incurred response costs, then all liable parties, with the exception of cities and towns, can be assessed up to three times those response costs.[18] Chapter 21H allows the use between private parties of hold harmless agreements and indemnification provisions covering liability under Chapter 21H, but it provides that such agreements and provisions cannot insulate any person from liability to the Commonwealth.[19]

ENFORCEMENT

Under M.G.L. c. 111, §150A, the following penalties can be imposed by a court for a violation of Section 150A or the requirements of a MassDEP order or regulation implementing Section 150A: (a) imprisonment for up to two years and/or a fine of up to $25,000 for each day of violation; or (b) a civil penalty of up to $25,000 for each day of violation[20] MassDEP's solid waste management regulations include provisions for the issuance of enforcement orders.[21]

NOTES

1. 310 C.M.R. 16.02.

2. The regulations reference the provisions of the beverage container deposit law, M.G.L. c. 94, §§321–326.
3. 310 C.M.R. 16.05.
4. 310 C.M.R. 16.08.
5. 310 C.M.R. 16.10.
6. 310 C.M.R. 16.20.
7. 310 C.M.R. 19.020, 19.030.
8. 310 C.M.R. 19.013. *See also* 310 C.M.R. 16.05.
9. 310 C.M.R. 19.020.
10. 310 C.M.R. 19.030(3).
11. 310 C.M.R. 9.032(3), 19.033, 19.037.
12. 310 C.M.R. 19.035(1).
13. 310 C.M.R. 19.036(4).
14. 310 C.M.R. 19.044.
15. 310 C.M.R. 19.050. The combustion facility located in Saugus and covered by Chapter 84 of the Mass. Acts of 1985 is subject to a different taxing provision. *See* 310 C.M.R. 19.050(4)(b).
16. 310 C.M.R. 19.050.
17. M.G.L. c. 21H, § 4.
18. M.G.L. c. 21H, § 4(t), (g), (h).
19. M.G.L. c. 21H, § 4(i).
20. M.G.L. c. 150A; 310 C.M.R. 19.081, 19.082.
21. 310 C.M.R. 19.081.

Chapter 9

Hazardous Waste Management and Facility Siting

The federal Resource Conservation and Recovery Act ("RCRA")[1] provides for the U.S. Environmental Protection Agency ("EPA") to authorize states to administer their own hazardous waste regulatory program in lieu of the federal program. The Massachusetts Department of Environmental Protection ("MassDEP") has been authorized by EPA to administer certain portions of the state hazardous waste regulatory program.[2]

Generally, the management of hazardous waste is regulated at the state level in Massachusetts under the provisions of the Massachusetts Hazardous Waste Management Act, M.G.L. c. 21C ("Chapter 21C") with MassDEP regulations at 310 C.M.R. 30.001 to 30.1103. While these provisions partly parallel those of EPA, MassDEP regulations are more stringent or more comprehensive than their federal counterparts in several respects. In addition, M.G.L. c. 21E, §6 authorizes MassDEP to regulate sites where a release of hazardous materials might occur. Facilities that treat, store, or dispose of hazardous waste are also subject to the siting requirements of the Massachusetts Hazardous Waste Facility Siting Act, M.G.L. c. 21D ("Chapter 21D"). In addition to the requirements of Chapter 21D, a facility that treats; stores., or disposes of hazardous waste generated off-site must have a site assignment from the local board of health under Section 150B of Chapter 111 of the Massachusetts General Laws. If the site of the facility is owned by a state agency, then the site assignment must be issued by MassDEP.

Significant differences between the state and federal requirements are noted in this chapter. Further, hazardous waste regulations undergo frequent amendments and the current regulations should be consulted in order to answer specific questions. In addition, MassDEP has issued a number of policy documents and fact sheets pertaining to hazardous waste issues.

HAZARDOUS WASTE MANAGEMENT REQUIREMENTS

Identification of Hazardous Waste

Chapter 21C, contains a broad definition of "hazardous waste":

> [A] waste or combination of wastes, which because of its quantity, concentration, or physical, chemical or infectious characteristics may cause or significantly contribute to an increase in mortality or an increase in serious irreversible, or incapacitating reversible illness or pose a substantial present or potential hazard to human health, safety or welfare or to the environment when improperly treated, stored, transported, used or disposed of, or otherwise managed, however not to include solid or dissolved material in domestic sewage, or solid or dissolved materials in irrigation return flows or industrial discharges which are point sources subject to permits under section 402 of the Federal Water Pollution Control Act of 1967 as amended, or source, special nuclear, or byproduct material as defined by the Atomic Energy Acts of 1954.[3]

A "waste" is defined under MassDEP's regulations as any discarded material not covered by a regulatory exemption.[4] The term encompasses solid, liquid, semisolid, and contained gaseous material, as well as any refuse or sludge. As in EPA's regulations, "discarded material" includes any material that is abandoned by being disposed of, burned, or incinerated, any material that is accumulated, stored, or treated in lieu of being disposed of, burned, or incinerated, and inherently waste-like material (which includes several categories of hazardous wastes specified in the regulations, as well as materials designated as such by the EPA Administrator or by ast that quasi-exemption as a result of non-compliance with the recycling provisions of the hazardous waste regulations.[5]

Hazardous wastes subject to MassDEP management requirements include (a) those exhibiting characteristics of ignitability, corrosivity, reactivity, or toxicity and (b) listed wastes.[6] In addition, DEP may designate a waste as hazardous if "in the course of inspecting any premises, [the Department] has reason to believe that the waste being generated, transported, stored, treated used, or disposed of meets the general criteria of a hazardous waste" set forth in the regulations and MassDEP "believes that an imminent threat . . . may exist."[7]

A listed waste is a waste MassDEP has specifically identified as hazardous, often based upon the source of or process generating the waste. Although slightly expanded upon, MassDEP's lists of hazardous wastes parallel the federal lists, including wastes from non-specific sources, wastes from specific sources, discarded commercial chemical products or off-specification batches of commercial chemical products or spill residues of either, and acutely hazardous wastes. Massachusetts also has listed: (a) waste oil not otherwise specified as a hazardous waste;[8] (b) wastes containing polychlorinated biphenyls ("PCBs") in concentrations of 50 parts per million or greater;[9] and (c) certain wastes generated in the manufacture of paint.[10]

Some wastes are exempt from the hazardous waste requirements. These include: domestic sewage and mixtures of domestic sewage and other waste that are legally discharged through a sewer system to a publicly owned treatment works; (b) industrial wastewater point source discharges authorized under the Massachusetts Clean Waters Act; (c) irrigation return flows; (d) certain nuclear materials; (e) certain mining and ore processing materials; (f) household waste, including waste from single and multiple family residences. hotels, and motels; (g) agricultural crops and animal manure used as soil fertilizer; (h) fly ash, bottom ash, slag waste, and flue gas emission control waste generated from the combustion of coal or other fossil fuels; (i) certain drilling fluids; (j) cement kiln dust waste; (k) certain wood wastes that fail the toxicity characteristic test; (1) samples collected for hazardous waste testing that comply with certain packaging and shipping requirements; (m) certain explosives; (n) wastes stored and burned by a resource recovery facility that does not accept hazardous waste and receives and burns only household waste and commercial and industrial solid waste without hazardous waste; (o) samples undergoing treatability studies at testing facilities that comply with certain requirements; (p) certain petroleum—contaminated material and debris; and (q) cathode ray tubes.[11] Hazardous wastes that are recycled and universal wastes (including certain batteries, thermostats, mercury—containing devices and lamps, and banned or suspended pesticides) are subject to special requirements.[12]

Generator Requirements

Generators of hazardous waste are subject to detailed requirements (set forth at 310 C.M.R. 30.301 to 30.399). Under these requirements, any person who produces a waste in, or imports a waste into, Massachusetts must determine whether the waste constitutes a hazardous waste.[13] If it does, the generator of that waste must calculate the volume of waste in order to determine whether it is subject to the variable requirements applicable to large, small or very small quantity generators.[14] A small quantity generator ("SQG") is defined as one that generates, in a calendar month, less than 1,000 kilograms of certain regulated recyclable materials or non-acutely hazardous wastes, less than one kilogram of certain acutely hazardous wastes, and no more than specified quantities of certain spill residues and container inner liners, and that accumulates no more than specified quantities of such materials on-site.[15] A generator of less than 100 kilograms per month of non-acutely hazardous waste or regulated recyclable material that does not accumulate 600 kilograms or more of such waste and material at any time qualifies as a very small quantity generator ("VSQG") and is subject to fewer requirements than a small quantity generator.[16]

Large and small quantity generators must obtain an EPA identification number,[17] and must comply with containerization, labeling, marking, placarding, recordkeeping, and reporting requirements, as well as with emergency preparedness and personnel training requirements (to ensure safe handling and storage of the waste on-site).[18] Very small quantity generators need not obtain EPA identification numbers, but must register with MassDEP.[19]

A large quantity generator ("LQG") may store its hazardous waste on-site for up to 90 days, if such waste is then transported or transferred to a facility that has an EPA or state license to treat, store, or dispose of hazardous waste or to a facility that has interim status granted by EPA to continue operation pending completion of the licensing process.[20] In addition, the LQG must complete a manifest (or shipping paper) before sending the waste off-site,[21] and must package[22] and transport the waste in compliance with various requirements.[23]

Small quantity generators are subject to less stringent storage, training and emergency preparedness and pre-transport requirements.[24] SQGs may accumulate waste for up to 180 days without a license from MassDEP, provided that each tank and container of hazardous waste is clearly marked and labeled with the date when accumulation in that tank or container began. The 180-day period begins to run when the total amount generated at the site during a calendar month or accumulated at any one time equals 100 kilograms of regulated recyclable material or of non-acutely hazardous waste, or any amount of acutely hazardous waste or regulated recyclable material identified in the list of acutely hazardous wastes.[25]

A VSQG is not subject to accumulation time limits or manifest requirements and may, under certain conditions, recycle or transport its own waste.[26]

Special requirements are imposed on generators who import hazardous wastes into Massachusetts from outside the United States, or export hazardous waste to another country.[27] There are also special provisions governing the accumulation of household hazardous waste and hazardous waste generated by VSQGs in order to facilitate so-called household hazardous waste collection days, and to encourage the establishment of centers for the accumulation of such waste.[28]

Transporter Requirements

Hazardous waste transporters also must operate in accordance with MassDEP's regulatory requirements (set forth at 310 C.M.R. 30.401 to 30.416). Under these requirements, a hazardous waste transporter must obtain an EPA identification number, a MassDEP license, an identification device for each vehicle, and a certification of compliance with respect to the relevant motor vehicle carrier requirements of M.G.L. c. 159B.[29] In addition, a hazardous waste transporter must comply with certain recordkeeping, reporting, and training requirements, must carry liability insurance for sudden and accidental occurrences, and must file a bond, a letter of credit, or other acceptable collateral with MassDEP in order to obtain the MassDEP license.[30] A hazardous waste transporter must carry an emergency procedures guide and certain emergency equipment.[31] A vehicle used in hazardous waste transport must be prominently marked with the identity of the hazardous waste transport licensee and must comply with other marking and placarding requirements.[32] The transporter may not accept hazardous waste without a manifest, and must deliver its cargo to the facility or transporter listed in the manifest, except in the case of certain air, rail, and bulk water shipments where alternative requirements apply.[33]

Certain shipments are exempt from some or all of the transporter requirements. Among the activities entirely exempt from these requirements are (a) transport of hazardous waste by the generator within the site where it is generated, and (b) transport of hazardous waste at a licensed facility that treats, stores, or disposes of such waste by the owner or operator of that facility.[34] The transport of recycled material also is exempt from the hazardous waste requirements, but is separately and extensively regulated.[35] In addition, partial exemptions are provided for shipments of waste from and by VSQGs.[36] Air and rail transporters, which are subject to U.S. Department of Transportation ("DOT") regulations, and bulk shippers by water, which are subject to U.S. Coast Guard regulations, are exempt from certain DEP transporter requirements.[37] A partial exemption is also provided for common or contract carrier transport of hazardous waste through Massachusetts, where the carrier has Interstate Commerce Commission approval, neither accepts nor delivers hazardous waste from or to a Massachusetts location, and carries waste generated in one state to another state where it will be treated, stored, used, or disposed of.[38]

The regulations also provide an exemption from the hazardous waste storage requirements in connection with certain waste transport activities. This exemption covers the storage of hazardous waste shipments in a vehicle at a transportation-related area for up to five days when certain conditions exist, such as delays due to inclement weather or pre-scheduled pickups of less than a truckload of waste.[39]

In some situations, a hazardous waste transporter must comply with the hazardous waste generator requirements. Such requirements are applicable to a transporter that conveys hazardous waste to Massachusetts from outside the Commonwealth or mixes hazardous wastes of different DOT shipping descriptions in a single container.[40]

Recycling Requirements

Requirements for hazardous waste recycling activities are set forth at 310 C.M.R. 30.201 to 30.298. The regulations apply to "regulated recyclable material" which includes recyclable material that is encompassed by DEP's hazardous waste identification regulations,[41] but not to nonhazardous materials being recycled.

The recycling regulations establish three classes of hazardous waste that can be recycled and set forth applicable permit requirements. The regulations also specify standards for generators and transporters of recyclable material. Generators, transporters and facilities that recycle or otherwise handle regulated recyclable material may comply with the recycling regulations and appropriate permit conditions in lieu of other state hazardous waste generator, transporter, or facility standards.[42] However, regulated recyclable material that is not handled in compliance with the recycling regulations is subject to other hazardous waste regulations (at 310 C.M.R. 30.000).[43]

Recyclable materials are classified based upon MassDEP's evaluation of the degree of regulation necessary to protect public health, safety, welfare and the environment. The first category of recyclable hazardous wastes is designated as Class A regulated recyclable material. MassDEP has determined that these materials (and the processes by which they are recycled) present a minimum hazard to public health, safety, and welfare. As a result, MassDEP does not impose facility-specific management standards on the recycling of materials that fall within this class. Class A covers: material that is not reclaimed and is used or reused as an ingredient in a product; (b) industrial ethyl alcohol; (c) scrap metal that would constitute hazardous waste if disposed of; (d) sludge having a hazardous waste characteristic when reclaimed; (e) a by-product having a hazardous waste characteristic when reclaimed; (t) a commercial chemical product listed in Section 30.133 or 30.136 of DEP's regulations which has never been used and is being reclaimed; (g) waste oil if recycled other than by burning for energy recovery; (h) specification used oil fuel burned for energy recovery and handled in accordance with specified procedures; (i) material that is recycled in a completely enclosed recycling system at the site of generation; and (j) material covered by an EPA variance from classification as a RCRA solid waste and approved by DEP as Class A regulated recyclable material.[44] Generators of Class A regulated recyclable material must apply to MassDEP for a permit which is deemed granted unless MassDEP sends written notification of deficiencies in the application within twenty-one days of receipt.[45] Permit conditions are set forth in the regulations.[46]

Class B regulated recyclable materials are those materials which MassDEP has determined should be subject to some management standards to ensure that they to not pose a significant hazard to public health, safety, or welfare. Class B includes: (a) regulated recyclable materials that are not intended, or used, for the production of heat-or power and are instead used in a manner constituting disposal so that the material or any of its constituents could enter the environment; (b) hazardous waste fuels and used oil fuels that are intended to be, and are, burned for the production of heat or power; (c) spent material and hazardous waste listed in Section 30.130 or 30.132 of MassDEP's regulations where such material or waste contains an economically recoverable quantity of a precious metal; and (d) spent lead-acid batteries from which lead is intended to be, and is, reclaimed.[47]

The regulations establish permit and handling requirements for each category of Class B regulated recyclable material.[48] Standards for the storage, blending, and burning of hazardous waste fuel, waste oil, and used oil fuel include requirements to procure generator and transporter identification numbers, and manifesting requirements.[49] In addition, the regulations impose special requirements on those who sell hazardous waste fuel, waste oil, or used oil fuel for burning, and on the burning of used oil fuel.[50]

Regulated recyclable materials which fall outside the scope of Class A and Class B are categorized as Class C recyclables. The examples specified in MassDEP's regulations are spent material that is being reclaimed, as well as a sludge or by-product listed in Section 30.131 or 30.130 of MassDEP's hazardous waste regulations and is being reclaimed. Each of these examples would constitute Class B regulated recyclable material if burned or used in a manner constituting disposal, but if reclaimed, fall outside of the descriptions for Classes A and B, and are therefore designated Class C.[51] Generators and transporters of Class C materials must comply with hazardous waste generator and transporter regulations.[52] Recycling standards and permit requirements for Class C materials are described in the regulations.[53]

In general, anyone who accumulates or recycles any regulated recyclable material except for small and very small quantity generators of Class A regulated recyclable material must obtain a recycling permit.[54] All permittees must store all recyclable material in tanks or containers, must comply with personnel training and emergency prevention and response plan requirements, must submit annual reports to DEP and must maintain all records for at least three years.[55]

Universal Waste Management Requirements

In order to streamline management and facilitate recycling of certain widely generated wastes, MassDEP has adopted regulations for managing wastes such as hazardous batteries, mercury containing devices and lamps, and certain pesticides. The regulations set forth at 310 C.M.R. 30.1001 to 30.1082 are modeled on the federal regulations at 40 C.F. R. Part 273.

Three categories of operations are subject to the regulations: (a) universal waste handlers who generate and accumulate but do not treat, dispose of or recycle universal wastes; (b) transporters, of universal wastes; and (c) destination facilities. Universal waste handlers are divided into two classes, with those who accumulate less than 5,000 kilograms of universal waste at one time qualifying as small quantity handlers who are exempt from many of the recordkeeping requirements. All handlers must comply with management, labeling and storage requirements. Management standards describe the recycling activities allowed and set forth standards for small quantity and large quantity handlers of each category of universal waste.[56] Small quantity handlers need not notify DEP of recycling activities, but must handle universal wastes in accordance with the regulations.[57] Large quantity handlers of universal waste must obtain an EPA identification number and comply with notification and recordkeeping requirements.[58] These requirements are not as detailed or stringent as those applicable to other types of hazardous wastes.

Universal waste transporters must comply with applicable U.S. Department of Transportation regulations at 49 C.F.R. Parts 171 to 180, and may only transport the waste to a handler, a destination facility or a foreign destination.[59] Destination facilities must comply with recordkeeping requirements and are subject to all applicable requirements of the hazardous waste regulations.[60]

Treatment, Storage, and Disposal Facility Requirements

A hazardous waste treatment, storage, or disposal facility ("TSDF") is subject to extensive, complex licensing and financial responsibility requirements and to detailed operating, closure and post-closure standards. These requirements are set forth at 310 C.M.R. 30.501 to 30.595 (specifying management standards for all TSDFs), 310 C.M.R. 30.601 to 30.699 (specifying technical standards for each type of TSDF), 310 C.M.R. 30.701 to 30.791 (specifying facility location standards and land disposal restrictions), 310 C.M.R. 30.801 to 30.890 (specifying licensing requirements and procedures), and 310 C.M.R. 30.901 to 30.910 (specifying financial responsibility requirements).

Under certain conditions, on-site accumulation of hazardous waste for 90 days or less at the site of generation is exempt from the aforementioned licensing requirements and from many of the operating standards.[61] These conditions include storage of the waste in tanks and containers that meet certain standards and labeling specifications, compliance with personnel training and emergency planning requirements, and transfer of the waste to a properly licensed facility.[62] Other exemptions apply to a treatment process or method which is an integral part of the manufacturing process, small quantity generators and universal waste handlers and transporters operating in compliance with regulations specific to those operations, and municipal or industrial wastewater treatment facilities permitted under the Massachusetts Clean Waters Act.[63] In addition, the storage, treatment, or disposal of hazardous wastes containing PCBs in concentrations of 50 parts per million or greater is exempt from MassDEP's TSDF requirements, if such activity occurs at a facility that complies with EPA's regulations at 40 C.F.R. Part 761 adopted under the federal Toxic Substances Control Act, and if any burning or incineration of the PCBs at such facilities complies with DEP's air pollution control regulations, which are discussed in Chapter 4 of this Handbook.[64]

As noted above, MassDEP's management standards for all TSDFs are set forth at 310 C.M.R. 30.501 to 30.595. Under these regulations, a TSDF must prepare and submit to MassDEP written plans on the following subjects: waste analysis, facility security, facility inspection, personnel training, emergency response contingency procedures and preventive measures, closure, and post-closure.[65] A TSDF must also obtain an identification number, and comply with requirements for waste analysis and notification to EPA and MassDEP regarding waste shipments.[66] Other operating requirements pertain to facility security, facility inspection, personnel training, emergency procedures, use of hazardous waste manifests, recordkeeping, reporting, and procedures for closure and post closure activities.[67]

MassDEP's technical standards for TSDF operating units are set forth at 310 C.M.R. 30.601 to 30.699. There are general standards applicable to all TSDFs, and additional specific standards for each type of unit. The regulations mandate groundwater monitoring for certain regulated units including surface impoundments, waste piles, miscellaneous units, land treatment units, and landfills.[68] The regulations also set forth requirements for facilities storing hazardous waste in tanks and containers.[69]

MassDEP's TSDF location standards and land disposal restrictions are set forth at 310 C.M.R. 30.701 to 30.791. In determining whether to issue a TSDF license, MassDEP must evaluate location factors including transportation risks, buffer zones, population density, and sensitive receptors.[70] The regulations forbid the location or expansion of a TSDF on land subject to flooding, and impose flood-proofing requirements on existing facilities in such areas.[71] Furthermore, TSDFs may not be located in the watershed of a surface water supply, on land overlying a present or potential underground drinking water source, or on land in the flow path of a ground water supply to an existing drinking water well.[72] The disposal of hazardous waste into bodies of water, salt domes, salt bed formations, underground mines, or caves is prohibited.[73] The MassDEP land disposal-restrictions (set forth at 310 C.M.R. 30.751 to 30.782) generally track EPA Regulations (at 40 C.F.R. Part 268). MassDEP restrictions do not cover all of the wastes regulated by their EPA counterparts.[74] The DEP regulations prohibit the placement of specified waste materials in a landfill or surface impoundment, or any other land disposal of such materials, unless a treatment standard or concentration threshold has been established and the waste meets that standard or is present at a concentration below the requisite threshold. Generators must analyze their waste to determine whether the waste is subject to disposal restrictions and must notify the receiving facility as to whether the waste meets the applicable treatment standard or is below the threshold concentration which triggers the land disposal restrictions.[75]

The procedures and requirements for licensing TSDFs and transporters are set forth at 310 C.M.R. 30.801 to 30.890. These provisions identify the activities exempt from the licensing requirements[76] and explain the license application and review procedures. They also identify the conditions to be included in a license and set forth license modification, suspension, and revocation procedures, and they describe license and vehicle identification fees, adjudicatory hearing procedures, and the application of the Massachusetts Environmental Policy Act ("MEPA").

The financial responsibility requirements for TSDFs are set forth at 310 C.M.R. 30.901 to 30.910. Owners or operators must submit closure and post-closure cost estimate and evidence of a financial assurance mechanism to MassDEP for approval. Such a mechanism may be a trust fund, surety bond, letter of credit, or insurance policy or a combination of these mechanisms.[77] TSDF owners or operators must also maintain a specified level of coverage for bodily injury and property damage to third parties arising from both sudden and non-sudden accidental occurrences. Compliance with the financial responsibility requirements can be met through use of the above described mechanisms.[78]

Finally, it should be noted that Chapter 21C prohibits the conveyance or lease of property on which hazardous waste has been disposed of until notice of such disposal has been recorded. Such notice is recorded in the registry of deeds or in the registry section of the land court if the property is registered land.[79]

HAZARDOUS WASTE FACILITY SITING REQUIREMENTS

Massachusetts Hazardous Waste Facility Siting Act

Chapter 21D of the Massachusetts General Laws establishes siting requirements for hazardous waste facilities. Chapter 21D defines hazardous waste "facility" very broadly as "a site or works for the storage, treatment, dewatering, refining, incinerating, reclamation, stabilization, solidification, disposal or other processes where hazardous wastes can be stored, treated or disposed of," but this definition does not include municipal or industrial wastewater treatment facilities permitted under the Massachusetts Clean Waters Act.[80]

Facilities that were licensed by MassDEP as of May 1, 1980 or exempt from licensing requirements of Chapter 21C and lawfully in existence as of May 1, 1980, are exempt from Chapter 21D unless the license has since been revoked or the facility seeks to increase capacity.[81] A facility that manages only hazardous waste generated on-site and does not dispose of the waste into or onto the land is also exempt from the siting requirements.[82]

The multi-step siting process begins with submission of a notice of intent to construct, maintain, and operate a hazardous waste facility.[83] The statute provides for briefing sessions in order to insure that the public and interested parties have an opportunity to participate in the process.[84] The developer must prepare a preliminary project impact report, and negotiate a siting agreement with a local assessment committee comprised of officials and residents of the community where the TSDF would be located.[85] The siting agreement must address certain subjects, including operating procedures for the facility and the services and compensation to be provided to the host community.[86] Upon successful completion of the siting agreement negotiations, the developer must prepare a final project impact report. Once the final project impact report has been approved, the siting agreement takes effect.[87]

Site Assignment Requirements

M.G.L. c.111, §150B prohibits the establishment, maintenance, or operation of a hazardous waste facility as defined in Chapter 21D without a site assignment from the board of health for the municipality where the facility is situated, or from MassDEP if the facility site is owned by a state agency. A hazardous waste "facility" is very broadly defined in Chapter 21D to encompass essentially any facility that treats, stores, or disposes of hazardous waste, other than a wastewater treatment facility permitted under the Massachusetts Clean Waters Act.

Before issuance of a site assignment under Section 150B, there must be both public notice and a public hearing. Construction, operation, or maintenance of the facility may not commence until the site assignment is recorded in the registry of deeds, or in the registry section of the land court if the facility site is registered land. Persons aggrieved by the issuance of a site assignment may appeal the decision to MassDEP, while the refusal to issue a site assignment is appealable to the Superior Court.[88]

ENFORCEMENT

Chapter 21C empowers MassDEP to issue orders to abate or prevent violations of that statute or of licenses, orders, approvals, or regulations issued thereunder.[89] Such violations are presumed to constitute irreparable harm to public health, welfare, and safety and the environment and are punishable by imprisonment for not more than two years and/or a fine of up to $25,000 for each day of violation, or by a civil penalty of as much as $25,000 for each day of violation. In addition, a person who knowingly commits such a violation or knowingly handles hazardous waste in a manner which could endanger human health, safety, or welfare can be imprisoned for a term of as much as twenty years and/or fined as much as $100,000 for each day of violation.[90] Finally, it should be noted that a person who violates Chapter 21C or a MassDEP regulation, order, or authorization issued thereunder can be subject to a penalty under the Massachusetts Administrative Penalties Act.

Neither Chapter 21D nor its implementing regulations contain enforcement provisions, but M.G.L. c. 111, §150B does contain such provisions. A violation of Section 150B or an order, rule, or regulation issued thereunder is punishable by imprisonment for up to one year and/or a fine of from $100 to $25,000, or by a civil penalty of up to $25,000 for each day of violation.[91] In addition, a person violating Section 150B or a MassDEP regulation, order, or approval issued thereunder can be subject to enforcement action under the Massachusetts Administrative Penalties Act.

NOTES

1. RCRA was enacted as part of the Solid Waste Disposal Act, 42 U.S.C. §§6901–6992k, and is set forth at 42 U.S.C. §§6921–6939b, 6971–6979b, 6991–699li.

2. *See* 50 Fed. Reg. 3344 (Jan. 24, 1985); 63 Fed. Reg. 52,180 (Sept. 30, 1998).

3. M.G.L. c. 21C, § 2. *See also* definition of hazardous waste at 310 C.M.R. 30.010.

4. 310 C.M.R. 30.010.

5. 310 C.M.R. 30.010.

6. 310 C.M.R. 30.102. *See* 310 C.M.R. 30.120 to 30.125 for hazardous waste characteristics and 310 C.M.R.

to 30.136 for listed wastes.

7. 310 C.M.R. 30.144.

8. 310 C.M.R. 30.130 to 30.136.

9. It should be noted that PCBs are also subject to regulation by EPA under the Toxic Substances Control Act. *See* 15 USC§§2601–2692; 40 CFR Part 761.

10. 310 C.M.R. 30.131.

11. 310 C.M.R. 30.104.

12. 310 C.M.R. 30.143.

13. 310 C.M.R. 30.301, 30.302.

14. *See* criteria at 310 C.M.R. 30.340, 30.351, 30.353.

15. 310 C.M.R. 30.351(1).

16. 310 C.M.R. 30.353(1).

17. 310 C.M.R. 30.303.

18. 310 C.M.R. 30.32 to 30.324; 30.331 to 30.334; 30.340; 30.351.

19. 310 C.M.R. 30.353(9).

20. 310 C.M.R. 30.340(1)(e), 30.305.

21. 310 C.M.R. 30.311.

22. 310 C.M.R. 30.321.

23. 310 C.M.R. 30.304; 30.321 to 30.324.

24. 310 C.M.R. 30.351(8-(11).

25. 310 C.M.R. 30.351(5). A small quantity generator may generate, in a calendar month, less than 100 kilograms of spill residue from certain regulated recyclable materials or acutely hazardous wastes listed or described in Section 30.136 of DEP's regulations, and less than ten kilograms of container inner liners or paper bags containing residue of such regulated recyclable materials or acutely hazardous wastes. A small quantity generator may accumulate less than 2,000 kilograms of non-acutely hazardous waste in containers and less than 6,000 kilograms of such waste in tanks, provided that if both containers and tanks are used, then the amount in containers shall not equal or exceed 2,000 kilograms and the total amount in containers and tanks taken together shall not exceed 6,000 kilograms. 310 C.M.R. 30.351(1).

26. 310 C.M.R. 30.353(6), (7), (11).

27. 310 C.M.R. 30.361.

28. 310 C.M.R. 30.390 to 30.394.

29. 310 C.M.R. 30.402.

30. 310 C.M.R. 30.406, 30.407, 30.409 30.410, 30.411.

31. 310 C.M.R. 30.415.

32. 310 C.M.R. 30.416.

33. 310 C.M.R. 30.403, 30.404, 30.405.

34. 310 C.M.R. 30.401(3)(a), (b).

35. 310 C.M.R. 30.401(8).

36. 310 C.M.R. 30.353(7), 30.401(6).

37. 310 C.M.R. 30.401(3)(d), (e).

38. 310 C.M.R. 30.401(4), (5).

39. 310 C.M.R. 30.408.
40. 310 C.M.R. 30.401(2).
41. 310 C.M.R. 30.010.
42. 310 C.M.R. 30.211. *See also* 310 C.M.R. 30.380, 30.401(8), 30.501(1).
43. 310 C.M.R. 30.211.
44. 310 C.M.R. 30.212.
45. 310 C.M.R. 30.221.
46. 310 C.M.R. 30.225. *See also* 310 C.M.R. 30.202(2), 30.205, 30.206, 30.221, 30.222, 30.250.
47. 310 C.M.R. 30.213.
48. 310 C.M.R. 30.230 to 30.280.
49. 310 C.M.R. 30.204; 30.221 to 30.297.
50. 310 C.M.R. 30.244, 30.245, 30.255, 30.261, 30.262, 30.263, 30.264.
51. 310 C.M.R. 30.214.
52. 310 C.M.R. 30.292, 30.293.
53. 310 C.M.R. 30.294 to 30.298.
54. 310 C.M.R. 30.221(3).
55. 310 C.M.R. 30.205.
56. 310 C.M.R. 30.1034 (small quantity handlers), 30.1044 (large quantity handlers).
57. 310 C.M.R. 30.1031, 30.1033.
58. 310 C.M.R. 30.1040 to 30.1049.
59. 310 C.M.R. 30.1050 to 30.1056.
60. 310 C.M.R. 30.1060 to 30.1063.
61. 310 C.M.R. 30.801(1), 30.501(2).
62. 310 C.M.R. 30.801(1), 30.501(2), 30.340(1).
63. 310 C.M.R. 30.501(2).
64. 310 C.M.R. 30.501(3).
65. 310 C.M.R. 30.513(2), 30.514(2), 30.515(2); 30.516(2), 30.521, 30.583, 30.593.
66. 310 C.M.R. 30.511, 30.512, 30.513.
67. 310 C.M.R. 30.514; 30.515; 30.516; 30.524; 30.530 to 30536; 30.540 to 30.544; 30.580 to 30.587; 30.590 to 30.596.
68. 310 C.M.R. 30.660 to 30.675.
69. 310 C.M.R. 30.680 to 30.689 (containers), 310 C.M.R. 30.690 to 30.699 (tanks).
70. 310 C.M.R. 30.705.
71. 310 C.M.R. 30.701.
72. 310 C.M.R. 30.702 to 30.704.
73. 310 C.M.R. 30.706 to 30.707.
74. 310 C.M.R. 30.750.
75. 310 C.M.R. 30.750 to 30.764. Treatment standards are set forth at 310 C.M.R. 30.771 to 30.782.
76. 310 C.M.R. 30.801.
77. 310 C.M.R. 30.903, 30.904, 30.905, 30.906, 30.907.

78. 310 C.M.R. 30.908.
79. M.G.L. c. 21C, §7.
80. M.G.L. c. 21D, §2.
81. M.G.L. c. 21D, §§18, 19.
82. M.G.L. c. 210, §18.
83. M.G.L. c. 21D, §7.
84. M.G.L. c. 210, §8.
85. M.G.L. c. 210, §§5, 13.
86. M.G.L. c. 210, §12.
87. M.G.L. c. 21D, §10.
88. M.G.L. c. 111, §150B.
89. M.G.L. c. 21C, §9.
90. M.G.L. c. 21C, §10.
91. M.G.L. c. 111, §150B.

Chapter 10

Underground and Aboveground Tanks

EPA has delegated authority to Massachusetts to administer the state underground storage tank program in lieu of the federal program. The Massachusetts Department of Environmental Protection (MassDEP) has proposed amendments to its Underground Storage Tank (UST) regulations at 310 CMR 80.00 to make them at least as stringent as EPA UST regulations at 40 CFR 280 and 281. As of August 19, 2021, the final version of the regulations has not been issued.[1] The state program also consists of the UST Cleanup Fund regulations adopted pursuant to M.G.L. c. 21J, and the requirements for reporting and responding to releases and threats of releases of oil and hazardous materials associated with underground tanks under the Massachusetts Contingency Plan ("MCP").[2]

The UST Cleanup Fund is funded by fees on bulk deliveries of petroleum products to dispensing facilities and on certain USTs at dispensing facilities. The Fund was created to provide: (a) partial reimbursement to certain parties who incur costs and damages as a result of releases from USTs containing petroleum products capable of being used as motor fuels; and (b) funds to MassDEP for its activities regarding administration of Chapter 21J and prevention of and response to releases of petroleum products from underground storage tanks.

Chapter 21J and its implementing regulations provide for reimbursement of investigation and cleanup costs, as well as for claims for bodily injury, property damage, and natural resources damages, associated with contamination from a petroleum product underground storage tank (including contamination from spilling and overfilling under some circumstances) at a site for which the owner or operator has paid delivery fees under M.G.L. c. 21J and provided notice of the release to Mass DEP. A "petroleum product" is defined as a product that is obtained from distilling and processing crude oil and that is capable of being used as fuel for propulsion of a motor vehicle, boat, or aircraft, and was in fact delivered to the UST facility for that purpose. The term does not include product destined for use in chemical manufacturing.

In order to be eligible for reimbursement from the und an owner or operator must comply with the following:

a. An owner or operator must have completed, as the case may be, all underground storage tank or underground storage tank system registration requirements as set forth in section 9002 of the Resource Conservation and Recovery Act of nineteen hundred and seventy-six as well as with all federal or state regulatory requirements relating to the registration of underground storage tanks or underground storage tank system;
b. be in full compliance with all regulatory requirements imposed upon an owner or operator, as the case may be, of an underground storage tank or underground storage tank system, which requirements relate to the maintenance and operation of the underground storage tanks or underground storage tank system and with all regulatory requirements related to the construction and installation of such underground storage tank or underground storage tank system, provided such requirements applied to such owner or operator at the time such underground storage tank or underground storage tank system was constructed or installed;
c. have incurred a cost, expense, or obligation, whether for cleanup or related matters or for claims of third parties resulting from a release of a petroleum product from an underground storage tank or underground storage tank system; and
d. in the case of claims for bodily injury, property damage, or damage to natural resources, the owner or operator submitting the claim shall have obtained a final judgement from a court of competent jurisdiction, all rights of appeal being exhausted, waived, or expired, that the bodily injury, property damage, or damage to natural resources was a result of a release of a petroleum product from the underground storage tank or underground storage tank system.

Chapter 21J and its implementing regulations provide for administrative and judicial review of a denial of, or other action on, a claim for reimbursement.

A person who violates any requirement of the tank regulations can be subject to: (a) a civil penalty of up to $25,000 for each day of violation; or (b) imprisonment for up to two years and/or a fine e of up to $25,000 for each day of violation. Upon the request of the head of the fire department, the local licensing authority and the town or city counsel must take any necessary actions to enforce MassDEP's tank regulations. As an alternative or in addition to such enforcement action, the head of the fire department or the State Fire Marshal may revoke or suspend a tank permit or mandate more frequent tank testing than would otherwise be required. If a permit is revoked or if a tank has been installed or maintained without a permit, the fire department head, or the Fire Marshal, may also order removal of the tank.

A person who violates a requirement relating to the Underground Storage Tank Petroleum Product Cleanup Fund can be subject to: (a) a civil penalty of up to $25,000 for each day of violation; (b) imprisonment for up to two years and/or a fine of up to $25,000 for each day of violation; or (c) prohibition from participation in any current or future reimbursement claim.[3]

NOTES

1. The draft regulations are available at https://perma.cc/NP84-KJNV.
2. 310 C.M.R. 40.0000.
3. M.G.L. c. 21J, §13.

Chapter 11

Oil and Hazardous Material

The Massachusetts Oil and Hazardous Material Release Prevention Act, M.G.L. c. 21E, §§1–19 ("Chapter 21E"), imposes liability on certain classes of persons for releases and threats of release of oil or hazardous material, and authorizes the Massachusetts Department of Environmental Protection ("MassDEP") to conduct response actions, including investigation and remediation, and to require other parties to conduct response actions, with respect to releases and threats of release of oil or hazardous material. Although patterned after the federal Superfund statutes, Chapter 21E is broader than the federal Comprehensive Environmental Response, Compensation and Liability Act ("CERCLA")[1] in several significant ways. Most importantly, (1) Chapter 21E imposes liability and cleanup requirements for releases and threats of release of oil, as well as hazardous material; (2) Chapter 21E imposes liability for property damage, as well as response costs and natural resource damages; (3) Chapter 21E, as implemented through the Massachusetts Contingency Plan, 310 C.M.R. 40.0000 to 40.1600 (the "MCP"), generally imposes on responsible parties an affirmative obligation to notify MassDEP of, to investigate and, if necessary, to remediate any site at which a reportable release or threat of release has occurred, under the oversight of an environmental consultant licensed by the Commonwealth; and (4) the 1998 amendments to Chapter 21E added innovative liability relief and funding provisions designed to encourage redevelopment of contaminated property, *i.e.,* "brownfields."

THE LIABILITY REGIME

The Chapter 21E liability scheme is generally similar to that under CERCLA, but Chapter 21E also imposes liability on certain classes of persons for releases and threats of release of oil. The MCP refers to these parties as "responsible parties" or "RPs," and refers to persons potentially liable under Chapter 21E as "potentially responsible parties" or "PRPs."[2]

Chapter 21E applies to releases or threats of release of oil or hazardous material ("OHM") into the environment. These terms are broadly. defined. In particular, OHM includes and is broader than "hazardous substances" under CERCLA: First, "hazardous material" includes "hazardous substances," as defined under CERCLA, "hazardous wastes" and "regulated recyclable materials" as defined under the Massachusetts Hazardous Waste Management Act, and waste oil.[3] Second, as described below, Chapter 21E appears to mimic the petroleum exclusion found in CERCLA by excluding oil from the definition of hazardous material. However, because releases or threats of release of oil are treated in basically the same fashion as releases of hazardous material under Chapter 21E, that exclusion is largely illusory. Furthermore, "oil" is itself broadly defined, and is not limited to petroleum-related materials. Instead, oil includes, *inter alia* insoluble or partially insoluble derivatives of mineral, animal or vegetable oils.[4]

"Release" and "environment" are likewise broadly defined under Chapter 21E. "Release" includes any spilling, leaking, pumping pouring, emitting, emptying, discharging, injecting, escaping, leaching, dumping, or disposing into the environment.[5] The definition of "release," however, contains significant exceptions, generally similar to those under CERCLA: (a) emissions from the exhaust of an engine; (b) certain releases of source, byproduct or special nuclear material; (c) the normal application of fertilizer; (d) the application of pesticides in accordance with their labeling; and (e) the application of residuals, *i.e.,* sludge and septage, in. accordance with 310 C.M.R. 32.00. Threat of release refers to a substantial likelihood of release requiring action to prevent or mitigate the damage to the environment that may result from such release. "Environment" is defined as the waters, land, subsurface strata, or ambient air of the Commonwealth.[6]

Classes of Responsible Parties

The classes of persons liable for a site at which there has been a release or threat of release of hazardous material are: (1) current owners and operators, (2) past owners at the time of storage or disposal of hazardous material, (3) persons who, directly or indirectly, arranged for transportation, disposal, storage, or treatment of hazardous material, (4) those who transported such material, and (5) "any person who otherwise caused or is legally responsible for a release or threat of release" of hazardous material at a site.[7] In relation to oil, the statute creates only two classes of liable parties: (1) current owners and operators, and (2) the "catch-all" category of "any person who otherwise caused or is legally responsible for a release or threat of release" of oil.[8] Interpreting this language, Massachusetts courts have held that current owners or operators are strictly liable for oil releases and threats of release based on their status, and that others are liable for the same only if they caused or are legally (*i.e.*, contractually) responsible for the release of the oil from the site that caused the contamination at issue.[9]

Responsible parties are jointly and severally liable to the Commonwealth for injury to or loss of natural resources and for cleanup costs, including the costs of assessing and evaluating the injury, when such are incurred or suffered as a result of the release or threat of release.[10] In order to encourage responsible parties to "voluntarily and without delay participate in carrying out and paying for response actions," a court can order a responsible party to pay up to treble damages, plus litigation costs and attorneys' fees, to the Commonwealth, if such responsible party failed to comply with a Mass DEP order to conduct response actions, or acted unreasonably or in bad faith in not carrying out a response action.[11] Additionally, responsible parties are liable for damage to real or personal property resulting from the release or threat of release, and for recovery of necessary and reasonable response costs incurred by private parties to investigate and remediate the site.[12]

Limits on Liability

Chapter 21E provides several limited defenses to liability. An otherwise responsible party is not liable if it can establish that the release or threat of release and the resulting damage were caused by (a) an act of God; (b) an act of war; or (c) an act or omission of a third party, other than an employee or agent of the otherwise liable party and other than in connection with a direct or indirect contractual relationship, provided that the otherwise liable party exercised due care with respect to the OHM, took precautions against foreseeable acts or omissions of third parties and the consequences of such acts or omissions, and complied with the Chapter 21E notification requirements.[13] Furthermore, if an otherwise liable party can establish that only a portion of the response costs or other damages is attributable to the release or threat of release for which that party is liable under Chapter 21E, that party is responsible only for such portion.[14] Of course, merely hiring a licensed site professional to conduct a response action consistent with the MCP does not cause anyone to be liable.[15]

Although not tested or interpreted in any Massachusetts case, Chapter 21E also states that an otherwise responsible party is not liable to the Commonwealth if he or she can establish that the "substance or amount thereof released or threatened to be released does not represent a long or short-term danger to the public health, safety, welfare or the environment."[16]

In addition to these general defenses to liability, there are several conditional limitations on and exceptions from liability for certain parties who are, in some sense, "innocent" with respect to the contamination. As discussed below, current landowners, lenders and fiduciaries, and those who acquire ownership or become tenants or operators and meet the requirements of "eligible persons" or "eligible tenant," usually as part of redevelopment of a brownfields site, may qualify for protection from Chapter 21E liability.

Liability Protections for Current Landowners

A current owner who did not own or operate the site at the time of the release of OHM, and did not cause or contribute to the release or threat of release, *i.e.*, an "innocent owner," and who meets certain other conditions, is shielded from most liability to the Commonwealth and other responsible parties, except for contractual liability. Where the Commonwealth has incurred costs for assessment, containment or removal of contamination, the "innocent owner" remains liable up to the post-cleanup value of the property.[17] The statute is ambiguous as to whether a current *operator* could take advantage of this provision.

Another liability limitation, and one with significant potential for benefitting "innocent" landowners, is "downgradient property status," which was initially created by DEP by regulation[18] but was codified by statute in 1998. In particular, the 1998 Amendments provide an exemption from liability under Chapter 21E and from common law property damage (but not from contractual or personal injury claims) to owners of downgradient or downstream property contaminated by a release from a *known* source, provided the owner did not cause or contribute to the contamination and meets certain requirements such as providing notice to DEP and access. to those conducting response actions. When the release is from an unknown source, the statute provides only a defense to liability.[19] There are also liability limitations available for resident-owners of one-to-four-family residences, and for public utility companies regarding contamination of a right-of-way.[20]

Liability Protections for Lenders and Fiduciaries

Chapter 21E provides protection from liability for secured lenders and fiduciaries who do not cause or contribute to releases of OHM and who meet certain other conditions, by excluding such parties from the definition of owner or operator.[21] In order to qualify for protection from liability, a secured lender or fiduciary must comply with specified conditions and requirements, such as notice to DEP, reasonable access to persons conducting response actions, reasonable efforts to contain and prevent exposure, and compliance with the MCP when undertaking any voluntary response actions. In addition, a secured lender or fiduciary must act to abate imminent hazards, but a fiduciary may instead notify DEP, where the assets of an estate or trust are not sufficient to perform these otherwise required response actions.

The 1998 Amendments significantly narrowed the circumstances under which a secured lender may be liable. As before, in order for a secured lender to maintain the exemption after foreclosing and taking title to or possession of a borrower's property, the secured lender must act diligently to sell or divest ownership or possession of the site. However, a secured lender no longer must sell or divest within five years. Instead, during the first 36 months, it is presumed that the secured lender is acting diligently to sell the contaminated property; after 36 months, the secured lender carries the burden of demonstrating adequate diligence. Further, the 1998 Amendments removed language (similar to that found in CERCLA) that had subjected a lender to liability if the secured lender had "participat[ed] in the management" of the site. A secured lender, however, is liable for any release or threat of release that first begins to occur during its ownership or possession of the site.[22]

Liability Protections for Eligible Persons at Brownfields Sites

Liability relief has been provided for certain "eligible persons" who either acquire previously contaminated property *after* a permanent solution or remedy operation status has been achieved, *or* who remediate the site[23] to achieve a permanent solution or remedy operation status. In order for a current (or prospective) owner or operator be eligible for this protection, *i.e.,* in order to be an "eligible person," one must not have owned or operated the site at the time of the release and must not have caused or contributed to the release. Additionally, one must comply with certain conditions, including notifying MassDEP of the release, providing reasonable access to parties conducting response actions, responding to MassDEP information requests in a timely manner, ensuring that response actions comply with the MCP and Chapter 21E, preventing new exposure, and settling any past response costs incurred by the Commonwealth.[24]

The liability relief provided protects an eligible person from claims of the Commonwealth or other persons for contribution, response costs, and statutory or common law property damage, but not from personal injury claims. The liability protection is an exemption from liability if the property is acquired after notification to MassDEP of the release; and a defense if acquired before such notification. An eligible person may transfer ownership to another eligible person, and, if certain conditions are met, both may obtain the liability protections described herein.

In order to encourage the development and reuse (*i.e.,* leasing) of previously contaminated properties, a similar protection is afforded to "eligible tenants." The conditions for eligible tenants parallel those for eligible persons, except that eligible tenants who use oil or hazardous material similar to those that were released at the site must demonstrate that they did not contribute to the contamination.[25]

Financial Assurances

Where necessary to assure the timely and proper performance and completion of response actions, MassDEP may require an RP, PRP, or other person to provide assurance that such person has sufficient financial resources to perform the response actions or a specific portion thereof. Among the financial assurance mechanisms that may be required are trust funds, stand-by trust funds, letters of credit, escrow deposits, and surety bonds.[26] Also an RP, PRP, or other person performing response actions must notify MassDEP promptly in writing if it has reason to believe that performance of the response actions is beyond its technical, financial, or legal ability.[27] Furthermore, the MCP provides that MassDEP may refuse to allow an RP, PRP, or other person to perform a response action if MassDEP is not persuaded that: (a) the person will comply with the deadlines and time periods for taking such action and other requirements imposed by Chapter 21E and the MCP; (b) the person's performance of the response action will not result in or cause a hazard, or exacerbate an existing hazard, to health, safety, public welfare, or the environment; or (c) the person has a satisfactory record of compliance with the statutes, regulations, and other requirements administered or enforced by MassDEP.[28]

RELEASE NOTIFICATION

Chapter 21E and the MCP generally require the owner or operator of a site or vessel and any other liable person to notify MassDEP of both current and historic releases or threats of release of OHM that exceed or would exceed regulatory thresholds. This notification requirement is triggered when such person obtains "knowledge" of a release or threat of release.[29] If a release or threat of release has occurred and it is unclear whether it involves OHM but $ere is a "substantial likelihood" that it does, the person otherwise responsible for notification must determine whether such release or threat of release triggers notification.[30] Chapter 21E imposes serious penalties for failure 'to report properly.[31]

MassDEP has established thresholds below which notification is not required as well as procedures for giving notice.[32] The MCP sets forth characteristics of a release or threat of release, such as whether it creates a sheen on water, equals or exceeds a reportable quantity ("RQ"), or equals or exceeds a reportable concentration ("RC"), that determine if notification is required. Further, the MCP specifies whether notice must within two hours, 72 hours, or 120 days, depending upon the type, location, and severity of the release or threat of release.[33]

The notification triggers include RQs and RCs. Reporting is required when it is determined that an amount of OHM meeting or exceeding the relevant RQ has been released (or is threatened to be released) within a 24-hour period, and this trigger is most often met in relation to new, sudden releases or spills. RQs have been established by MassDEP for many substances and are listed in the MCP.[34] Many are substantially lower than the corresponding federal RQs promulgated under CERCLA.[35] RCs, by contrast, apply generally to OHM contamination in soil or ground water, whether the result of a new or a historic release.[36] In essence, RCs are *de minimis* thresholds below which risks are presumed to be minimal and regulatory involvement is not required. Each OHM listed in the MCP has an RC for each of two categories of soil and two categories of ground water, with the stringency of the RC dependent upon the nature and uses of the soil or ground water in that category. For example, RCs for ground water in category RCGW-1, which includes ground water that may affect a potential public or private drinking water supply or a high quality surface water body, are more stringent than those for ground water in RCGW-2, which includes all other ground water.[37]

Generally, the two-hour notice requirement applies when the release or threat of release of OHM has or would cause either an "imminent hazard" or an exceedance of an RQ. A release will also trigger the two-hour notification requirement if it causes, *inter alia,* a sheen on surface waters, or a measurement from a private drinking water supply exceeding an RCGW-1 standard.[38] An "imminent hazard" is a hazard that would pose a significant risk of harm to health, safety, public welfare, or the environment if it were present for even a short period of time,[39] and the MCP identifies certain categories of releases that are deemed to pose imminent hazards.[40]

Releases considered by MassDEP to warrant less immediate attention must be reported either within 72 hours or 120 days. The 12-hour notice requirement applies to releases exceeding certain RCs within Zone I of a public water supply well or 500 feet of a private water supply well, certain releases and threats of release related to underground storage tanks, the presence of subsurface non-aqueous phase liquid ("NAPL") greater than or equal to a specified thickness, and the presence of certain contaminant levels in specified locations near a school or occupied residential structure where the ground water table is within 15 feet of the surface of the ground.[41] The 120-day notice requirement applies to all other soil and ground water contamination exceeding RCs and to the presence of subsurface NAPL of a specified thickness.[42]

In the case of a 120-day notification, a person may not begin to undertake response actions at the site, except Limited Removal Actions as discussed below, without first making the required notification to MassDEP.[43]

The time period for notification begins to run when the person required to notify "obtains knowledge" of the release or threat of release, or when a person with knowledge obtains the status of a person required to notify, whichever is later.[44] The MCP defines "knowledge" as either "actual knowledge" or the "knowledge a person acting in a reasonably prudent and intelligent manner would have but for that person's willful, knowing or negligent avoidance of learning about the fact or facts in question. In determining whether a person has acted in a reasonably prudent and intelligent manner, any specialized knowledge or training possessed by that person and the circumstances surrounding the fact or facts in question shall be taken into account.[45]

Certain categories of releases do not require notification. These include, *inter alia:* (a) a release of OHM that is discharged from a point source which is regulated under a valid permit, license, or approval, unless the release violates the limits set forth in such permit, license, or approval; (b) a release that was previously reported and is the subject of ongoing response actions; and (c) a release where a Limited Removal Action, which is discussed in Section 11.7.2 of this Chapter, has reduced the soil concentration of OHM to an amount less than the RC within the time period allowed for notification.[46]

SITE LISTING

MassDEP is required under Chapter 21E and the MCP to maintain and update annually a list of suspected and confirmed "disposal sites," *i.e.,* locations where OHM has come to be located as a result of a release.[47] MassDEP is not required to list a site where sufficient response actions have been completed, or for which no response actions were necessary.[48]

LICENSED SITE PROFESSIONALS

Those conducting response actions must hire hazardous waste site cleanup professionals, generally known as "licensed site-professionals" ("LSPs") who oversee decisions regarding site investigation and remediation and submit required reports to MassDEP, subject to MassDEP audit and enforcement.[49] While LSPs are retained and paid by the parties conducting response actions, they are independently licensed and regulated by the Commonwealth by the Board of Registration of Hazardous Waste Site Cleanup Professionals (the

"LSP Board"). Further, they are subject to discipline by the LSP Board for failure to meet specified rules of professional conduct.[50]

The MCP requires LSPs to render opinions regarding their clients' compliance with a variety of site investigation, cleanup, and reporting requirements.[51] Submission of an LSP opinion is a representation that the professional services associated therewith were provided in accordance with the applicable standards of care, that the response actions that are the subject of the opinion were performed in accordance with the applicable provisions of Chapter 21E and the MCP, and that the conclusions expressed in the opinion are based upon the LSP's professional judgment and reflect his or her knowledge, information, and belief.[52] LSPs must meet the "Response Action Performance Standard" ("RAPS") in performing response actions,[53] which is defined as the "level of diligence reasonably necessary to obtain the quantity and quality of information adequate to assess a site and evaluate remedial action alternatives, and to design and implement specific remedial actions at a disposal site to achieve a level of No Significant Risk for any foreseeable period of time and, where feasible, to reduce to the extent possible the level of oil and/or hazardous materials in the environment to background levels."[54]

CLEANUP STANDARDS AND RESPONSE ACTION OUTCOMES

The MCP is intended to facilitate expeditious voluntary site cleanups by private parties. The types of response actions that may or must be performed range from preliminary response actions, which may lessen or eliminate future obligations and are discussed below, to comprehensive response actions, which must be conducted in phases under the direction of DEP or an LSP and are discussed below.

For each site, Chapter 21E requires, if feasible, implementation of one or more "permanent solutions" as necessary to achieve a level of "no significant risk." "No significant risk" is defined as "a level of control of each identified substance of concern at a site or in the surrounding environment such that no such substance of concern shall present a significant risk of harm to health, safety, public welfare, or the environment during any foreseeable period of time.[55] For purposes of determining whether a permanent solution will achieve the "no significant risk" standard, current and foreseeable uses of the site and the surrounding environment, as well as applicable and suitably analogous public health and environmental standards, must be considered.[56]

Chapter 21E further provides that, where feasible, a permanent solution must include measures designed "to reduce to the extent possible the level of [OHM] in the environment to the level that would exist in the absence of the site of concern," *i.e.,* to background.[57] The MCP defines "background" as "those levels of [OHM] that would exist in the absence of the disposal site of concern which are: (a) ubiquitous and consistently present in the environment at and in the vicinity of the disposal site of concern; and (b) attributable to geologic or ecologic conditions, atmospheric deposition of industrial process or engine emissions, fill materials containing wood or coal ash, releases to [ground water] from a public water supply system and/or petroleum residues that are incidental to the normal operation of motor vehicles."[58]

Chapter 21E provides that where a permanent solution is not feasible, a temporary solution must be implemented to eliminate to the extent feasible any substantial hazard to health, safety, public welfare, or the environment. In addition, a plan must be developed, including a timetable of "definitive and enterprising" steps to be taken to identify, develop, and implement a feasible permanent solution at the site.[59]

The MCP uses the term "Response Action Outcome" ("RAO") to indicate achievement of a cleanup endpoint, *i.e.*, a permanent or temporary solution. There are three basic classes of RAOs that may be achieved at a disposal site. A Class A RAO applies to a site where a permanent solution has been achieved.[60] A Class B RAO applies to a site where a level of no significant risk exists and thus no remedial actions are necessary or were taken.[61] A Class C RAO applies to a site where a temporary solution has been achieved and any substantial hazard has been eliminated, but a level of no significant risk cannot be demonstrated.[62]

At almost any time during the site investigation and remediation process, if the conditions for an RAO have been met, the person conducting response actions can submit to MassDEP a statement. containing the LSP's opinion that an RAO has been achieved (an "RAO Statement").[63] An RAO Statement can be submitted for an entire site or for a portion of a site.[64] In order to ensure that future uses of the site are in accordance with the assumptions on which the RAO is based, a property use restriction may be imposed, limiting future land uses and activities, as discussed below.[65] Such limitations "lock in" the foreseeable land use (*e.g.,* industrial), and may justify a less extensive cleanup than would be required for unrestricted future use (*e.g.,* residential).

Subject to certain conditions and extensions, an RAO must be achieved no later than five years after either the effective date of a Tier I permit or the submission of a Tier II classification, which are discussed in Section 11.8 of this chapter.[66]

PRELIMINARY RESPONSE AND RISK REDUCTION MEASURES

General Provisions

The MCP provides incentives and opportunities for RPs, PRPs, and other persons to take early response actions to reduce risks and, in many cases, to reduce or avoid further obligations under the MCP. The MCP allows, and in some cases requires, persons subject to the release notification requirements to carry out certain response actions promptly and with minimal MassDEP involvement. These actions include limited removal actions ("LRAs"), initial site investigation activities, immediate response actions ("IRAs"), release abatement measures ("RAMs"), and utility-related abatement measures ("URAMs"). The data gathered during preliminary response and risk reduction measures guide determinations regarding required and appropriate future response actions, and may be used to identify RPs and PRPs, or as a basis for an RAO.

Limited Removal Actions

LRAs involve excavation and off-site recycling, reuse, treatment, or disposal of limited volumes of contaminated soil that equal or exceed applicable RCs, and therefore are subject to the 120-day release notification requirement. An LRA can be undertaken to remove such soil prior to expiration of the 120-day notification period and thereby to eliminate the need to notify MassDEP. LRAs are limited to the following volumes of soil removed from a site: (a) 20 cubic yards of soil contaminated with hazardous material or with a mixture of hazardous material and oil or waste oil; or (b) 100 cubic yards of soil contaminated only with oil or waste oil. Under most circumstances, an LRA may be performed without hiring an LSP.[67]

Immediate Response Actions

Immediate response actions ("IRAs") are mandatory, early actions required in order to abate or investigate certain releases or threats of release that may pose an imminent hazard to health, safety, public welfare, or the environment. IRAs may involve assessment of a release or threat of release and, where appropriate, actions to contain, isolate, remove, or secure the release or threat of release. IRAs must be undertaken: (a) in response to releases and threats of release subject to the two-hour and seventy-two-hour release notification requirements; (b) in response to conditions of "substantial release migration," which are defined as conditions where the mechanism, rate, or extent of transport has resulted in or, if not promptly addressed, has the potential to result in (i) health damage, safety hazards, or environmental harm or (ii) a substantial increase in the extent or magnitude of the release, the degree or complexity of future response actions, or the amount of response costs;[68] and (c) at any other site or vessel where MassDEP has determined that immediate or accelerated response actions are necessary to prevent, eliminate, or minimize damage to health, safety, public welfare, or the environment.[69]

IRAs may include assessment of whether an imminent hazard exists, installation of drainage controls, construction of berms or dikes, installation of waste or product recovery systems, installation of ground water treatment systems, removal of contaminated soils, installation of soil vapor recovery systems, temporary capping, and other assessment, containment, and removal actions. IRAs are presumed to entail containment or removal actions, although under certain circumstances they may be limited to investigation or assessment of a release or threat of release.

The MCP requires that DEP be provided with notice that an IRA is to be conducted and provides that, with certain exceptions, an IRA involving remedial actions cannot be conducted until DEP has granted approval. In addition, with certain exceptions, the MCP requires submission of an IRA plan and includes requirements for quarterly IRA status reports and for an IRA completion report. Completion of an IRA may result in filing of a Class A or B RAO, initiation of a RAM, or continuation of preliminary or comprehensive response actions.[70]

Release Abatement Measures

Release abatement measures ("RAMs") are remedial actions that may be voluntarily undertaken to remediate a limited or localized release or to mitigate the impacts of a larger release until such time as more comprehensive remedial actions can be instituted. Among the actions that may be carried out as RAMs are: (a) excavation and off-site disposal of up to 500 cubic yards of contaminated soil that equals or exceeds applicable RCs; (b) excavation and on-site or off-site treatment, recycling, or reuse of up to 1,500 cubic yards of contaminated soil that equals or exceeds applicable RCs; (c) initiation of a ground water or non-aqueous phase liquid recovery system that discharges to a closed container or pursuant to required discharge permits; and (d) implementation of a soil vapor extraction system or a ground water sparging system with certain controls.

The MCP provides that, with certain exceptions, a RAM cannot be conducted until a RAM plan has been received by MassDEP, and MassDEP has granted approval or has failed to issue approval or denial within a specified period of time. The MCP also includes requirements for quarterly RAM status reports and for a RAM completion report. Completion of a RAM may result in filing of a Class A RAO or continuation of preliminary or comprehensive response actions.[71]

Utility-Related Abatement Measures

Utility-related abatement measures ("URAMs") are voluntary actions taken on public rights-of-way, utility easements, and private property to respond to soil or ground water contamination that equals or exceeds applicable RCs and that is encountered during the installation, repair, replacement; or decommissioning of sewer, water, and drainage systems-, natural gas pipelines, and electric, telephone, telecommunication, and other conduits, as well as related appurtenances. URAMs may be undertaken by persons overseeing or directly responsible for utility construction activities, or site preparation work requested by a utility company or a governmental authority prior to utility construction activities, and these measures are limited to those assessment, containment, and removal actions necessary to complete such construction. The MCP requires that DEP be provided with notice that a URAM is to be conducted but does not require DEP approval unless DEP determines that approval is necessary. In addition, the MCP includes requirements for semi-annual URAM status reports and for a URAM completion report.[72]

Phase I Initial Site Investigation Report

A Phase I initial site investigation report ("Phase I Report") is prepared within one year of notification to MassDEP of the release or threat of release and documents the results of preliminary response actions conducted at a site. These preliminary response actions facilitate evaluation and tier classification or, where appropriate, filing of an RAO Statement prior to tier classification.[73] Activities conducted during the initial site investigation include record reviews, evaluation of monitoring data, evaluation and testing of underground storage tanks, and limited soil and water sampling and analysis.[74] The Phase I Report should include: (a) general site information; (b) preliminary information about site hydrogeological conditions; (c) preliminary findings concerning the nature and extent of contamination, migration pathways, and exposure potential; and (d) an evaluation of the need for IRAs.[75] Phase I can result in one of the following outcomes: (a) a determination that comprehensive response actions are necessary; or (b) filing of a Class A or Class B RAO based on a determination that the requirements have been met.[76] The MCP's tier classification and comprehensive response action requirements are described below.[77]

TIER CLASSIFICATION, PERMITS AND FEES

The MCP contains detailed provisions regarding the classification of sites into tiers based on their relative risk and complexity. Complex, higher-risk sites are classified as Tier IA, IB, or IC, and other, lower-risk sites are classified as Tier II. The tier classification determines the level of MassDEP oversight at the site, whether a permit is required, and the amount of annual compliance fees assessed for the site.[78]

Tier classification is required if an RAO Statement for a site has not been submitted to DEP within one year of the initial release notification to MassDEP, or within one year of certain other dates in some cases.[79] A site's classification is determined by completing a numerical ranking system ("NRS") scoresheet, with scoring based on exposure pathways, human populations, land and water uses, ecological factors, and certain site-specific mitigating factors.[80]

Permits are required in order to perform comprehensive response actions at Tier I sites, but not for Tier II sites.[81] Comprehensive response actions at Tier IA sites are subject to ongoing MassDEP oversight, review, and approval requirements.[82] By contrast, comprehensive response actions may be performed at Tier IB and IC sites under LSP supervision without MassDEP's prior approval once a Tier I permit is issued.[83] Comprehensive response actions may be performed by an LSP at Tier II sites once the tier classification is submitted to MassDEP.[84]

Certain fees are assessed for all Tier I and II sites, which are used to help fund MassDEP's waste site cleanup program. MassDEP has established schedules for action on permit applications and must refund a permit fee if MassDEP does not act on an _application in a timely manner.[85] MassDEP has promulgated timely action permit and fee regulations at 310 C.M.R. 4.01 to 4.10.

COMPREHENSIVE RESPONSE ACTIONS

The MCP contains detailed provisions applicable to the performance of comprehensive response actions after preparation of a Phase I Report. Comprehensive response actions must be conducted under the oversight of an LSP and are conducted in phases as follows:

Phase II: comprehensive site assessment;
Phase III: identification and selection of remedial action alternatives;
Phase IV: implementation of the selected remedial action alternative; and

Phase V: operation, maintenance, and/or monitoring.[86]

The MCP allows a party conducting comprehensive response actions to forgo or modify one or more of the requirements for Phases II through V if the party can demonstrate a "technical justification" establishing that site-specific conditions make the requirement unwarranted.[87] The "technical justification" provision is in keeping with MassDEP's goal of making the scope and level of detail of response actions commensurate with the complexity of the specific disposal site[88] and provides a key element of flexibility in the MCP process.

The results of each phase must be summarized in a report to MassDEP by the appropriate deadline specified by the MCP.[89] The LSP is generally required to submit a completion statement with each report certifying that the phase was completed in accordance with applicable requirements.[90] In addition, the MCP imposes public information and involvement requirements in connection with comprehensive response actions, and these are discussed below. If, at any time during comprehensive response actions, the LSP determines that an RAO has been achieved and sufficient information has been developed to support the RAO in accordance with the MCP, an RAO completion statement may be filed.[91]

Phase II

The Phase II comprehensive site assessment is intended to gather sufficient information to support LSP opinions regarding remedial action, particularly information regarding the source, nature, extent, and potential impacts of the release, and the risk of harm posed by the disposal site. Prior to initiation of Phase II, a Phase II scope of work must be submitted to MassDEP. However, except for Tier IA sites, MassDEP's approval of the scope of work is not required. Phase II culminates in the submission of a report ("Phase II Report") to MassDEP. A Phase II Report includes a more complete evaluation of site information than is provided in the Phase I Report, including the nature and extent of contamination, a thorough discussion of the environmental fate and transport of the OHM at the site, and a risk 'characterization for all relevant human and environmental receptors identified at and near the site. The Phase II assessment can result in one of the following outcomes: (a) a determination that additional remedial actions are necessary to achieve an RAO; or (b) a determination that a Class A or Class B RAO has been achieved.[92]

Phase III

Phase III involves the identification and evaluation of remedial action alternatives that are reasonably likely to achieve a level of "no significant risk" under the circumstances present at the site, as well as the recommendation of a remedial action alternative. Phase III must include an evaluation of the feasibility of achieving a permanent solution and reducing contaminants to background levels. The Phase III evaluation must recommend a specific remedial action and provide appropriate support for this choice, and the plan must be submitted to MassDEP.[93]

Phase IV

Phase IV involves design, construction, and implementation of the remedial action alternative selected in Phase III. A remedy implementation plan must be prepared, which includes, as appropriate: (a) construction plans and specifications; (b) an operation, maintenance, and monitoring plan; and (c) a health and safety plan.[94] The MCP contains detailed provisions regarding the management of remediation waste and the control of air emissions associated with remedial actions. Phase IV also entails the preparation and submission to DEP of a final inspection report and, for certain sites, an as-built construction report. Phase IV can result in: (a) achieving a Class A or Class C RAO, without the need for additional operation, maintenance, or monitoring to ensure the integrity of the RAO; (b) achieving a Class C RAO, with post-RAO operation, maintenance, or monitoring to ensure that the conditions upon which the RAO is based are maintained and/or to ensure progress is being made toward a permanent solution; or (c) concluding that operation, maintenance, and/or monitoring under Phase Vis required in order to-achieve an RAO.[95]

Phase V

Phase V consists of operation, monitoring, and/or maintenance of the remedial action required to achieve an RAO. The operation, monitoring, and maintenance activities must comply with the plan developed in Phase *N* unless the plan is revised due to changed site conditions. Phase V inspection and monitoring results must be submitted to DEP. Phase V must result in the achievement of an RAO, although additional operation, monitoring, or maintenance may be needed to maintain the conditions on which the RAO is based or to make progress from a Class C RAO toward a Class A RAO.[96] In particular, where achievement of a Class A RAO cannot be accomplished within the five year deadline and active operation and maintenance is required to obtain a permanent solution, "Remedy Operation Status" may be achieved, thereby extending the deadline.[97]

RISK CHARACTERIZATION AND CLEANUP STANDARDS

The MCP sets forth detailed provisions for conducting risk characterizations to determine cleanup objectives for response actions.[98] which are intended to simplify and provide some consistency in the risk characterization process. The MCP provides three methods for characterizing risk of harm to health, public welfare, and the environment to determine cleanup objectives. Method 1 and Method 2 are chemical-specific approaches under which concentrations of OHM in soil or ground water at a site are compared with specified numerical soil and ground water cleanup standards for common contaminants to determine whether a condition of no· significant risk exists or has been achieved.[99] Method 3 involves a detailed quantitative characterization of cumulative risk, and requires analysis of each chemical and exposure pathway of concern at the site. Each method is discussed in more detail-below. In addition to establishing risk-based cleanup objectives, the MCP requires the characterization of the risk to safety (*i.e.*, the risk of physical harm or bodily injury) presented by the site.[100] Further, the MCP provides a risk characterization method for evaluating site conditions that may pose an imminent hazard.[101]

Method 1 involves a direct comparison between site conditions and the numerical soil and ground water cleanup standards, while Method· 2 involves the use of the Method 1 standards, supplemented and modified by site-specific and chemical-specific information.[102]

Method 3 involves performing a more extensive quantitative risk characterization for each of the chemicals and exposure pathways of concern at a site. Method 3 may be used at any site, but it *must be* employed if OHM is present in or will foreseeably migrate to an environmental medium other than ground water or soil, such as sediments, surface water, or ambient air.[103] For a complex or heavily contaminated site, a Method 3 risk characterization may be preferable to Method 1 or Method 2 because it may justify less stringent cleanup standards based on a more detailed site-specific analysis of exposure and risk. The objective of a Method 3 risk characterization is to provide a conservatively protective estimate of the cumulative impact that the OHM may have on the human and environmental receptors at the disposal site and in the surrounding environment, assuming exposure scenarios based on all current and reasonably foreseeable site activities and uses. Quantitative estimates of cancer and non-cancer health risks and quantitative and qualitative evaluations of risk to public welfare and to the environment are used to determine whether remedial action is needed or whether a condition of no significant risk exists or has been achieved.[104] In addition, upper concentration limits ("UCLs") for soil and ground water generally cannot be exceeded. UCLs are elevated contaminant levels, which are deemed to indicate the potential for significant risk of harm to human health, public welfare and the environment under future use conditions,[105] and thus precludes achieving a permanent solution, *i.e.*, a Class A RAO.

PROPERTY USE RESTRICTIONS

The MCP provides for the following three types of property use restrictions:[106] (a) a notice of activity and use limitation("AUL"); (b) a grant of environmental restriction ("Environmental Restriction") to MassDEP; and (c) an Environmental Restriction imposed by MassDEP.[107] AULs are by far the most common type of use restriction. An AUL can be implemented by a landowner without MassDEP involvement and does not require a subordination agreement from all holders of prior interests in the property. The AUL must be accompanied by an LSP's opinion, and must include: (a) a description of the property and the area to be restricted; (b) a description of permitted activities and any conditions for conducting those activities; (c) a description of activities and uses that are inconsistent with the RAO; (d) procedures to be followed to ensure that changes in activities and uses do not lead to a level of significant risk; and (e) an agreement to reference the AUL in all instruments that convey an interest in or a right to use the property. The AUL must be recorded or registered with the appropriate registry of deeds or land registration office.[108] An Environmental Restriction must be accompanied by an LSP's opinion specifying: (a) why the Environmental Restriction is appropriate to achieve or maintain a level of no significant risk; (b) the site activities and uses to be permitted, prohibited, or restricted; and (c) the conditions necessary to maintain a level of no significant risk. The Environmental Restriction must be reviewed by DEP and signed by the DEP Commissioner, although this does not signify DEP approval regarding the adequacy of the response actions at the site. It must be recorded or registered with the appropriate registry of deeds or land registration office, and a certified registry copy must be filed with DEP. Significantly for secured lenders, the MCP requires a property owner to obtain and record a subordination agreement (using a prescribed DEP form) from all holders of prior interests in the property to ensure that their respective interests are subordinated to the Environmental Restriction.[109] The DEP may impose an Environmental Restriction on any site at which the Department conducts a response action, but the MCP specifies additional requirements, such as a DEP notice of its intent and procedures for challenging the imposition of such a Restriction.[110]

Once a property use restriction on which an RAO is based becomes effective, any contemplated site use or activity that is not specifically permitted by the property restriction, and which may invalidate a finding of no significant risk, must be evaluated by an LSP. The LSP must provide an opinion as to whether the proposed changes would cause an exceedance of a reporting threshold and whether a condition of no significant risk would still exist, and, if not, any additional response actions necessary to maintain or achieve compliance with the standard. If such actions are necessary, they must be completed before the new or altered site uses and activities commence. In addition, the property use restriction may be amended or released, as appropriate, to include the new or altered uses activities, and a revised RAO reflecting such changes must be filed with MassDEP.[111] The MCP contains detailed provisions, including prescribed forms, for amending and releasing AULs and Environmental Restrictions.[112]

A property use restriction, once implemented, must be adhered to by the owner of the property, as well as by any person holding an interest in or right to use the property and any person conducting response actions at the property.[113] Indeed, the MCP broadly prohibits *any person* from violating, allowing, or causing a violation of, a property restriction or other covenant pursuant to Chapter 21E.[114]

ENFORCEMENT AND COMPLIANCE ASSISTANCE

Chapter 21E generally requires responsible parties[115] to conduct response actions to address releases or threats of release to the environment, and provides mechanisms for MassDEP both to enforce Chapter 21E and the MCP if RPs fail to take response actions or if response actions do not comply with law, and (2) provide compliance assistance in various forms. There are three primary forms of enforcement by the Commonwealth and MassDEP: (1) audits of response actions conducted by RPs, PRPs or other persons and resulting notices of deficiencies or violations; (2) orders mandating RPs and PRPs to conduct response actions; and (3) actions for "cost recovery," injunctive relief, civil or criminal penalties, and natural resource damages. MassDEP's compliance assistance role ranges from providing guidance documents and compliance advice to providing access to land for the purpose of response actions where the landowner has denied access to those conducting the response actions.

Orders

MassDEP may order any person potentially liable for the release or threat of release to conduct response actions.[116] Chapter 21E specifies procedures for issuance of such an order and for appeal of the order pursuant to the Massachusetts Administrative Procedure Act1.[117] When MassDEP orders abatement of an imminent hazard, however, such order is effective and enforceable immediately and cannot be appealed, although a party who has complied with such an order and can show it was not liable may petition MassDEP for reimbursement of its response costs.[118] Where MassDEP has ordered an RP to take response actions and that RP fails or refuses to comply, MassDEP is entitled in a cost recovery action to recover two to three times its costs, unless the non-complying party demonstrates non-liability or a good faith basis for its failure to comply.[119]

Actions for Cost Recovery, Injunctive Relief, Civil or Criminal Penalties, or Natural Resource Damages

Although most response actions are conducted by PRPs and RPs, MassDEP may conduct response actions itself, and then bring a cost recovery action against RPs. The Commonwealth may be awarded up to treble damages, plus litigation costs and attorneys' fees, where it has incurred costs for response actions and can demonstrate that the liable party acted unreasonably or in bad faith in failing to carry out response actions, even in the absence of an order.[120] Where MassDEP conducts response actions, or otherwise selects response actions, it may develop an administrative record, which allows the participation of interested parties, response to significant comments, and preparation of a detailed statement of the basis for and purpose of the selected response action.[121]

MassDEP may also issue an administrative order or bring an enforcement action for civil or criminal penalties where a violation of Chapter 21E or the MCP has occurred. Any person who violates a provision of Chapter 21E or an order or regulation issued thereunder can be subject to: a civil penalty of up to $25,000 for each day of violation; or (b) imprisonment for up to two years and/or a fine of up to $25,000 for each day of violation. Penalties for failing to notify MassDEP of a release or threat of release of OHM are significantly greater: up to twenty years imprisonment and/or a fine of up to $100,000 for each day of violation.[122]

Regardless of who performs or funds response actions, the Commonwealth additionally may recover from responsible parties "all damages for injury to and for destruction or loss of natural resources."[123]

Incentives to Settle with the Commonwealth

Chapter 21E authorizes DEP to provide incentives to encourage settlements. One such incentive is an express grant of contribution protection to parties who settle with the Commonwealth, which protects such parties from claims by non-settling parties for additional cleanup costs at a site. Contribution protection. under Chapter 21E is effective only against non-settling parties that received notice and an opportunity to comment on the settlement. Chapter 21E also permits the Commonwealth to covenant not to sue when in the public interest.[124] The 1998 Amendments authorized a new, discretionary covenant not to sue as part of encouraging Brownfields redevelopment. This covenant not to sue provides to certain persons protection from liability to the Commonwealth and from claims by persons with a notice of an opportunity to join in the settlement. The protection is against contribution claims, response costs, property damage under Chapter 21E, and common law property damage, to the extent such are covered matters under the covenant not to sue agreement. In particular, the Commonwealth may grant a covenant not to sue to certain parties who are current or prospective owners or operators of a Brownfields site, who propose redevelopment or reuse that will contribute to the economic or physical revitalization of the area, and who submit a redevelopment plan for the site. Such a covenant may be given only to a party who achieves and maintains (1) a permanent solution, (2) a remedy operation status, or (3) who is an eligible person and can prove that a solution is not feasible.[125]

PRIVATE CLAIMS

Chapter 21E creates private causes of action for recovery of past and future response costs and property damage.[126] Chapter 21E includes a number of procedures and standards applicable to private party claims for cost recovery and contribution. A party may also sue for property damages.[127] For a permanent injury, the measure is the "difference in the fair market value of the injured premises before and after the injury." For a temporary injury, the measure is the cost of repairs (*i.e.*, cleanup) plus consequential damages such as lost rental value during cleanup.[128] It is not clear if the Section 4A pre-litigation procedure must be followed for property damage claims.[129]

STATUTES OF LIMITATIONS

Chapter 21E specifies time periods within which various claims must be brought. Cost recovery and lien enforcement claims by the Commonwealth must be commenced within five years from the date that all such costs are incurred or the date of discovery of the identity of the liable party, whichever is later. Claims for natural resources damage or property damage brought by the Commonwealth must be commenced within three years from the date of discovery of the damage or the date of discovery of the identity of the liable party, whichever is later.[130]

Private actions for cost recovery or contribution must be commenced within three years from the later of the date of incurring of costs, the date of discovery of the identity of the liable party, or the date of sending a Section 4A notice letter. Private property damage claims must be commenced within three years of the date of discovery of the damage or the date of discovery of the identity of the liable party, whichever is later.[131]

LIENS

Chapter 21E authorizes MassDEP to impose a lien on the real and personal property of any person liable to the Commonwealth under the statute to secure such person's debt to the Commonwealth. A lien on the site where the OHM is located takes priority over all prior encumbrances on that property. However, this "superlien" provision does not apply to real property "the greater part of which is devoted to single or multi-family housing." As to such property, as well as any property of the liable party other than the site where the OHM is located, the lien is subject to ordinary rules of priority.[132]

The lien provisions apply to a site or vessel owned or possessed by a secured lender. In such a case, the Commonwealth may foreclose upon the lien and subsequently sell the property in question in accordance with specified requirements; however, if the property is sold for less than the amount of the lien, the secured lender will not be liable for any deficiency, provided that it has complied with certain requirements.[133]

The statute and the MCP specify procedures that must be followed to effectuate a Chapter 21E lien and provide for release or dissolution of a lien. When MassDEP intends to record, register, or file a Chapter 21E lien on real or personal property, notice must be provided to any owner of the site and to any other person with a recorded, registered, unrecorded, or unregistered property interest in the site.[134] The MCP provides that the aforementioned persons have a right to an adjudicatory hearing on MassDEP's intent to impose a lien. The regulations also include requirements regarding the content and service of the lien notice, the actions to be taken by a person receiving a notice to avoid waiving the right to an adjudicatory hearing, and the conduct of the adjudicatory hearing.[135]

PUBLIC NOTICE AND PARTICIPATION

Chapter 21E and the MCP impose numerous requirements concerning notice to the public and to municipal officials about the existence of a contaminated site, the availability of information concerning the site, the investigative and cleanup actions to be taken, and milestones in the cleanup process.[136] In addition, they require that MassDEP or the private party conducting response actions consider the concerns and comments of the public in making decisions regarding such actions. If MassDEP determines that additional public involvement activities are warranted by conditions at a site, or if a petition is submitted by ten or more residents of the municipality in which a site is located or of a municipality potentially affected by a site, MassDEP or the private party conducting response actions must designate the site as a "public involvement plan" ("PIP") site and must prepare and implement a plan for ensuring public involvement during the investigation and cleanup process.[137]

NOTES

1. 42 U.S.C. §§9601 to 9675.

2. *See* 310 C.M.R. 40.0006(12).

3. M.G.L. c. 21E, §2; 310 C.M.R. 40.0006(12); *see* 42 U.S.C. § 9601(14); M.G.L. c. 21C. The MCP contains a list of OHM (Oil and Hazardous Material) and describes methods and criteria for identifying and designating substances as OHM. 310 C.M.R. 40.0340 to 40.0347 and 40.1600.

4. M.G.L. c. 21E, §2; 310 C.M.R. 40.0006(12).

5. M.G.L. c. 21E, §2

6. M.G.L. c. 21E, §3; 310 C.M.R. 40.0006(12).

7. M.G.L. c. 21E, §5(a)(l) to (5); *cf.* 42 U.S.C. § 9607.

8. M.G.L. c. 21E, §5(a)(l) and (5). *But cf.* M.G.L. c. 21E, §§ 5C and 5D, as amended by, 1998 Mass. Acts c. 206, § 25 (although prior owner or operator would not be liable for a release or threat of release of oil, if an "eligible person" remediates the site, the prior owner or operator becomes liable, unless certain limited defenses apply).

9. *See Marenghi v. Mobil Oil Corp.*, 420 Mass. 371,374, 649 N.E.2d 764 (1995); *Griffith v. New England Telephone & Telegraph Co.*, 420 Mass. 365, 366–70, 649 N.E.2d 766 (1995).

10. M.G.L. c. 21E, §5(a)(i) and (ii).

11. M.G.L. c. 21E, §5(e).
12. M.G.L. c. 21E, §§4 and S(a)(iii).
13. M.G.L. c. 21E, §5(c). The current landowner remains liable to the Commonwealth for up to the post-cleanup value of the property, as described below. *See* M.G.L. c. 21E, §5(d).
14. M.G.L. c. 21E, §5(b).
15. M.G.L. c. 21E, §5(g).
16. M.G.L. c. 21E, §5(c)(4).
17. M.G.L. c. 21E, §5(d). *See* M.G.L. c. 21E, § *SC* as created by 1998 Mass. Acts c. 206, § 25.
18. 310 C.M.R. 40.0180 to 40.0187.
19. M.G.L. c. 21E, §5(d), *See* 310 C.M.R. 40.0180 to 40.0187.
20. M.G.L. c. 21E, §5(h) and (g).
21. M.G.L. c. 21E, §2.
22. M.G.L. c. 21E, §2.
23. Although "site" is defined under the MCP as wherever the contamination from the release comes to be located, 310 C.M.R. 40.0006(12), if the release affects only soil, the permanent solution or remedy operation status need only be achieved within the property bounds. However, if the release affects ground water, the remedy must address the entire site *(i.e.,* plume).
24. M.G.L. c. 21E, §2, as amended by 1998 Mass. Acts c. 206, § 9 (defining eligible person); M.G.L.
c. 21E, §5(c).
25. M.G.L. c. 21E, §2.
26. 310 C.M.R. 40.0170(6).
27. 310 C.M.R. 40.0172(1).
28. 310 C.M.R. 40.0170(8).
29. M.G.L. c. 21E, §7, §27; 310 C.M.R. 40.0331.
30. 310 C.M.R. 40.0331(2). Even if a release or threat of release does not require notification, response actions must be undertaken if the release or threat of release poses a significant risk to health, safety, public welfare, or the environment. A person undertaking response actions for such a release or threat of release is not subject to the MCP's requirements regarding submittals, approvals, and fees. 310 C.M.R. 40.0370.
31. M.G.L. c. 21E, §11.
32. 310 C.M.R. 40.0310 to 40.0317; *see also* M.G.L. c. 21E, §7.
33. 310 C.M.R. 40.0310 to 40.0317, 40.0332, 40.0350 to 40.0362, and 40.1600.
34. 310 C.M.R. 40.0350 to 40.0352, and 40.1600.
35. *Compare* 40 C.F.R. 302.4 to 310 C.M.R. 40.1600.
36. Please note that whenever one evaluates whether notification for a release or threat of release is required, regardless of whether the release is a current release or a historic release, one must evaluate the possibility of an exceedance of an RQ, an RC, or any of the other notification criteria listed in the MCP. 310 C.M.R. 40.0310 to 40.0315.
37. 310 C.M.R. 40.0361, 40.0362 and 40.1600.
38. 310 C.M.R. 40.0006(12) and 40.0321; *see also* 310 C.M.R. 40.0951 to 40.955.

39. 310 C.M.R. 40.0006(12).
40. 310 C.M.R. 40.0311.and 40.0312.
41. 310 C.M.R. 40.0313 and 40.0314.
42. 310 C.M.R. 40.0315.
43. 310 C.M.R. 40.0332(3).
44. 310 C.M.R. 40.0311 to 40.0315, and 40.0332(7).
45. 310 C.M.R. 40.0006(12).
46. M.G.L. c. 21E, §7; 310 C.M.R. 40.0317 (listing 21 categories of non-reportable releases).
47. M.G.L. c. 21E, §§2 and 3A(b); 310 C.M.R. 40.0168.
48. M.G.L. c. 21E, §3A(b)(5).
49. M.G.L. c. 21A, §§ 16 and 19 to 19J, as amended by 1998 Mass. Acts c. 206, §§ 1 to 6; 310 C.M.R. 40.0015(3).
50. *See* 309 C.M.R. 2.00 to 8.00.
51. *See* 310 C.M.R. 40.0015(3).
52. 310 C.M.R. 40.0015(4); *see also* M.G.L. c. 21E, §2 (defining standard of care).
53. 310 C.M.R. 40.0191.
54. 310 C.M.R. 40.0006(12).
55. 310 C.M.R. 40.0006(12).
56. M.G.L. c. 21E, §3A(g); *see* 310 C.M.R. 40.0006(12); *see also* 310 C.M.R. 40.0900 to 40.0996.
57. M.G.L. c. 21E, §3A(g); *see* 310 C.M.R. 40.1020.
58. 310 C.M.R. 40.0006(12).
59. M.G.L. c. 21E, §3A(f) and (g); *see* 310 C.M.R. 40.0580 and 40.1050(5).
60. 310 C.M.R. 40.1035.
61. 310 C.M.R. 40.1045.
62. 310 C.M.R. 40.1050. *See* 310 C.M.R. 40.0580.
63. 310 C.M.R. 40.0406, 40.0840, 40.0861, 40.0862, 40.0881. and 40.0896; *see* 310 C.M.R. 40.1056.
64. 310 C.M.R. 40.1003(3).
65. 310 C.M.R. 40.1070.
66. 310 C.M.R. 40.0550(1) and (5), 40.0560(1), (5), and (7).
67. 310 C.M.R. 40.0317(15) and 40.0318.
68. M.G.L. c. 21E, § 2.
69. 310 C.M.R. 40.0405(2) and 40.0410 to 40.0413.
70. 310 C.M.R. 40.0414 to 40.0429.
71. 310 C.M.R. 40.0405(3) and 40.0440 to 40.0448.
72. 310 C.M.R. 40.0460 to 40.0467.
73. 310 C.M.R. 40.0480 to 40.0486.
74. 310 C.M.R. 40.0480 to 40.0489; *see* 310 C.M.R. 40.0405(1).
75. 310 C.M.R. 40.0483.
76. 310 C.M.R. 40.0486.
77. 310 C.M.R. 40.0403(3) and (4), 40.0404(3), and 40.0406.
78. 310 C.M.R. 40.0500 to 40.0590.
79. 310 C.M.R. 40.0501(3) and (4).

80. 310 C.M.R. 40.0520 and 40.1500 to 40.1516 (these regulations contain the NRS scoresheet itself).

81. 310 C.M.R. 40.0560, 40.0702, 40.0703(2) and (3), and40.0706; *see generally* 310 C.M.R.40.0703 to

40.0770.

82. 310 C.M.R. 40.0550(4)(a).

83. 310 C.M.R. 40.0550(4)(b).

84. 310 C.M.R. 40.0560.

85. M.G.L. c. 21E, §3B.

86. 310 C.M.R. 40.0800 to 40.0896.

87. 310 C.M.R. 40.0810(7).

88. 310 C.M.R. 40.0810(6).

89. 310 C.M.R. 40.0810(2).

90. 310 C.M.R. 40.0836, 40.0862, 40.0879, and 40.0894.

91. 310 C.M.R. 40.0406, 40.0840, 40.0861, 40.0862, 40.0881 and 40.0896; *see* 310 C.M.R. 40.1056 (except a Class C RAO may not be filed unless Phases II and III have been completed).

92. 310 C.M.R. 40.0840(1).

93. 310 C.M.R. 40.0850 to 40.0861.

94. 310 C.M.R. 40.0870 to 40.0874.

95. 310 C.M.R. 40.0875, 40.0878, and 40.0881

96. 310 C.M.R. 40.0890 to 40.0896.

97. 310 C.M.R. 40.0893.

98. 310 C.M.R. 40.0900 to 40.0996.

99. 310 C.M.R. 40.0941(3)(a) and (b), 40.0942(1) and (2).

100. 310 C.M.R. 40.0960, 40.0971(5), 40.0981, and 40.0992(4).

101. 310 C.M.R. 40.0950 to 40.0955.

102. 310 C.M.R. 40.0980 to 40.0988.

103. 310 C.M.R. 40.0942(1)(b) and (2).

104. 310 C.M.R. 40.0941(3)(c), 40.0942(3), and 40.0990 to 40.0995.

105. 310 C.M.R. 40.0994(4)(b), 40.0995(5), and 40.0996.

106. Please note that the MCP and Chapter 21E refer to all property restrictions as “activity and use limitations” and one of the specific kinds of property restrictions is a *notice of* activity and use limitation.

107. 310 C.M.R. 40.1070(1).

108. 310 C.M.R. 40.1074(1) to (3). The regulations require use of MassDEP forms. *See* 310 C.M.R. 40.1099.

109. 310 C.M.R. 40.1071 and40.1072.

110. 310 C.M.R. 40.1073.

111. 310 C.M.R. 40.1080(1) and (2); *see* 310 C.M.R. 40.1012(5).

112. 310 C.M.R. 40.1081 to 40.1084; *see* 310 C.M.R. 40.1099 (forms). DEP forms generally cannot be modified. 310 C.M.R. 40.0009(5).

113. 310 C.M.R. 40.1012(6) and 40.1070(2); *see* M.G.L. c. 21E, § 6, as amended by 1998 Mass. Acts c. 206, § 26.

114. 310 C.M.R. 40.0019(1) and (2); see 310 C.M.R. 40.0019 and 40.1020.

115. *See, e.g.*, M.G.L. c. 21E, §§ 4 (authorizing DEP to take response actions and authorizing cost recovery actions) and §4 (defining liable parties and authorizing Commonwealth to recover response costs it incurs). The MCP distinguishes between RPs, who *must* perform response actions, and PRPs and other persons, who *may* perform response actions. 310 C.M.R. 40.0403(1).

116. M.G.L. c. 21E, §§ 4 and 9.

117. M.G.L. c. 21E, § 10; *see* M.G.L. c. 30A.

118. M.G.L. c. 21E, §§ 5(e) and 10. *See* 310 C.M.R. 40.1260 to 40.1265.

119. M.G.L. c. 21E, § 5(e).

120. M.G.L. c. 21E, §§ 4, 5 and 5A.

121. M.G.L. c. 21E, § *SA; see* M.G.L. c. 21E, § l0(b); *see* 310 C.M.R. 40.1300 to 40.1306.

122. M.G.L. c. 21E, §11.

123. M.G.L. c. 21E, §5(a)(ii); *cf* 42 U.S.C. § 9607(a).

124. M.G.L. c. 21E, §3A(j)(2), as amended by 1998 Mass. Acts c. 206, § 19.

125. M.G.L. c. 21E, §3A(j)(3).

126. See M.G.L. c. 21E, §§ 4 and 4A (contribution and cost recovery); M.G.L. c. 21E, §5 (property damage).

127. M.G.L. c. 21E, §5(a)(iii).

128. For a discussion of temporary versus permanent damages, *see Black* v. *Coastal Oil New England, Inc.*, 45 Mass App. Ct. 461, 465–66, 699 N:E. 2d 353 (1998); *see also* Robert D. Cox, Jr., and Barry A. Bachrach, Damages for Contaminated Property, 37 Boston Bar Journal, July/August 1993, at 19.

129. *Black* v. *Coastal Oil New England, Inc.*, 45 Mass App. Ct. 461, 465–66, 699 N.E. 2d 353 (1998).

130. M.G.L. c. 21E, § 11A(l) and (3).

131. M.G.L. c. 21E, § 11A(2) and (4).

132. M.G.L. c. 21E, § 13.

133. M.G.L. c. 21E, § 13.

134. 310 C.M.R. 40.1250, 40.1251, and 40.1254.

135. 310 C.M.R. 40.1252, 40.1253, and 40.1255 to 40.1257.

136. 310 C.M.R. 40.1403.

137. M.G.L. c. 21E, §14; 310 C.M.R. 40.1400 to 40.1406.

Chapter 12

Chemical Use and Exposure

Two Massachusetts environmental statutes impose requirements in connection with the use of and exposure to chemicals in places of employment. The first, the Massachusetts Right-to-Know Act, Massachusetts General Law Chapter 111F, governs the dissemination of information about exposure to toxic and hazardous substances in the workplace and the community. The second, the Massachusetts Toxics Use Reduction Act, Massachusetts General Law Chapter 211, requires the submission of information to state authorities regarding the use of toxic substances and planning to reduce the levels of such use. In addition, certain Massachusetts agencies have responsibilities under the federal Emergency Planning and Community Right-to-Know Act, 42 U.S.C. §§ 11001 to 11050.

MASSACHUSETTS RIGHT-TO-KNOW ACT

The Massachusetts Right-to-Know Act ("MRTKA"), more formally known as the Hazardous Substances Disclosure by Employers Act, imposes requirements regarding the dissemination of information concerning toxic or hazardous substances to certain agencies and public officials and to members of the public pursuant to the statute's community right-to-know provisions.[1] Three state agencies share responsibility for implementation and enforcement of the MRTKA.3 These are the Massachusetts Department of Public Health ("DPH"), which has adopted implementing regulations at 105 C.M.R. 670.000 to 670.030; the Massachusetts Department of Environmental Protection ("MassDEP"), which has adopted implementing regulations at 310 C.M.R. 33.00 to 33.09; and the Massachusetts Department of Labor and Workforce Development ("DOL"), which has adopted implementing regulations at 454 C.M.R. 21.00 to 21.09.

Scope

MRTKA defines "toxic or hazardous substance" as any chemical substance or mixture of substances in a gaseous, liquid, or solid state which is listed on the Massachusetts Substance List ("MSL") and which is manufactured, processed, used, or stored in the workplace.[2] MRTKA charges DPH with compiling, amending and publishing the MSL.[3] The MSL includes substances listed in various public and private source lists and currently contains more than two thousand substances. These substances are designated, where applicable, as carcinogens, mutagens, neurotoxins, teratogens, and extraordinarily hazardous substances.[4]

MRTKA provides that a toxic or hazardous substance is present in a mixture for purposes of the Act if it constitutes one percent or more of the mixture, or two percent if it is an impurity in the mixture.[5] DPH is authorized to increase the concentration requirement thresholds for substances that are not toxic or hazardous at these threshold levels, and to lower concentration requirements for carcinogens, mutagens, teratogens, and neurotoxins for which there is valid and substantial scientific evidence that the substance is extraordinarily hazardous.[6] The definition of "toxic or hazardous substance" excludes alcoholic beverages, articles intended for personal consumption by employees in the workplace, consumer articles packaged for distribution to and used by the general public, articles sold or used in retail establishments (excluding articles used in processing and repair areas), and substances being transported in interstate commerce.[7]

Data Submission and Availability; Community-Right-to-Know

MRTKA requires any employer that manufactures, processes, uses, or stores toxic or hazardous substances in the workplace to file a material safety data sheet ("MSDS") for each such substance with the appropriate MassDEP regional office and to file an updated MSDS as new information is obtained.[8] Upon request, such an employer also must provide the MSDS to the municipal right-to-know coordinator for the municipality in which the workplace is located.[9] In addition, a manufacturer or seller of a toxic or hazardous substance must provide the MSDS to direct purchasers and must keep the MSDS updated.[10]

MRTKA and its implementing regulations provide exemptions from the MSDS filing requirements for toxic or hazardous substances that are present in a workplace as part of, or in the form of, various products or materials, provided that the substances satisfy certain standards regarding exposure risk. The specified exempt products and materials are: (a) consumer goods in containers weighing five pounds or less or having volumes of one gallon or less (unless the substance is designated on the MSL as a carcinogen, teratogen, mutagen, neurotoxin, or extraordinarily hazardous substance); (b) office supplies; (c) food stuffs; (d) gasoline, oils, and other additives used in passenger vehicles or light duty trucks; and (e) certain fuels used for space heating or power generation purposes.[11]

MSDSs submitted pursuant to MRTKA do not automatically become available to the public, but MRTKA does provide for limited public access to MSDS information in response to a petition submitted by a community resident. A community resident who has reason to believe that use of a toxic or hazardous substance in a workplace is or may be endangering public health or safety may file with the municipal coordinator a petition stating the grounds for such belief and requesting an investigation. The filing of such a petition triggers a review process which can lead to investigation by the municipal coordinator and action by MassDEP. The MassDEP Commissioner may provide an employer's MSDS to a petitioner "where appropriate," provided that the Commissioner determines that the petitioner's request is not frivolous or intended to harass the employer.[12]

Under certain circumstances, MassDEP may provide MSDSs to other state agencies, and municipal coordinators may provide MSDSs to other municipal officials.[13] In addition, an MSDS must be provided to a physician treating a community resident when certain preconditions are met.[14]

Research Laboratories

The requirements of MRTKA do not apply to a workplace or work area that constitutes a research laboratory as defined under the Act, unless there is reason to believe that operation of the workplace or work area poses a threat to the health or safety of employees who work therein.[15] "Research laboratory" is defined as a workplace or a work area of a workplace used primarily for research, development, non-routine testing, or experimentation in which toxic or hazardous substances are used by or under the direct supervision of a technically qualified individual. A research laboratory may not be involved in the production or manufacture of goods for direct commercial sale.[16]

To qualify, an employer must provide information sufficient to enable DPH to determine that the workplace or work area constitutes a research laboratory for purposes of MRTKA and that there is no reason to believe the operation of such workplace or work area poses a threat to employee health or safety. The employer also must provide DPH with assurance that it has notified the employees of the workplace or work area that the employer is claiming an exemption as a research laboratory. If DPH determines that a work area or workplace does not qualify as a research laboratory, the employer may appeal

DPH's determination to an adjudicatory hearing, and a decision after that hearing may be appealed to the Superior Court pursuant to the Massachusetts Administrative Procedures Act.[17] Pending DPH's final determination regarding a research laboratory exemption claim, the workplace or work area will be deemed to qualify for the exemption.[18]

Trade Secrets

The preparer of an MSDS may omit from the MSDS the chemical name, common name, and Chemical Abstracts Service number of the toxic or hazardous substance if release of that information would disclose a trade secret as defined under MRTKA. All other information concerning the properties and effects of the toxic or hazardous substance must be provided in the MSDS.[19] A "trade secret" is defined for purposes of MRTKA as a formula, pattern, device, or compilation of information which is used in an employer's or manufacturer's business and which gives the employer or manufacturer an opportunity to obtain an advantage over competitors who do not know or use it.[20]

To take advantage of this trade secret protection, an MSDS preparer must submit to DPH a sworn statement providing a "complete justification and statement of the grounds" for the trade secret claim. If DPH; rejects the trade secret claim, the Department's decision may be appealed to the Superior Court for review pursuant to the Massachusetts Administrative Procedure Act.[21] Pending a final determination regarding the trade secret claim, the MSDS preparer is not obligated to supply the claimed trade secret information.[22]

Trade secret information withheld from an MSDS must be provided to the treating physician of a past or present employee or of a current community resident under certain circumstances. However, the physician must sign an agreement regarding maintenance of the confidentiality of the information contained in the MSDS.[23]

Workplace Standards

MRTKA imposes a number of employee protection requirements on public sector employees.[24] Public sector employers must: (a) use diligent efforts to obtain MSDSs for all listed toxic or hazardous substances manufactured, processed, used, or stored in the workplace and, if the MSDSs are not then provided by the manufacturer or intermediate seller, request the DOL to obtain the MSDSs on the employer's behalf;[25] (b) label containers of such substances;[26] (c) make available at a central location in the workplace all MSDSs prepared or obtained by the employer;[27] (d) revise MSDSs as new information becomes available;[28] (e) post notices and provide training to inform employees of their rights under the MRTKA;[29] (f) train employees in the proper handling of toxic or hazardous substances and emergency procedures[30] and (g) provide employees with MSDSs within four days of request.[31]

A public sector employee who has requested an MSDS for a toxic or hazardous substance from his or her employer and not received it within four working days may refuse to work with such substance if the employer has not exercised diligent efforts, as defined under MRTKA, to obtain the MSDS.[32] An employee who is provided with an incomplete or outdated MSDS may similarly refuse to work with the substance.[33] Employees of the Commonwealth and of its political subdivisions must, however, continue to perform those services determined to be essential pursuant to MRTKA and its implementing regulations.[34]

A public sector employer is prohibited from discharging or otherwise disciplining or discriminating against an employee because that employee exercised any rights or filed or participated in a claim, complaint, or suit under MRTKA. MRTKA sets forth procedures for filing and review by DOL of a claim of such discharge, discipline, or discrimination and for appeal of DOL's determination to the Superior Court pursuant to the Massachusetts Administrative Procedure Act.[35]

Enforcement

If the agency responsible for administering an applicable requirement of MRTKA believes that an employer or manufacturer has violated wrongfully that requirement, the agency must attempt to eliminate the violation by "conference, conciliation, and persuasion." If that process fails, the agency may order appropriate remedial action including the issuance of a cease and desist order against any recurrence and may request the Attorney General to enforce such an order and to seek penalties. A person who violates MRTKA can be subject to a civil penalty of up to $250 for each day of violation.[36]

If the agency believes that the employer or manufacturer has willfully and intentionally violated an applicable requirement of the MRTKA, the agency may request the Attorney General to bring an action to restrain the violation and to seek penalties. Willful and intentional violation of MRTKA is a misdemeanor punishable, for a first offense, by a fine of up to $500, or imprisonment for up to thirty days, or both, for each day of violation.[37] In addition, a person who violates any portion of MRTKA administered by MassDEP may be subject to an administrative penalty pursuant to the Massachusetts Administrative Penalties Act.[38]

MASSACHUSETTS TOXICS USE REDUCTION ACT

The purpose of the Massachusetts Toxics Use Reduction Act ("TURA"),[39] is to minimize risks associated with the handling, treatment and disposal of toxic chemicals by reducing or eliminating their use. "Toxics use reduction" is defined under the statute as in-plant changes in production processes or raw materials that reduce, avoid, or eliminate the use of toxic or hazardous substances or generation of hazardous by-products per unit of product, without shifting risks to consumers, other workers or different environmental resources. Toxics use reduction techniques include: (a) input substitution; (b). product reformulation; (c) production unit redesign, modification, or modernization; (d) improved operation and maintenance of production unit equipment and methods; and (e) recycling, reuse, or extended use of toxic or hazardous substances through use of equipment or-methods that become an integral part of the production unit, including filtration and other closed-loop methods.[40]

MassDEP's responsibilities under TURA include: (a) adoption of implementing regulations; (b) standardization and coordination of state reporting requirements pertaining to chemical use, release, and disposal; (c) compilation of information on the manufacture, distribution, processing, sale, storage, disposal, release, and other use of toxic or hazardous substances; (d) development of guidelines for, and coordination of, multi-media facility inspections; (e) enforcement of the statute; and (t) promotion of toxics use reduction as a means for achieving compliance with environmental laws and regulations.[41] MassDEP has adopted TURA regulations at 310 C.M.R. 50.00 to 50.072.

Facilities Subject to Act

In general, TURA applies to any facility that "manufactures, processes or otherwise uses" a "toxic or hazardous substance" and that falls within any of specified industrial categories ("toxics users"). These categories are those covered by Standard Industrial Classification Codes 10 through 14, 20 through 40, 44 through 51, 72, 73, 75, and 76.[42]

"Toxic or hazardous substances" ("toxics") are identified on a list promulgated by the Administrative Council. This list includes the toxic chemicals listed pursuant to Section 313 of the federal Emergency Planning and Community Right-to-Know Act ("EPCRA"), 42 U.S.C. §11023, and the hazardous substances listed pursuant to Sections 101(14) and 102 of the federal Comprehensive Environmental Response, Compensation, and Liability Act ("CERCLA"), 42 U.S.C. §§9601(14), 9602, and the Council must add or delete chemicals from its list as those chemicals are added to or deleted from the EPCRA and CERCLA lists.[43] In addition, the Council has limited authority to add or delete other chemicals pursuant to recommendations from DEP and DPH, after consultation with the Institute.[44]

Excluded from the definition of toxics are chemical substances (a) present in manufactured articles not manufactured at the facility; (b) used as facility structural components; (c) present in routinely used janitorial or facility grounds maintenance products; (d) present in foods, drugs, cosmetics or other personal items used at the facility; (e) present in products used for maintaining motor vehicles used by the facility; (t) present in pesticides or herbicides when used in agricultural applications; or (g) present in process water or non-contact cooling water as drawn from the environment or municipal sources or in air used either as compressed air or in combustion.[45]

Most of the substantive requirements of TURA are triggered only by the manufacture, processing, or other use of a toxic or hazardous substance in an amount equal to the applicable "threshold amount" in a calendar year at a facility.[46] In effect, therefore, the statute provides an incentive to reduce toxic and hazardous substance volumes to below these threshold levels. The threshold amount for a toxics user that manufactures or processes a toxic or hazardous substance is 25,000 pounds per year at one facility. The threshold amount for a toxics user which uses such a substance for purposes other than manufacturing or further processing is 10,000 pounds per year at a facility. A user who equals or exceeds these thresholds is defined as a large quantity user." For those substances for which EPA has established a lower reporting threshold under the reporting provisions of EPCRA, the threshold amount of such substances triggering large quantity user status is decreased to correspond to the EPCRA reporting threshold.[47]

Annual Reporting of Toxics Use

Each large quantity user, with certain exceptions, must prepare and file with MassDEP an annual report covering each toxic or hazardous substance manufactured or processed at a facility in an amount at least equal to the applicable threshold amount or 10,000 pounds, whichever is less, and for each toxic or hazardous substance otherwise used at the facility in an amount at least equal to the applicable threshold amount.[48] Annual reports must be filed by July 1 of each year. An annual report must include certain information specified in the statute and regulations, including information on the quantities of toxic or hazardous substances manufactured, processed, or otherwise used, generated as by-products, and shipped as or in product from the facility. The facility also must report its progress in reducing toxics generated as by-products and toxics emitted to the environment or transferred off-site as waste.[49] Certain activities and facilities, including laboratory activities and facilities with the equivalent of fewer than ten full-time employees, are exempt from some or all of the annual toxics use reporting requirements described above. MassDEP, however, may require a small quantity toxics user or a toxics user whose facility has the equivalent of fewer than ten full-time employees to file an annual toxics use report if such user falls within a priority user segment.[50]

Toxics Use Reduction Plans

Each large quantity user must prepare a toxics use reduction plan for any facility subject to the annual reporting requirement by July 1 each year. The plan must contain certain information specified in the statute and regulations, including information on planned reductions in toxics use and generation and toxics reduction goals, the costs and liabilities associated with the generation or use of toxics, and technologies, procedures, and training programs that could be used to reduce toxics use and generation.[51] The plan must be certified by a toxics use reduction planner and must be updated and recertified every two years.[52] A summary of the plan must be filed with MassDEP, and certain information regarding the plan and toxics use reduction must be provided to employees.[53] In addition, MassDEP may require a small quantity toxics user or a toxics user whose facility has the equivalent of fewer than ten full-time employees to prepare a toxics use reduction plan if such user falls within a priority user segment.[54]

Toxics Use Reduction Performance Standards and Goals

TURA does not, in general, require toxics users to implement the toxic use reduction plans discussed above. MassDEP may, however, seek authorization from the Administrative Council to establish performance standards, in the form of levels of by-products generated per unit of product, that are to be achieved by toxics users within a priority user segment. The Council may authorize the establishment of such requirements if a majority of users in the user segment fall significantly below regional, national, or international achievements of by-product generated per unit of product based on reasonably proven, public domain technologies and/or industry practices.

The Council also may authorize the establishment of such performance standards if a number of toxics users in the user segment fall significantly below a Massachusetts-based norm for by-product generated per unit of product based on such technologies and practices. The performance standards must be based on reasonably proven, public domain technologies and/or industry practices applicable to the user segment and must be complied with to the extent "economically feasible." Under certain circumstances, a toxics user in a user segment for which such performance standards have been established may be exempt from such standards.[55]

Toxics Use Reduction Waivers

A toxics user may petition MassDEP for the temporary waiver of any statutory or regulatory requirement administered by Mass DEP, including any requirement of TURA, if the toxics user proposes to comply with such requirement through implementation of a toxics use reduction technique or combination of such techniques or through use of innovative toxics use reduction· techniques. MassDEP must make certain findings regarding the effectiveness of, and the benefits and lack of risks associated with, the proposed technique before granting such a waiver. A waiver can be granted for a period of up to two years and may be extended. In addition, a toxics user may request MassDEP assistance in seeking a waiver on similar grounds from a federal requirement administered by MassDEP.[56]

Trade Secrets

The Act provides procedures for a toxics user to file a claim with MassDEP that disclosing information required to be disclosed under TURA will reveal a trade secret.[57] Under these procedures, the information for which the claim is being made still must be filed with MassDEP, but MassDEP must abide by certain disclosure prohibitions and by requirements to maintain the information in a secure location.[58] The statute specifies standards which have to be met for a trade secret claim to be valid and provides for a MassDEP determination on the trade secret claim upon the initiative of the MassDEP Commissioner or upon receipt of a petition from any resident of the Commonwealth seeking disclosure of the claimed trade secret information.[59]

A determination that information constitutes a trade secret may be appealed by the petitioner to the Superior Court. A determination that information does not constitute a trade secret may be appealed by the trade secret claimant to an adjudicatory hearing, and an adverse decision after that hearing may be appealed to the Superior Court pursuant to the Massachusetts Administrative Procedure Act.[60] Pending the outcome of such an appeal by the trade secret claimant, DEP must maintain the claimed trade secret information in accordance with the disclosure prohibitions and information maintenance requirements referred to above.[61]

Toxics Use Fees

TURA establishes toxics use fees for large quantity users whose operations come under certain Standard Industrial Classification ("SIC") codes.[62] These fees are based on the number of employees at a facility and the number of toxics for which annual reporting is required. In addition, the statute directs the Administrative Council to adopt regulations to implement the fee requirements and to adjust the amounts of toxics use fees annually in accordance with certain criteria.[63] The Council has adopted regulations governing such fees at 301 C.M.R. 40.00 to 40.05. The toxics use fee is not imposed on a facility with the equivalent of fewer than ten fulltime employees and may be waived in whole or in part for a toxics user that has the equivalent of fewer than 100 full-time employees and is facing severe economic hardship, if the Secretary of Environmental Affairs determines that there is good cause to waive the fee.[64]

Employee Protection

An employer or an employer's agent is prohibited from discharging, refusing to hire, or otherwise discriminating against an employee who has exercised any right under TURA. An employee claiming a violation of this prohibition may initiate proceedings in the Superior Court. An employer found to have violated these prohibitions must pay the employee lost wages, give the employee suitable employment, and pay the employee's reasonable attorney fees.[65]

Enforcement

MassDEP may refer a toxics user to the Office of Toxics Use Reduction Assistance and Technology when the Department believes there has been a violation of TURA or a regulation or approval issued thereunder.[66] In addition, MassDEP may issue an administrative compliance order or an administrative penalty, or request the Attorney General to seek injunctive relief in response to such a violation.[67]

Any person who violates TURA or a regulation or approval issued or adopted thereunder also is subject to a civil penalty of up to $25,000 for each day of violation.[68] An individual or toxics user who willfully violates any requirement of the large quantity toxics user annual toxic or hazardous substance report requirements, M.G.L., c. 211, §10, the toxics use reduction plans requirements, M.G.L. c. 211, §11, any regulation or approval issued or adopted thereunder, or any requirement of the trade secret protection requirements, M.G.L. c. 211, §20, is subject to a fine of not less than $2,500 and not more than $25,000, or by imprisonment for up to one year, or both, for each violation.[69] If a person fails to provide information required under the statute on the grounds that such information constitutes a trade secret and the MassDEP Commissioner determines that the trade secret claim is frivolous, such person can be subject to a civil penalty of up to $25,000 per claim.[70] In addition, a person who violates the statute or a MassDEP regulation or order issued thereunder may be subject to an administrative penalty pursuant to the Massachusetts Administrative Penalties Act.[71] Finally, in certain situations, if a toxics user violates a statutory or regulatory standard limiting a release or threat of release of toxic or hazardous substances to the environment, MassDEP may order the toxics user to prepare a certified toxics use reduction plan meeting certain standards for the production unit where the violation occurred.[72]

TURA allows citizens to review annual toxics use reports and toxics use reduction plan summaries tiled with MassDEP. Any ten residents living within ten miles of a facility required to prepare a toxics use reduction plan may petition MassDEP to review and determine the adequacy of the plan, the plan summary and any required backup data, after which MassDEP must report its determination to the petitioners and the toxics user within a reasonable time.[73] TURA also allows any ten residents of the Commonwealth to bring an action in the Superior Court alleging that a toxics user is in violation of the statute or that a public official has failed to perform a duty under the statute.[74]

MASSACHUSETTS ROLE UNDER FEDERAL EMERGENCY PLANNING AND COMMUNITY RIGHT-TO-KNOW ACT

The federal Emergency Planning and Community Right-to-Know Act ("EPCRA") requires each state to establish a system for responding to releases of hazardous substances and for public access to information about hazardous substances in the community.[75] The Governor of Massachusetts has established a State Emergency Response Commission ("SERC"). SERC is responsible for designating emergency planning districts within the state and for appointing a local emergency planning committee for each district.[76]

SERC has designated each municipality in the Commonwealth as an emergency planning district. The local emergency planning committees are comprised of local law enforcement, firefighting, civil defense, and health personnel, representatives of community groups, and owners and operators of facilities subject to the emergency planning requirements of EPCRA. Each local emergency planning committee is responsible for preparing and maintaining an emergency plan covering specified topics for its district. These topics include the following: (a) the facilities at which extremely hazardous substances are present; (b) the methods and procedures to be followed by facility owners and operators and emergency personnel in responding to releases of extremely hazardous substances; (c) the community and facility coordinators who will make decisions necessary to implement the plan; (d) the procedures to be used to notify the public of a release; (e) the methods for determining that a release has occurred and the extent of its impact; (f) the emergency equipment and facilities available in the community; (g) training programs for response to releases; and (h) evacuation plans.[77] SERC is responsible for reviewing the district plans and making recommendations to ensure coordination among the districts.[78]

NOTES

1. MRTKA also requires employers to provide employees with information about toxic or hazardous substances present in the workplace, and to train employees regarding the proper handling of, and risks associated with, such substances. However, several federal court decisions have held that application of such state regulations to private sector employers and employees is preempted by the Hazard Communication Standard promulgated pursuant to the federal Occupational Safety and Health Act, 29 C.F.R. §1910.1200. The Massachusetts agencies responsible for implementation of MRTKA do enforce the acts provisions with respect to public sector employers.

2. M.G.L. c. 111F, §1; 105 C.M.R. 670.005; 310 C.M.R. 33.02.

3. M.G.L. c. 111F, §4.

4. M.G.L. c. 111F, §4(c); 105 C.M.R. 670.01O(C). *See* 105 C.M.R. 670.000, Appendix A.

5. M.G.L. c. 111F, §4(d). *See* 105 C.M.R. 670.010, 670.000 (Appendix A).

6. M.G.L. c. 111F, §4(d). A substance designated as "extraordinarily hazardous" is deemed to be present in a mixture if the concentration of such substance is greater than one part per million. 105 C.M.R. 670.010(0). *Id.*

7. M.G.L. c. 111F, §1; 105 C.M.R. 670.005; 310 C.M.R. 33.02; 454 C.M.R. 21.01(3)(b).

8. M.G.L. c. 111F, §16; 310 C.M.R. 33.04. *See* definitions and descriptions of MSDS in 105 C.M.R. 670.005, 310 C.M.R. 33.02, and 454 C.M.R. 21.06, and of MSDS filing procedures in 310 C.M.R. 33.04.

9. 310 C.M.R. 33.03(2).

10. M.G.L. c. 111F, §§8,9.

11. 310 C.M.R. 33.08(2).

12. M.G.L. c. 111F, §18; 310 C.M.R. 33.06. Section 21(b) of MRTKA precludes a person who receives information through the petition process from disclosing it "to any person not specifically authorized to receive it" under the statute. In *Lawlor v.*

Shannon No. 85–2516-MC, 18 Envt'l L. Rep. (Envt'l L. Inst.) 21,496 (D. Mass. Aug. 29, 1988), this provision was invalidated on First Amendment free speech grounds.

13. M.G.L. c.111F, §§17, 19; 310 C.M.R. 33.05(2), (3).

14. M.G.L. c. 111F, §20; 105 C.M.R. 670.025.

15. M.G.L. c. 111F, §6; 105 C.M.R. 670.015.

16. M.G.L. c. 111F, §1; 105 C.M.R. 670.005.

17. M.G.L. c. 111F, §6; 105 C.M.R. 670.015. The Massachusetts Administrative Procedures Act is codified.

at M.G.L. c. 30A.

18. 105 C.M.R. 670.015(B).

19. M.G.L. c. 111F, § 5; 105 C.M.R. 670.020. *See* 310 C.M.R. 33.04(1).

20. M.G.L. c. 111F, § 1; 105 C.M.R. 670.005.

21. M.G.L. c. 111F, § 5; 105 C.M.R. 670.020.

22. M.G.L. c. 111F, § 5(d); 105 C.M.R. 670.020(D)(5)(c).

23. M.G.L. c. 111F, §§12, 20; 105 C.M.R. 670.025.

24. As noted above, application of these provisions to private sector employers is preempted by federal regulations promulgated under OSHA.

25. M.G.L. c. 111F, §§9(b), 11.

26. M.G.L. c. 111F, §7; 454 C.M.R. 21.05. MRTKA labels are not required for certain small volume containers and for containers already labeled in accordance with certain federal regulations. *See* 105 C.M.R. 670.030.

27. M.G.L. c. 111F, §11(a). *See* 310 C.M.R. 33.04(1).

28. M.G.L. c. 111F, §8.

29. M.G.L. c 111F, §11(d).

30. M.G.L. c. 111F, §15; 454 C.M.R. 21.07.

31. M.G.L. c. 111F, §11(c).

32. M.G.L. c. 111F, §11(d).

33. 454 C.M.R. 21.04(4).

34. M.G.L. c. 111F, §11(d); 454 C.M.R. 21.04(2).

35. M.G.L. c. 111F, §13.

36. M.G.L. c. 111F §3(a); 310 C.M.R. 33.07(2).

37. M.G.L. c. 111F, §3(b); 310 C.M.R. 33.07(a). Subsequent violations are punishable by a fine of up to $1000, or imprisonment for up to 90 days, or both, for each day of violation. M.G.L. c. 111F, §3(b).

38. 310 C.M.R. 5.03. MassDEP is responsible for administration of M.G.L. c. 111F §§16 to 19, which relate to filing of information on toxic or hazardous substances and disclosure of such information to governmental agencies and officials and to the public.

39. M.G.L. c. 21I.

40. M.G.L. c. 21I, §2; 310 C.M.R. 50.10.

41. M.G.L. c. 21I, §3.

42. M.G.L. c. 21I, § 2 (definition of "toxics user"); 310 C.M.R. 50.10 (same). *See* 301 C.M.R. 41.02.

43. M.G.L. c. 21I, §§2, 9(A), (B); 301 C.M.R. 41.03, 41.05(2).

44. M.G.L. c. 21I, §9(C); 301 C.M.R. 41.05(1), (3) to (5).

45. M.G.L. c. 21I, §2; 301 C.M.R. 41.02; 310 C.M.R. § 50.10.

46.M.G.L. c. 21, §9A.

47. M.G.L. c. 21I, §2; 310 C.M.R. 50.10.

48. M.G.L. c. 21I, §10.

49. M.G.L. c. 21I, §10; 310 C.M.R. 50.30 to 50.36.

50. M.G.L. c. 21I, §10(D), (I); 310 C.M.R. 50.31(3), (4), 50.32(12).

51. M.G.L. c. 21I, §11; 310 C.M.R. 50.40 to 50.46, 50.49.

52. M.G.L. c. 21I, §11(B), (D); 310 C.M.R. 50.41(5), 50.42(3), 50.48, 50.49. TURA and MassDEP's regulations specify detailed requirements for qualification as a toxics use reduction planner. M.G.L. c. 211, §12; 310 C.M.R. 50.50 to 50.61.

53. M.G.L. C. 21I, §11(E), (F); 310 C.M.R. 50.42(5), 50.47.

54. M.G.L. c. 21I, §11(G); 310 C.M.R. 50.41(2), (3).

55. M.G.L. c. 21I, §§14(B), (C), (D), (F), 15.

56. M.G.L. c. 21I, §17. *See* M.G.L. c. 21I §§14(E), 16.

57. TURA defines "trade secret" as any formula, plan, pattern, process, production data, device, information, or compilation of information which is used in a toxics user's business, and which gives said toxics user an opportunity to obtain an advantage over competitors who do not know or use it. M.G.L. c. 21I, §2.

58. M.G.L. c. 21I, §20(A), (B), (J).

59. M.G.L. c. 21I, §20(A) to (C), (E), (F), (J).

60. M.G.L. c. 21I, §20(F).

61. M.G.L. c. 21I, §20(F)(4), (6).

62. The applicable SIC codes are 10 through 14, 20 through 40, 44 through 51, 72, 73, 75, and 76. 301 C.M.R. 40.03(1)(a) & (b).

63. M.G.L. c. 21I §19.

64. M.G.L. c. 21I, §19(C), (G); 301 C.M.R. 40.03(1)(c), 40.05.

65. M.G.L. c. 21I §23.

66. M.G.L. c. 21I. §16.

67. M.G.L. c. 21I, §§16, 22.

68. M.G.L. c. 21I, §21(A). This penalty does not apply to violations of the toxics use fee provisions, which provisions establish a maximum fee of $1000 for failure to timely file a complete and accurate toxics survey and a sliding scale penalty structure for late payment of toxics use fees. M.G.L. c. 21I, §§19(F), 21(A).

69. M.G.L. c. 21I, §21(B).

70. M.G.L. c. 21I, §21(C).

71. 310 C.M.R. 5.03.

72. M.G.L. c. 21I, §16.

73. M.G.L. c. 21I, §18(B).

74. M.G.L. c. 21I, §18(C).

75. 42 U.S.C. §11001

76. 42 U.S.C.§11001.

77. 42 U.S.C. §11003(c).

78. 42 U.S.C. §11003(e).

Chapter 13

Regulation of Hazardous Building Materials

Several Massachusetts statutes and regulatory programs contain provisions designed to limit exposure to asbestos and lead paint, which were used widely in the construction of industrial, commercial, and residential buildings.

ASBESTOS

Any action that disturbs even a *de* minimis quantity of asbestos requires notification to the Environmental Protection Agency, the Massachusetts Department of Environmental Protection ("MassDEP"), and the state and local Board of Health. Under federal law, asbestos is considered a hazardous air pollutant,[1] a water pollutant,[2] a hazardous chemical and a toxic and hazardous substance,[3] a hazardous material,[4] and a hazardous substance.[5]

Three Massachusetts agencies have promulgated regulations governing inspection for, and maintenance and removal of, asbestos-containing materials. These agencies are the Department of Labor Standards ("DLS"),[6] the Department of Environmental Protection ("MassDEP"),[7] and the Department of Public Health ("DPH").[8]

MassDEP's air pollution control regulations include provisions governing demolition and renovation operations at facilities where asbestos or asbestos-containing material is present.[9] "Asbestos-containing material" is defined as friable asbestos and any material containing one percent or more asbestos by weight, including but not limited to sprayed-on and troweled-on materials applied to ceilings, walls, and other surfaces; insulation on pipes, boilers, tanks, ducts, and other equipment; structural members; tiles; shingles; and asbestos-containing paper. "Friable" materials are those which can be crumbled, pulverized, or reduced to powder by hand pressure when dry. "Demolition/renovation" is defined as any operation which involves the wrecking, taking out, removal, stripping, altering in any way, or construction of one or more facility components or of facility component insulation.[10]

MassDEP's regulations require notice to the Department prior to commencement of demolition or renovation involving asbestos-containing material. In most cases, the notice must be provided at least ten working days prior to commencement of work, and the notice must include information specified in the regulations and on MassDEP's notice form.[11] MassDEP's regulations also impose work practice standards for the conduct of demolition and renovation activities involving asbestoscontaining material to prevent emissions to the ambient air.[12] In addition, the regulations impose requirements for disposal of asbestos-containing waste material, including a requirement that such material be disposed of at a site approved to receive such material and operated in accordance with Massachusetts solid waste requirements or, if the site is outside Massachusetts, operated in accordance with applicable federal and state asbestos requirements.[13] "Asbestos-containing waste material" is defined as friable asbestos-containing material removed during a demolition/renovation project and anything contaminated in the course of such work, including asbestos waste from emission control devices, contaminated clothing, and debris.[14]

MassDEP's asbestos regulations contain a general prohibition on allowing demolition, renovation, installation, reinstallation, handling, transport, storage, or disposal of a facility or facility component that contains asbestos, asbestos-containing material, or asbestos-containing waste material in a manner that causes or contributes to a condition of air pollution.[15] MassDEP's asbestos regulations, other than the notice requirement, are enforceable by the municipal police department, fire department, board of health officials, or building inspector or designee thereof, as well as by MassDEP.[16]

Massachusetts law requires a DLS license prior to engaging in the business of removing, containing, or encapsulating asbestos or materials containing asbestos[17] and directs the Department of Labor and Workforce Development ("DLWD") to promulgate regulations for the protection of the general public and workers engaged in the use, handling, removal, or disposal of asbestos or materials containing asbestos.[18] DLWD has promulgated such regulations at 453 C.M.R. 6.01 to 6.20. DLWD's regulations define "asbestos-containing material" as any material containing more than one percent asbestos, but do not specify whether the percentage is determined by weight or by volume.[19]

DLWD's regulations set forth licensure requirements, and they require DLWD certification of workers engaging in any activities connected with asbestos abatement.[20] DLWD certification also is required for asbestos consultants, asbestos analytical services providers and asbestos training providers.[21]

A person who violates the DLWD asbestos requirements can be subject to a fine of between $500 and $1,500 for each offense and can have a DLWD asbestos abatement contractor license denied, revoked, or suspended. The DLWD Commissioner is authorized to order closure of a work site upon a determination that there is a violation of the DLWD asbestos requirements.[22] DPH has promulgated, as part of the State Sanitary Code, a regulation which requires that every owner must maintain all asbestos materials in good repair, and free from any defects including holes, cracks, tears or any looseness which may allow the release of asbestos dust or any powdered, crumbled or pulverized asbestos.[23] For purposes of the DPH regulation, "asbestos material" is defined simply as "asbestos or any material containing asbestos," with no minimum percentage of asbestos specified.[24] Violations of the DPH regulation must be corrected in accordance with the DEP and DLWD requirements discussed above.[25]

LEAD PAINT

The Lead Poisoning Prevention and Control Act, as amended (the "Act"),[26] directs DPH to establish a program for prevention, screening, diagnosis, and treatment of lead poisoning, including elimination of sources of such poisoning. Among the provisions of the Act are requirements regarding the abatement and containment of paint and other materials containing lead in certain residential premises and the disclosure of information about the presence of such materials. DPH has promulgated regulations to implement the Act's requirements at 105 C.M.R. 460.010 to 460.900. In addition, DLWD's Division of Industrial Safety has promulgated at 454 C.M.R. 22.01 to 22.92 regulations regarding the abatement and containment of paint and other materials containing lead.

The Act prohibits (i) the application of any lead-based paint, glaze or other substance to any toy, furniture, cooking, drinking, or eating utensil, or interior or exterior surface or fix.tu.re of any dwelling and (ii) the sale, delivery or gift of such products to which any lead-based paint, glaze or other substance has been applied.[27] Violation of this prohibition is punishable by a fine of $100 to $500 for each violation; each article, surface or fixture to which a lead-based substance is applied is a separate violation. Willful violation of this prohibition is punishable by imprisonment for up to three months for each violation.[28] In addition, the owner of any residential property is liable for all damages caused by his or her violation of this prohibition.[29]

The Act also prohibits the sale, delivery, gift, or possession with the intent to sell, deliver or give, any lead-based paint; glaze or other surface covering. Violation of this prohibition is punishable by a fine of $200 to $500 for each violation; each can, bottle or other container of any prohibited substance is a separate violation. Willful violation of this prohibition is punishable by imprisonment for up to six months for each violation.[30] Certain lead-based paints and products used for hobby, artistic and marine applications are exempt from these restrictions.[31]

The Act requires the owner of a residential premises to abate or contain paint, plaster, or other accessible structural material containing a dangerous level of lead[32] when a child under six years of age resides in the premises or when ordered to do so by DPH.[33] Abatement" is defined as the removal and replacement of paint, plaster, or other accessible structural material containing a dangerous level of lead or the replacement of an architectural fixture or element that contains paint or other accessible structural material containing a dangerous level of lead.[34] "Containment" is defined as the encapsulation, covering, or enclosing, by means authorized by DPH, of paint, plaster, or other accessible structural material containing a dangerous level of lead.[35] Repainting with non-lead-based paint without abatement or containment of the lead-containing material does not satisfy the lead abatement and containment requirements.[36] When a residential premises containing any paint, plaster, or other accessible structural material with a dangerous level of lead undergoes a change of ownership, and as a result a child under six years of age will become or will continue to be a resident therein, the new owner has 90 days to comply with the abatement and containment requirements.[37]

The Act generally requires that abatement or containment of materials containing lead be performed by a de-leading contractor licensed by DLWD.[38] The Act imposes requirements to notify building occupants, DPH, DLWD, local health officials, and certain other parties prior to conducting lead abatement or containment work.[39] In addition, the Act specifies in detail the building surfaces on which lead-containing materials must be abated or contained and the manner in which such work must be carried out to protect human health and safety and the environment.[40] The Act provides that a lead inspector licensed by DPH must issue a letter of full compliance for a residential premises upon such inspector's determination that the premises fully complies with the lead abatement and containment requirements.[41] The Act also specifies the conditions under which a residential premises may be reoccupied after the work has been completed.[42]

An owner of residential property otherwise obligated to abate or contain lead based materials in a residence in which a child under six years of age resides may delay full compliance for up to one year by implementing an Emergency Lead Management Plan and obtaining a Letter of Interim Control.[43] Implementation of an Emergency Lead Management Plan begins with a detailed inspection of the premises by a lead inspector who also is licensed as a risk assessor, to identify conditions which must be immediately abated or contained as interim control measures.[44] After implementation of the interim control measures, and following a risk assessment reinspection, the owner may obtain a Letter of Interim Control.[45] During the interim period, the owner must continue to contain and control paint, plaster or other accessible structural materials containing dangerous levels of lead in accordance with measures defined in an Emergency Lead Management Plan.[46] A Letter of Interim Control expires one year after issuance and may be renewed only once, for an additional one-year period, at the expiration of which the owner must have brought the property into full compliance.[47] DPH may waive or alter the lead abatement and containment requirements under certain circumstances.[48]

Certain holders of title to residential property and certain types of residential property are exempt from compliance with the foregoing abatement and containment requirements. A secured lender—a bank, lending institution, mortgage company, or other mortgagee which holds indicia of ownership of a residential property primarily to protect a security interest in the property—is not considered an owner for purposes of the lead abatement and containment requirements unless and until the lender acquires legal title pursuant to applicable law and takes actual physical possession of the premises.[49] Within ninety days after acquiring legal title to a premises in which a child under the age of six resides, a secured lender must either bring the premises into compliance with the Act or transfer the property in a manner that complies with the Act's disclosure requirements (discussed below).[50] Most of the requirements of the Act do not apply to the owner of a dwelling unit that is leased, rented, or occupied for vacation or recreational purposes for a period of 31 days, provided that the unit has no peeling or chipped paint and that the tenant has received the appropriate lead paint disclosure notification.[51] The Act also does not apply to dwelling units having fewer than two hundred and fifty square feet of floor area or which are used as a rooming house, provided that no child under the age of six occupies such premises.[52]

When DPH is informed of a case of lead poisoning, it is required to inspect the premises in which the victim resides, including any other premises in which the victim has resided within the prior twelve months. DPH and local officials also may inspect a residential premise subject to a Letter of Interim Control in response to a reported case of lead poisoning. Upon a finding of a dangerous level of lead, notice of the presence of lead in the premises must be provided to the owner, affected occupants of the building, and mortgagees and lienholders of record. In addition, the owner may be ordered to comply with the lead abatement and containment requirements.[53]

The requirements of the Act and regulations are enforceable by DPH and by local health officials. A person who fails to comply with the lead abatement and containment requirements or an order issued under the Act or regulations can be subject to a fine of from $10 to $500 for each day of non-compliance.[54] The owner of a residential premises is liable for all damages to a lead poisoned child who was under six years of age at the time of poisoning where such damages are caused by the owner's failure to comply with the lead abatement and containment requirements, regardless of whether the owner was aware of the presence of a dangerous level of lead. Where the owner has been notified of a dangerous level of lead or received an order regarding such a condition and has willfully failed to take required action to remedy the condition, the owner is also subject to punitive damages of treble the actual damages.[55] However, no claim of strict liability under the Act may be brought against an owner who has obtained a letter of interim control that was in effect at the time of injury, unless the damages were caused by the owner's breach of the duty to exercise reasonable care to ensure that the premises remain in compliance with the interim control measures. Nor can a claim of strict liability under the Act be brought against an owner who has obtained a letter of full compliance that remains in effect.[56] A new owner of a residential premises is not strictly liable for such damages if the owner achieves compliance with the lead abatement and containment requirements within ninety days after becoming owner.[57] In addition, a secured lender is not liable under the Act if, within ninety days of acquiring title to a residential premises, the lender obtains a letter of full compliance or a letter of interim control or transfers the premises in compliance with the property transfer disclosure requirements discussed below.[58] The Act requires a seller or lessor of, and a real estate agent for, a residential premises constructed before 1978 to provide a prospective purchaser or lessee, prior to the signing of a purchase and sale agreement or lease, with a notification form containing specified information regarding lead-containing materials and lead poisoning, as well as all available information and documentation regarding the presence of materials containing a dangerous level of lead in the premises. In addition, a prospective purchaser, or a lessee with an option to purchase, must be provided with an opportunity to have the premises inspected for lead.[59] An owner who fails to comply with the disclosure requirements may be held liable for all damages caused by such non-compliance and may be subject to a civil penalty of up to $1,000. A person engaged in trade or commerce who fails to comply with these requirements can be liable for an unfair or deceptive act or practice under the Massachusetts consumer protection statute, M.G.L. c. 93A.[60] An owner or other party is prohibited from refusing to sell, rent, or lease a residential premises to any person, and from discriminating against any person in the terms, conditions, or privileges of the sale, rental, or lease, because the premises contains or may contain a material with a dangerous level of lead, because the transaction would trigger requirements under the Act and regulations, or because such person chooses to exercise a right under the Act or regulations.[61] In addition, bank, lending institution, credit union, or mortgagee is prohibited from discriminating in the financing or refinancing of the purchase, improvement, repair, or maintenance of a residential premises solely because the premises contains or may contain a material with a dangerous level of lead.[62]

NOTES

1. 40 C.F.R. 61.140–.157.
2. 40 C.F.R. 427.10–.16.
3. 29 C.F.R. 1910.1001, 1910.1200, 1915.1001, 1926.1101, and 1926.59.
4. 49 C.F.R. 172.101.
5.6. 42 U.S.C. §§9601 – 9675; 40 C.F.R. 302.4.
7. See https://perma.cc/6APF-D2XW.
8. See https://perma.cc/H9YP-FLK4.
9. 105 C.M.R. 410.353, .470, and .410.
10. 310 C.M.R. 7.09, 7.15.
11. 310 C.M.R. 7.00, Definitions. "Altering," as used in the definition of "demolition/renovation," includes repairing, restoring, drilling, cutting, sawing, sanding, scratching, scraping, or digging into a facility component or facility component insulation. *Id.*
12. 310 C.M.R. 7.15(1)(b). "Emergency demolition/renovation operations," defined as unplanned operations resulting from a sudden unexpected event (including the non-routine failure of equipment) which requires the demolition/renovation of a structurally sound or unsound facility or facility component, may be undertaken upon one working day of notice to DEP. 310 C.M.R. 7.00, Definitions; 7.15(1)(b)2.b.
13. 310 C.M.R. 7.15(1)(c), (d).
14. 310 C.M.R. 7.15(1)(e).
15. 310 C.M.R. 7.00, Definitions.
16. 310 C.M.R. 7.15(1)(a).
17. 310 C.M.R. 7.15(2), 7.52.
18. https://perma.cc/BHN5-EAE2.
19. M.G.L. c. 149, §§6B, 6C.
20. 453 C.M.R. 6.02.
21. 453 C.M.R. 6.03(3) *See* 453 C.M.R. 6.06 (certification requirements).
22. 453 C.M.R. 6.03(4)-(6). *See* 453 C.M.R. 6.07-.09 (certification requirements).
23. M.G.L. c. 149, §§6E, 6F; 453 C.M.R. 6.16, .17.
24. 105 C.M.R. 410.353.
25. 105 C.M.R. 410.020.
26. 105 C.M.R. 410.353.
27. MGL c. 111, §§189A—199B.
28. The Act defines deems a paint, glaze or other substance to be "lead-based" if it contains more than 0.06 percent lead by weight or, for substances manufactured

before June 23, 1977, 0.5 percent lead by weight. M.G.L. c. 111, §196. However, DPH's implementing regulations specify that a glaze or enamel on a glass, ceramic, porcelain or porcelain-coated cooking, eating or drinking utensil or porcelain-coated household appliance or fixture is "lead-based" if it contains greater than 2 ppm lead when tested by ASTM Standard Method C 738. 105 C.M.R. 460.020.

29. M.G.L. c. 111, § 196(a).; 105 C.M.R. 460.200(A), (B), .210.

30. 105 C.M.R. 460.230.

31. M.G.L. c. 111, §196(b); 105 C.M.R. 460.200(C), .220.

32. M.G.L. c. 111, §196(b); 105 C.M.R. 460.300 to .340.

33. The Act does not define "dangerous level of lead," but authorizes DPH to determine the amount of lead in paint, plaster or other accessible structural material that produces the danger of lead poisoning, in accordance with sound medical practice and current technical knowledge. M.G.L. c. 111, §194. DPH has adopted a regulatory definition of "dangerous level of lead in paint or other coating, putty or plaster" as "the level of lead . . . which materially endangers the health of children or adults by producing a substantial and serious danger of lead poisoning" and by specifying thresholds for atomic absorption spectrophotometry, sodium sulfide solution reaction tests and mobile x-ray florescence analysis above which the presence of lead will be considered "dangerous." 105 C.M.R. 460.020.

34. M.G.L. c. 111, §197(a); 105 C.M.R. 460.100(A). *See* M.G.L. c. 111, §197(b), (c).

35. M.G.L. c. 111, §189A; 105 C.M.R. 460.020.

36. M.G.L. c. 111, §189A; 105 C.M.R. 460.020.

37. M.G.L. c. 111, §197(f); 105 C.M.R. 460.110(A).

38. M.G.L. c. 111, §197(a); 105 C.M.R. 460.100(B), .720(A).

39. M.G.L. c. 111, §§197(d), 197B(b)(2), (3); 105 C.M.R. 460.110(C). DLWD's regulations specify licensing, worker certification, training, medical monitoring, notification, work practice and record keeping requirements applicable to deleading contractors. 454 C.M.R. 22.03 to .10. *See* M.G.L. c. 111, §197B(b)(1), (e); 105 C.M.R. 460.420, .430.

40. M.G.L. c. 111, §§197(c). *See also* 105 C.M.R. 460.150, 454 C.M.R. 22.07.

41. M.G.L. c. 111, §197(c); 105 C.M.R. 460.110(B), .120 to .170; 454 C.M.R. 22.08, .11.

42. M.G.L. c. 111, §197(c). *See also* 105 C.M.R. 460.760(E)(2)(b). DPH's regulations include provisions regarding licensure, training and registration of lead inspectors. 105 C.M.R. 460.400 to .430. *See*

M.G.L. c. 111, §197B(a), (t) (authorizing DPH to make and implement such regulations).

43. M.G.L. c. 111, §197(g); 105 C.M.R. 460.160(E), .760.

44. M.G.L. c. 111, §197(b); 105 C.M.R. 460.105.

45. M.G.L. c. 111, §197(b); 105 C.M.R. 460.020, .015(A).

46. M.G.L. c. 111, §197(b); 105 C.M.R. 460.105(B) to (D).

47. 105 C.M.R. 460.105(E).

48. M.G.L. c. 111, §197(b); 105 C.M.R. 460.105(F).

49. M.G.L. c. 111, §197(e). In addition, DLWD is authorized by its regulations to grant exceptions therefrom under certain circumstances. 454 C.M.R. 22.01(3).

50. M.G.L. c. 111, §197D; 105 C.M.R. 460.l00(C)(l).

51. M.G.L. c. 111, §197D(a); 105 C.M.R. 460.100(C)(2).

52. M.G.L. c. 111, §199B; 105 C.M.R. 460.100(0). The owner of such a dwelling unit must comply with annual inspection and maintenance regulations. 105 C.M.R.·460.lO0(D)(l).

53. M.G.L. c. 111, § 199B; 105 C.M.R. 460.lOO(E). The exemption for a "rooming house" includes boarding houses, hotels, inns, lodging houses, dormitories and other similar dwelling places. M.G.L c. 111, § 199B; 105 C.M.R. 460.020.

54. M.G.L. c. 111, §194; 105 C.M.R. 460.710. *See also* M.G.L. c. 111, § 193 (establishing program for early identification of lead poisoning cases); 105 C.M.R. 460.700 (requiring local code enforcement agency to inspect for lead paint whenever conducting inspection for violations of State Sanitary Code).

55. M.G.L. c. 111, §198; 105 C.M.R. 460.190(A). Additionally, threatening or taking reprisals against a tenant for exercising his or her rights under the Act, or refusing to rent to or evicting families with children under the age of six is a violation of M.G.L. c. 186, § 18 and c. 93A. 105 C.M.R. 460.190(8), (C).

56. M.G.L. c. 111, §199(a), (b); 105 C.M.R. 460.lS0(A), (B).

57. M.G.L. c. 111, §§197(b), (c), 197C, 199(a); 105 C.M.R. 460.180(A)(3), (4).

58. M.G.L. c. 111, §199(d); 105 C.M.R. 460.180(A)(l), (B)(l).

59. M.G.L. c. 111, §197D(a); 105 C.M.R. 460.180(A)(2), (B)(2). As indicated above, a secured lender is not considered an "owner" of a residential premises for purposes of the Act and regulations, including the liability provisions, unless and until the secured lender acquires legal title and takes actual physical possession of the premises. M.G.L. c. 111, §197D(a).

60. M.G.L. c. 111, §197A(a), (b), (d); 105 C.M.R. 460.720(B) to (D). If the required information and materials have been provided to a prospective purchaser, or a lessee with an option to purchase, by a real estate agent, the agent must obtain written acknowledgment from the prospective purchaser or lessee that such notification has been provided. M.G.L. c. 111, §197A(b)(2); 105 C.M.R. 460.720(D). Where a sale will occur as a result of a foreclosure proceeding, the seller must provide each potential purchaser with the required notification and information and obtain an acknowledgment that the potential purchaser understands that there will not be an opportunity for a lead inspection prior to the sale. 105 C.M.R.651.014.

460.720(C)(2).

61. M.G.L. c. 111, §197A(e).

62. M.G.L. c. 111, §199A(a).

63. M.G.L. c. 167, § 48.

Index

About the Author

Theda Braddock has been an environmental and securities attorney for more than twenty years. She is author of *California Environmental Law and Natural Resources Handbook*, thirteenth edition, the fifth and sixth editions of *Washington Environmental Law Handbook*, the fifth edition of the *Maryland Environmental Law Handbook*, and *Wetlands: An Introduction*, third edition. Braddock is admitted to practice before the state and federal courts in California, Maryland, Massachusetts, and Washington State. She is also admitted to practice before the U.S. Court of Federal Claims and the U.S. Supreme Court. Braddock attended the Great Books Program at St. John's College in Annapolis, Maryland, and received her B.A. from Mills College in Oakland, California. She received her J.D. from Golden Gate University in San Francisco, California.

www.ingramcontent.com/pod-product-compliance
Lightning Source LLC
LaVergne TN
LVHW090403210926
848480LV00002B/433
9781641434270